THE MODERN LIBRARY
OF THE WORLD'S BEST BOOKS

AN ANTHOLOGY OF MEDIEVAL LYRICS

AN ANTHOLOGY OF MEDIEVAL LYRICS

Edited by ANGEL FLORES

THE MODERN LIBRARY

NEW YORK

 PUBLISHED IN NEW YORK BY RANDOM HOUSE, INC., AND IN TORONTO, CANADA, BY RANDOM HOUSE OF CANADA, LIMITED.

MANUFACTURED IN THE UNITED STATES OF AMERICA

LIBRARY OF CONGRESS CATALOG CARD NUMBER: 62-9688

ACKNOWLEDGMENTS ARE DUE TO THE FOLLOWING PUBLISHERS AND TRANSLATORS:

BANTAM BOOKS, INC., FOR ANTHONY BONNER'S VERSION OF VILLON'S "THE BELLE HEAULMIERE TO THE DAUGHTERS OF JOY" FROM *The Complete Works of François Villon* (NEW YORK: BANTAM BOOKS, 1960; © 1960 BY BANTAM BOOKS, INC.

OLIVER & BOYD, FOR DR. MARGARET F. RICHEY'S TRANSLATIONS, FROM *Medieval German Lyrics* (LONDON: OLIVER & BOYD, 1958; © 1958 MARGARET F. RICHEY.

THE HUDSON REVIEW, FOR ROBERT LOWELL'S VERSION OF THE POEM BY DER WILDE ALEXANDER, FROM *The Hudson Review*, VOL. XII, NO. 1, SPRING 1959. COPYRIGHT, 1959, BY THE HUDSON REVIEW, INC.

Random House IS THE PUBLISHER OF

THE MODERN LIBRARY

BENNETT CERF DONALD S. KLOPFER

PREFACE

In the period vaguely described as the "middle ages" a vast body of lyric poetry was produced which the present anthology endeavors to mirror in as many aspects as possible. Considerations of unity and expediency, however, as well as of space, have imposed certain limitations. Since English medieval writing is familiar to most cultured readers of English, and as adequate English versions of poets who wrote in Latin do abound, it was decided to devote these pages to the birth of the lyric in Continental Europe, with particular attention to the rise of new languages and techniques.

Poets conversant with medieval languages and distinguished scholars gifted with creative ability have assisted in this task, and, except for a few poems, all the translations were done especially for this anthology. A considerable number of these lyrics are presented here in English for the first time.

The editor wishes to thank his critics and advisors: Thomas G. Bergin (Yale), Andrew Chiappe (Columbia), A. Closs (Bristol), Margaret F. Richey (formerly of London), Martin Riquier (Barcelona), Maurice Valency (Columbia) and James B. Wadsworth (Penn State), as well as Kenneth Freyer, Eleanor C. Eldot, Margaret A. Webb and Frieda Baroway, of the Paul Klapper Library, Queens College; and most especially Berenice Hoffman for her intelligent and painstaking reading of the entire manuscript.

ANGEL FLORES

Queens College,
Flushing 57, New York

1-11
15-25
29-35
41-2
50-62
72-4
104-5
108-115
140-7
152-8
159-63
174-91

CONTENTS

Individual Table of Contents precedes each section.
Notes and Biographical Sketches are at the end of each section.

PROVENCE

ANONYMOUS

In an Orchard, under the Leaves of a Hawthorn

En un vergier sotz folha d'albespi

In an orchard, under the leaves of a hawthorn,
The lady kept her lover by her side
Until the watchman cried that the day had come:
Oh God, Oh God, the dawn! How soon it comes!

"Oh God, if only the night were not over,
And my friend were not going away,
And the watchman had never seen the dawn or the day!
Oh God, Oh God, the dawn! How soon it comes!

"Fair sweet friend, let us kiss once again,
In the depths of this field where the birds are singing,
Let us have our joy in despite of the Jealous One!
Oh God, Oh God, the dawn! How soon it comes!

"Fair sweet friend, let us play one more game
In this garden where the birds are singing,
Until the watchman begins to play on his pipe.
Oh God, Oh God, the dawn! How soon it comes!"

"In the sweet breeze that comes from yonder
Where my friend is, courteous and gay,
I have drunk a sweet draught of his breath—
Oh God, Oh God, the dawn! How soon it comes!"

The lady is gracious and charming,
And many look at her because she is beautiful,
And she has set her heart on a loyal love:
Oh God, Oh God, the dawn! How soon it comes!

MAURICE VALENCY

ANONYMOUS

Nightlong, Daylong, as the Sweet

Quan lo rosignol escria

Nightlong, daylong, as the sweet
Nightingale his love doth greet,
I lie at my sweet heart's feet
    Neath the flower
Till the watchman from his tower
Cries: " 'Tis dawn! Fair lovers, rise!
Soon bright day will gild the skies!"

JACQUES LECLERCQ

WILLIAM IX, COUNT OF POITIERS

I'll Make Some Verses Just for Fun

Farai un vers de dreyt nien

I'll make some verses just for fun,
Not about me nor any one,
Nor deeds that noble knights have done,
    Nor love's ado—
I made them riding in the sun
    (My horses helped, too.)

When I was born I cannot say;
I am not sad, I am not gay,
I am not stiff nor dégagé;
    What can I do?
Long since enchanted by a fay
    Star-touched I grew.

Dreaming for living I mistake
Unless I'm told when I'm awake.

My heart is sad and nigh to break
With bitter rue—
And I don't care three crumbs of cake,
Or even two.

So ill I am that death I fear;
I nothing know but what I hear;
I hope there is a doctor here,
No matter who,
If he can cure me I'll pay dear.
If not, he's through.

I have a lady, who or where
I cannot tell you, but I swear
She treats me neither ill nor fair
But I'm not blue—
Just as the Normans stay up there
Out of Poitou.

I have not seen yet I adore
This distant love; she sets no store
By what I think and furthermore
('Tis sad but true)
Others there are, some three or four,
I'm faithful to.

I've made this verse; if you'll allow
I think I'll send it off right now
To one who'll pass it on somehow
Up in Anjou
He'd tell me what it means, I vow,
If he but knew.

THOMAS G. BERGIN

⚜

Under the Sun I Ride Along

Farai un vers pos mi sonelh

Under the sun I ride along
And tell this story in a song;
Ladies there are who do great wrong,
I mean such dames
As turn a cruel and heedless ear
To lovers' claims.

Those who will dally and demur
And on their knights no grace confer
Do mortal sin; worse I judge her
That loves a priest;
By rights she should be hunted down
Like any beast.

But hear me: silent and discreet
Through our Auvergne mild and sweet
I rode and happened there to meet
Sir Guarin's dame,
And Bernard's too; they spoke me fair
And asked my name.

"God save you, pilgrim, as you fare,"
Thus cried one of the comely pair,
"Gentle you seem and debonair,
If I may judge;
Yet many vagabonds and rogues
Our highway trudge."

Now mark the style of my reply:
I spoke no truth, I told no lie,
But answered only with a sigh
(I had my plan):
"Babariol, babariol,
Babarian."

Then said Dame Ermesses in glee
To Lady Agnes: "Mute is he;
Let's take him home and lodge him free;
    When we're alone
Such sport as we'll devise with him
    Will ne'er be known."

So then one cast her mantle o'er
My back, and through her chamber door
Led me, and I could ask no more.
    A cozy fire
Burned in the hearth; a man had all
    He might desire.

A lordly meal did they prepare
And two fat capons were my share
All hotly spiced: the wine was rare
    And all for me.
No steward served, no cook was there
    But just we three.

"Sister, this fellow is too shy
To say a word while we stand by;
Lest he be scheming on the sly
    Let our cat come;
I'll warrant we shall straightway learn
    If he be dumb."

So Agnes went to fetch the cat;
Ne'er had I seen a beast like that,
I fell to trembling where I sat
    And with good cause:
Long-whiskered was he, big and fierce,
    With cruel claws.

Those prudent ladies first undressed
Their mute and unsuspecting guest,
Then on his back the cat they pressed—
    Keen could I feel

Its talons ripping down my flank
From haunch to heel.

As Agnes dragged it by the tail
My body's length I felt each nail,
And with the anguish I turned pale
Yet stood all meek;
By God, they could have flayed me there
Ere I would speak.

"Sister," I heard Dame Agnes say,
"He's mute indeed; I think we may
Prepare ourselves for sport and play:
Draw the bath hot."
More than a week I spent with them,
Such was my lot.

Now hear the tally I'll relate:
A hundred fourscore times and eight
I laid 'em—and a woeful state
They left me in,
With harness torn and broken blade—
Aye, 'twas a sin.

Good Squire, if I feel no worse
Tomorrow, take this little verse
To those fair ladies, with my purse,
And—tit for tat—
Ask them in memory of me
To kill that cat!

THOMAS G. BERGIN

In the Fair Times of New-born Spring
Ab la dolchor del temps novel

In the fair times of new-born spring
The trees leaf out and small birds sing;

Each in his own tongue greets the day
And all songs mingle in union sweet.
Time now it were to tune my lay
Toward that which makes my joy complete.

Alas, from whence each good thing
No message comes, sealed with her ring—
How can my heart be happy—nay,
I fear me it may cease to beat
Before I learn—if I learn I may—
If Love has won or met defeat.

For love with us has followed the way
Of the hawthorn tree whose branches sway
Trembling under the night's cold sleet,
Whipped by the wind and shivering,
Till light of morn and the soft sun's heat
Fresh bloom and life to the young buds bring.

And I recall as but yesterday
When we called truce to our affray,
Pledging our love without deceit—
This will I swear, God witnessing:
Let my hands 'neath her mantle meet
And I'll have done with sorrowing.

From slanderers' malice I'll not stray
From my true love; in vain they'll bray.
I know how gossip fills the street,
I know how jealous tongues can sting:
Let starvelings snarl—we have the meat,
The salt, the knife and everything.

THOMAS G. BERGIN

CERCAMON

With Mournful Tones My Verses Start

Lo plaing comenz iradamen

With mournful tones my verses start,
with words that rise from grieving heart,
as anguish raging past my art
tears youth and courtesy apart,
and evils come and joys depart,
because the Poitevan is dead.

The praise is killed and all reclaim
that always out of Poitou came.
What mourning they in France proclaim!
That I yet live is cause for shame.
Oh, Lord, the baron whom I name,
may he to Paradise be led.

The Count of Poitou I lament,
who was of merit complement;
since charity and worth are spent,
here I cannot be long content.
Oh, Lord, do not his soul torment:
the earthly life was good he shed.

Glorious God, to you I call,
who made this grief on earth befall:
as we must die for Adam's fall,
do not his soul with dread appall,
with bonds of fire in Satan's thrall.
This life has held us all misled.

I hold this world as mean and vain,
for good the poor nor rich attain.
My noble friends have dead long lain
while we in wretchedness remain,

although we know that right will reign
the day the Final Judgment's read.

Noble Gascons, worthy your renown,
you are deprived of honor's crown.
Fierce you must be and meekness drown,
since youth is wretchedly cast down,
unwelcomed now in court or town,
except from Alphonse, whom joy has fled.

The French and Normans share our woe
and well the Kin might sadness show
on whom he did his lands bestow,
and since his lands and honors grow,
he would do well to riding go
to strike the Saracens with dread.

They may rejoice, his enemy
in Engolmes and Limozi.
If he could live and God agree,
he would check their liberty,
but he is dead and they left free.
In Aunis there is dole instead.

The plaint is made with words worked right
by Cercamon, who grieves our plight.
Our Gascon joy is put to flight;
from Spain and Aragon goes delight.
Saint James, remember you that knight
for whom I kneel and prayers have said.

HARVEY BIRENBAUM

True Love Warms My Heart

Per fin' amor m'esjauzira

True love
warms my heart,

no matter if he run hot or cold.
My thoughts attract on her always,
but can't know yet
if I can finish the job, stay
firm with joy, that is
if she wants to keep me hers
which my heart most desires.

I quit all lords and all ladies
if she wants me to serve her in it:
and who speaks to me of separation
will have me die tonight. I
place my hope in no other one,
sunup, sunset, night or day,
my heart dreams no other happiness.

I'd hardly have spoken out so soon
if I'd known how hard she softened. No
thing but does not humble itself toward Love—
        her? she is fierce toward him!
But a lady can have no valor, not
by riches and not by power, if
the joy of Love blow not within her.

I'd not leave her feet, if it pleasure her
if she consent to it.
If she wanted to she could enrich me, saying
she were my woman.
All the rest whatever, at her pleasure,
were it truth or lies, no matter,
        that word
would be all the wealth I'd need.
        I've sat between joy and pain since
        goodbyes were said, for I've not seen
        her since that day. She said if I loved her
        she would love me. Beyond that, I
        know nothing of her intent.
        But she ought to know well enough that I
        will die if she keeps me in torment.

The fairest woman ever used a mirror never
saw anything soft and white as ermine,
as she is,
fresher than lily or rose—any flower!
And nothing makes me despair more. God!
may I enjoy the hour
when I can make love-play beside her!
No. I, no. She does not turn toward me.

My lady would fill to overflow
all my desires, if she but now
would grant—if only one—to
ease me, just one kiss.
How I'd fight then!
war against any neighbor, give largely,
make myself feared and know, hurl
enemies down, keep my possessions, my
goods, my own.
And may my lady know that, for my part,
no man of my rank could serve her
with better heart.
And if she pleasure me next her,
if she let me lie next to her level,
sure I would not die of this evil.

PAUL BLACKBURN

MARCABRU

In April around Easter the Streams Grow Clear

En abriu s'esclairo il riu contra'l Pascor

In April around Easter the streams grow clear
and in the groves, leaves burgeon above the blossoms.
Gentle, with gentle pleasure, gently
Pure Love comforts me.

Who has an acknowledged lover of one sort
should take him as white if he be not rubbed dark:

pied love, always, the best I can see it
being traitor from habit.

Pretends it's good bettering itself, gently
serving, while evil is what it's after. When
favor's given you'll see the heads broken
in many places, and muddied reputations.

God down and damn eternally pied love and curse forever
all it stands for! The drunk at least takes pleasure
in his letch—though if he drink too much
it drains his vigor.

If my love will disbelieve the muck that liars
make and snakes construct, my garrulous accusers,
I'll be hers if she wants me,
without loud-talk or falsity,
without lies or illusions.

But she doesn't believe me. I waste my time
reproaching her without a belt.
She makes her peace with hell and helling:
so the tongue turns toward the swelling
tooth, where the pain is felt.

Three of them pass before where I sit in the passage: I'm silent
until the fourth has finished fucking her and the fifth
comes tearing up.
That's where Amor is now, in foulness and filth. These cunts

are nymphos in bed
seducers when they talk
and thieves when they sleep,
and these male sluts not only want their piece—
but some back in theirs as well, and the best thing!
how shepherds make it with a sheep . . . ka . .
how describe this "culture"?

He takes the skin off a hard bird, who flays
and skins a vulture . . .

PAUL BLACKBURN

⚜

No Doubt At All, I'll Take Him on as Critic
Per savi'l tenc ses doptansa

No doubt at all,
I'll take him on as critic,
who'll call the meaning, in my song,
of each word,
who's analytic, who
can see the structure of the vers unfold.
I know it'll sound absurd, but
I'm often doubtful and go wrong myself
in the explication of an obscure word.

These simple-minded troubadours get off
on tangents which have the excellent merit
of leading nowhere.
And they turn into compulsion what
plain truth has accorded them.
Out of what truth has set in order, they
make compulsory laws
and by a certain reflection
they fit their words to fill the chinks and flaws.

Without demarcation
they set Love and the several ways
of letching-after-love on equal footing.
And he who's on the make for simple bedding
will find it is himself he covers up.
When his purse is empty as a street in winter
he'll see the sport of sledding hard
will serve for consolation.

I get sore and I show it, when I hear
from some poor sonofabitch that Love
has misled and betrayed him, when
it's lechery has thrown him out.
It's to themselves such lovers lie,
      for a lover's treasure
is in measure, patience, and in Joy.

      Some couplings make known
when two paths join and do not redivide,
that of two desires, one
will may be made,
and Fine Love walk beside
and live and stay
where trust lives, within
the honest loving whiteness of their days.

      For Love has the sign
      of emerald and sard,
      is Joy's peak and basis,
      and of Truth, the teacher,
      and has power over
      every creature.

To judge from the semblance
when he speaks acts, Love
arises from the heart of things
when he lays down his gage and does
not qualify his giving for a rule.
The man who does not advance
straitly toward Love
's a fool.

But it is not worth an egg, my preaching at him, whose
already miserable heart is strapped by madness.
For I, too, think that sensual love
proceeds from the affections,
although too often it proves false and thieving.

The fool sings out everything he has in mind.
He follows no intelligence but
tinkers the job and botches it:
his love lives on a kind of extortion,
his life is a constant makeshift.
I agree on principle, then: love
loves itself,
constantly is steadfast,
and probity has slimyness for breakfast.

The end of this vers uncoils against
and sets the weights to balance
this vicious, villainous crew of mutts
whose stars are red with malice,
who puff themselves up with crazy thoughts
and have great adventures summarily,
that is, they decide to have them . . .

May the thought that inflates them
bring them bad luck only.

PAUL BLACKBURN

Winter Goes and Weather Betters

L'iverns vai e'l temps s'aizina

Winter goes and weather betters,
hedgerows green, hawthorns flower,
for which sensible reason the birds rejoice

Even man grows gay with love
each drawing toward his private choice
yeah,
pursuing his heart's pleasure.

The cold and drizzle clink against
the gentle season to arrest it.

From the hedges and from thickets
I hear the lancing song contest it

Put down my name in the entry-books,
I'll sing of Love and how it goes,
yeah,
if I want to, *and* how it grows.

Letching love gets started, then it grabs
and cheats with a greedy, dire will.
Had just once, a cunt's softness
combusts, lights the damned traitorous fire

And no one who falls into that blaze,
if he really mean it, or just to try it
yeah,
will come out with his hair on Fridays.

Fine Love carries a medicine
intended to heal his companion.
Lechery binds and cramps his well
then shoves him down into a kind of hell

Long as there's the smell of money
it'll wear love's face both front and rear
yeah,
but when the cash runs low, you'll hear
"the road, sonny, the road."

Luring, enticing with sweet bait
to get the poor gull into the trap
until they have him, head and shoulders,
signal "yes" while saying "no":

I prefer as lover a man who's dark
or light-skinned, or nicely tanned,
I'll make it with you—no I won't
yeah,
crazy for a skinny behind!

The lady doesn't know Love's face
when she loves a servant of the house:
and if he covers her at her will
then it's the mongrel with the greyhound bitch

That's how these rich alloys are got
who will not lay out feasts or silver
yeah,
and it's Marcabru who says so.

The guardian gets into the back
and hurries to blow up the fire a bit,
then drinks the smoke from the waterbutt
of his Lady Goodandexcited.

I know how well he rests when he lies down
and gets the grain out of the sack
yeah,
and perpetuates his master's name.

Who has Amor as a neighbor
and lives on the allowance he gets,
good name, spunk and integrity
incline to him without complaint

He who acts as straight as he talks
will not have the same laments as
yeah,
sir Eglain, that balancing grain-sack.

For myself, I hold no more
with sir Eble's theory of *trobar*
that's made a stack of foolish decisions
and upholds them against all reason.

I say, and've said, and will again:
they feed us only rationalization.
Love weeps to be differentiated
from lechery. Plain, it's plain

that he who whines against Fine Love
's a botch. Let him complain
yeah.

PAUL BLACKBURN

I'll Tell You in My Own Way
Dirai vos en mon lati

I'll tell you
in my own way
what I've seen
and what I see.
I think the world will hardly last
according to scripture, for nowadays
the son fails toward the father,
father toward son equally.

Youth, turned from the road toward full decline
and Gift, who was his brother,
slip off in the night together.
And our sir Constans, the Great Deceiver,
would never have missed them.

Often, a rich man's bread and wine
feed a bad neighbor, and if he
has a hard face, it's sure to be
a hard morning, if what the farmer
says is true,
or that's how the proverb goes.

In the mill, the miller judges:
"What's well bound should be well loosed."
And the labourer behind his plowshare:
"Good harvest comes from a good field"
"Evil son from evil mother"
"The lickorous mare breeds a mean-
hearted little beast."

Two colts are born—mettlesome, handsome,
with blond manes that will turn from
blond to mouse and make them resemble two asses.
Youth and Joy have turned into swindlers
        and Malice sent in as replacement.

You married men, you act like goats.
You plump the cushions up a bit,
the cunts all wink and get undressed.
But it cuts both ways—and when you say

        "My sons laugh at me"
and you've had nothing to do with it,
that is, the birth of your sons, what goats!
You have a spirit that would look better sheepish.
Worth nothing to me to lecture at 'em.
The errors they make are always the same.
And one thing Marcabru's never seen,
and that's these merry married men
        give up their cheating
        when love's the game.

Always you cut instead of shaving, lads,
        when love's the game.

PAUL BLACKBURN

Since My Courage Is Clarified

Pus mos coratges s'es clartits

Since my courage is clarified
by the Joy I'm given, and I
see Love parcel out and choose,
wherein I hope to be a richness to her,
I do a good job and winnow out my song
so no one can put me in the wrong,
since for a little thing
a man can be contradicted when he sings.

The one whom Fine Love singles out
lives happy, courteous and wise.
And he to whom Joy is refused, is
undone, sent out to ruin. For he
who carps at Love is made to hang
his mouth wide like a fool and think
it was his own artifice destroyed him.

Such are false-hearted judges, thieves,
false-witnesses and cheating husbands,
back-biters, painted-up young men,
lip-servicers and convent-crackers,
and these flaming whores who'll do
agreeable things with other women's
husbands, all will earn their hell.

Homicides, traitors, the crud that sells
church preferments, the magicians,
usurers, in sex the aestheticians
who make livings from their dirty trade,
those who submit themselves to charms
and the fetid hags who make them, will
all share unrelenting flames.

Seducers, drunkards, false priests, false
abbots, nuns, the false recluse
will get theirs then, says Marcabru.
For each one has his seat reserved,
Fine Love has promised it will be thus:
great lamentation and gnashing teeth.

O noble Love, source of all giving,
by whom the whole world is illumined,
I cry mercy!
Keep these whiners from me! and
may I be defended against the fire!
On every side I hold myself your prisoner,
and comforted by you in all things, hope
that you shall be my guide and all my light.

With this vers I curb my heart
and direct the reproach at myself,
for he who would be a critic
is in, if he can guard himself, not
blot himself with the same crime
he charges the lady with, and think
he's in the right to rate her down.

And if it is a well-chosen bit,
what I know to say well, and say,
he can if he like, remember it.

PAUL BLACKBURN

JAUFRÉ RUDEL

When the Waters of the Spring
Quan lo rius de la fontana

When the waters of the spring
Run clear once more,
And the flower of the eglantine blooms,
And the little nightingale on the branch
Turns and repeats and modulates
Its song, and refines it,
It is right that I too should sing of my love.

Love of a far-off land,
For you my whole heart is aching,
And I can find no relief
Unless I hear your call
To a sweet meeting of love
In an orchard, or behind a curtain,
With a beloved companion.

Since always this chance is denied me,
I do not wonder that I consume myself,
For never, as God wills,

Was there seen a lovelier woman,
Christian, Jewess, or Saracen,
And the man is fed with manna
Who with aught of her love is rewarded.

The desire of my heart ever tends
Toward her whom most I love,
And I think that my wish abuses me
When by its vehemence it deprives me of her;
For more poignant than a thorn
Is the pain that only joy can cure,
And for that I ask no man's sympathy.

Without brevet of parchment
I send this song that we sing
In plain roman language
By Filhol to Don Hugo Brun:
It is good to hear that the people of Poitou,
Of Berry, and of Guyenne
Rejoice because of him, and those of Brittany.

MAURICE VALENCY

When Days Grow Long in May
Lanquan li jorn son lonc en may

When days grow long in May
I like to hear the birds sing far away
And when I leave or stray
I bring to mind a loved one far away:
Then I'm gloomy, pensive, and dismayed
And then no song of birds or hawthorn spray
Can please me more than winter's frozen gray.

Indeed I deem the lord is true
Through whom I'll view my loved one far away;
And for one good that forces me to rue

I have two evils, for she's too far away.
Ah, were I to tread the pilgrim's way
Then I'd go with bell and cape
To have her lovely pupils meet my gaze.

What joy I'll have when first I say
For love of God, lodge one from far away:
And, if she please, I'll lodge and stay
Near to her, though now I'm far away:
Then sweet converse will hold sway
When her distant lover stays
So close, and speaks his praise!

Sad and joyous, I'll slip from view
If e'er I see her, my love from far away:
But when I'll see her, I've no cue
For our two lands are far away:
As roads and byways wander,
About it all I say:
God's will be done, and praised!

Ne'er in love can I be gay
If I don't gain my love from far away,
For nobler or better holds no sway
In any place, though near or far away;
So true in merit and in grace
That I would go to Arrabace
And be their captive, if she called!

May God who made all walking, creeping things
And formed this love from far away
Give me power, for my heart stings
To see my love from far away.
Truly, when dwelling in that place
My mind makes room and garden
A palace to my gaze!

He speaks true who calls me wilful
Seeking love from far away:

For no happiness so thrills me
As joy in love from far away
But what I long for most, denies me
For I bear a godsire's curse
Who made me love though loveless in return.
But what I long for most, denies me,
So I curse the wicked godsire
Who made me love though loveless in return!

WILLIAM M. DAVIS

He Has Not Sung Who's Made No Sound

No sap chantar qui so non di

He has not sung who's made no sound,
nor with no words, a verse begun;
he cannot rhyme who can't expound
the rules with which it must be done.
For my songs—the more you hear them,
the more, indeed, you will revere them.

I have not lost my senses clean
to love one I shall not behold:
except for her I've never seen,
my heart no joy of love can hold.
No pleasures now can make me smile,
and I cannot hope for help meanwhile.

I die of wounds from blows of bliss,
while stings of love, which dry the flesh,
my health and all my strength dismiss,
and nothing makes my spirits fresh.
I never knew such misery,
for it is not right and should not be.

I never slept with so much ease,
my soul and body far apart,

and my great grief beyond the seas,
because I lay without my heart.
But in the morning when I waken,
by all my peace am I forsaken.

I'll never hold her in embrace
and she will have no joy of me;
I'll not be blessed with her good grace
or promised that I yet may be.
She tells me nothing false nor true,
and both, I think, she will not do.

My song is good, without mistake:
each word is in its proper place.
My messenger will dare not break
it up or any lines deface,
so Bertran and the Count Toulouse
may hear it sung without abuse.

My song is good and soon will bring
delight to those who like to sing.

HARVEY BIRENBAUM

BERNART DE VENTADORN

Friend Bernard de Ventadorn

Amics Bernartz de Ventadorn

Friend Bernard de Ventadorn,
Why have you stopped singing
When the nightingale's cry rings
From day to night to morn?
Listen to his happy refrain!
All-night song, with flowers too.
He knows more about love than you.

Peter, I'd rather sleep and rest
Than listen to a nightingale.

Certainly *you'll* never rail
Me back to love's foolishness.
Thank God I escaped those chains!
Though you and other fine men who love
Carry on like turtledoves.

Bernard, it's neither kind nor right
For a man to lose love's grip.
Forget about your hardships.
Love, more than any other delight,
Compensates for its pains.
No good comes without some sorrow.
Today's tears dry joyously tomorrow.

Peter, if I'd the world two years or three
To do with exactly as I please,
This is how I'd treat the ladies:
No man would ever grovel on his knees,
And women would be so pained
They'd perform all love's tasks,
Throwing us what we want—unasked.

Bernard, how could you be so cruel
To make them beg? Better a man
Plead or clamor for what he can.
Why, I believe that any fool
Who seeds a sandy plain
Is better than some lady-hater
Dumbly following the wrong *cher maître.*

Peter, my heart beats sadly
When I think how a woman's lies
Killed me. She'd no reason why,
For I never loved her badly.
A love-fast I've maintained,
Knowing that if I still don't eat,
None of this pain will retreat.

Bernard, you're folly's slave,
For the love you painstakingly flee
Fathers all worth and integrity.

Peter, a man who loves is depraved,
For the sweet cheats have conspired to destroy
All worth and integrity and joy.

JAMES J. WILHELM

When I See the Skylark Winging

Can vei la lauzeta mover

When I see the skylark winging
Joyfully toward the sun, how
Her heart filled with tender feelings
She freely, easily glides
Ah! I overflow with envy
For all those who are joyous!
How I marvel that my heart
Does not forthwith burst with longing.

Alas! I who thought I knew love
Barely do know love at all!
For I cannot keep from loving
One whose gifts I'll never share;
She has stolen from me my self
My heart, and my whole world;
When she smote me thus she left
But my longing and desire.

No longer was I my own master
Nor from that time ever free
Since she granted me a glance
From her eyes that mirrored joy.
Glass, since I saw my reflection
My heart's deep sighs left me dying,
For I have lost myself as once
Fair Narcissus in the fountain.

Women bring to me despair;
Nevermore will I trust them;

As much as I used to adore them
Nor will I abhor them
For no one will ever save me
From her who confounds me and slays me;
All fill me with doubt and with fear,
For well I know that thus they are.

In this my lady proves to be
True woman, so I tell this tale;
She does not wish what she should want
And does what is forbidden her.
I have fallen into disfavor,
Behaved like a fool on a bridge,
And know not why this befell me.
Perhaps the prize was too lofty.

DAISY ALDAN

Fair Now to Behold the Outgreening

Can l'erba fresch'e'lh folha par

Fair now to behold the outgreening
Of woodland fresh and green
With tender branches outleaving
While the nightingale under the leaf
Pours forth his longing and grief;
Yet might I find joy in grieving
If she were at one with my willing
Who knows my heart and my will.

Heart is hers although she be prideful
To one who ne'er showed her pride;
She must know I am hers for the taking
Whom I would so lovingly take;
All else I will gladly forsake
So I be by her unforsaken,
And my heart is hers for the holding
If only her love I may hold.

I hold to her love that binds me;
Aye, cruelly love's fetters bind;
For she is wont to accuse me
Whereof she does ill to accuse;
She errs but I freely excuse;
How could I forbear from excusing
When she is so fair and so kindly
That even her wounding is kind?

Sweet wounds yet not easy of healing
Though hers is the power to heal:
Let her lend me her lips for the sharing
Of the draught my soul would share—
Alas, this were too much to dare
And she chides me for overdaring,
When I would go thus discoursing,
And bids my verse alter its course.

Verse then must needs go veering
But from her I shall never veer
For my heart is fixed and desirous
Of her, past all other desire
And for her love alone I sigh
While she, a stranger to sighing,
Proves that my death I am seeking
When her beautiful face I seek.

Death must come of it and not joy
Since I may not hope for enjoyment
Yet my hope is that service painful
May with love's help solace my pain.

THOMAS G. BERGIN

It Is Worthless to Write a Line

Chantars no pot gaire valer

It is worthless to write a line
if the song proceed not from the heart:

nor can the song come from the heart
if there is no love in it.

Maligning fools, failing all else, brag,
but love does not spoil,
but countered by love, fills,
fulfilling grows firm.
A fool's love is like verse poor in the making,
only appearance and the name having,
for it loves nothing except itself, can
take nothing of good,
corrupts the rhyme.

And their singing is not worth a dime
whose song comes not from the heart.
If love has not set his roots there
the song cannot put forth shoots there: so
my song is superior, for I turn to it
mouth eyes mind heart
and there is the joy of love in it.
And the binding glance is food for it
and the barter of sighs is food for it
and if desire is not equal between them
there is no good in it.

God grants me no strictness to counter my desire
yet I wonder if we afford its acceptance,
responsible for what we have of it. Though
each day goes badly for me.
Fine thought at least will I have from it
though no other thing:
for I have not a good heart and I work at it,
a man with nothing.

Yet she has made me rich, a man with nothing.
Beautiful she is and comely, and the more
I see her openness and fresh body, the more
I need her and have smarting.
Yet so seldom her fine eyes look on me

one day must last me a hundred.
Yet her fine body—
when I gaze on it, I
grow like a canso, perfect.
And, if desire is equal between us
and the darkness enters my throat?

PAUL BLACKBURN

RAIMBAUT D'AURENGA

Full Well I Know How to Speak of Love

Assatz sai d'amor ben parlar

Full well I know how to speak of love
For the good of other lovers,
But for my own good, which means more to me,
I can find no word to say.
For neither presents nor praise,
Nor curses nor hard words avail me,
Yet I am true to love,
Sincere and frank and loyal,

So I shall teach the art of love
To other good lovers of women,
And if they follow my instructions,
I shall make them conquer in a trice
As many hearts as they desire—
And let him go hang or burn
Who believes not what I say,
For all honor shall come to those
Who hold the key to this art.

If you wish to win women,
And when you want them to do you honor
They give you a discourteous answer,
Turn at once to menaces,
And if that does not improve their manners,

Land them a fist across the nose.
If they are rude with you, be rude—
Through sheer brutality you will gain peace.

And now I shall show you further
How to conquer the most difficult—
Make bad verses and sing them yourself
As badly as you can, with much self-vaunting;
Honor the worst of them the most,
And make them for their faults equal to the best;
And see that your houses
Seem neither like churches nor ships.

In this way you will gain your desire, I think,
But I shall behave very differently,
For I care nothing for women's love,
And I shall never change my ways
On their account, any more than if they were all my sisters,
Therefore I shall ever be true and loving to them,
Humble, simple, and loyal,
Sweet, tender, sincere and faithful.

But be sure to keep away from this,
For what I do is purest folly,
Do not do what seems sheer madness,
But cherish my teaching carefully
If you desire not to suffer pain,
Grief and long weeping:
For I too would be cruel and contrary with them
If their houses pleased me more.

But I have certainly the right to mock them,
Since I—and it is a great dishonor to me—
Love none, nor even know what love is.
Only my ring I love, which keeps me pure,
For it was on the finger—now, voice, you go too far!
Tongue: no more! For too much talk
Does more harm than mortal sin,
Wherefore I shall keep my heart locked up.

But my Bel-Jongleur will easily know,
For it is of such worth and is so dear to me,
That no harm will ever come to me from it.
And she will have my song, which now I end,
At Rodez, where I was born.

MAURICE VALENCY

⚜

My Lords, I Pray You Now, Give Ear

Escotatz, mas no say que s'es

My lords, I pray you now, give ear,
Though I don't know and cannot guess
What sort of thing I've started here—
Vers, estribot, or *sirventès,*
It's none of these; it has no peer,
Nor any ending, I confess,
Save such an one as never yet was used by man or woman of this age or of
the other that has ended.

You'll think me mad if I express
This strange desire but, never fear,
I shall conclude it none the less:
I value what I see and hear,
And all the rest is foolishness—
It isn't worth a sou, that's clear,
And I shall tell you why: Because once I began this thing for you, if I
didn't bring it to an end, you would take me for an idiot. And I'd
rather have a sixpence in my fist than a thousand pounds in the sky.

Fear not to do what may distress
Me, friend, but be sincere,
And if this day you're powerless
To help, help me another year.

For none will cheat me, so I guess,
As she has whom I hold most dear:
All this I say because of a lady who makes me languish with fine words
and long delays, I really don't know why. Can she be good for me, my masters?

A good four months have passed—Oh yes,
To me each moment seems a year—
Since first, in all her loveliness,
She told me what I wished to hear.
Since all my heart you now possess,
Ah, lady whom I most revere,
Why not make sweet my bitterness?
God, help me! *In nomine patris et filii et spiritus sancti!* Lady, how is it to be?

You make me gay in my distress:
Small wonder that my song is queer.
And from those three, quite pitiless,
You sever me, whose only peer
You are. So strongly you possess
Me that a *jongleur* I appear:
Lady, you may do as you like about it, as Lady Ayma did with the shoulder
which she stuck wherever it pleased her.

My what-you-call-it's done, I guess;
No other name will do, that's clear—
No other poet or poetess
Has ever written aught so queer—
And may he sing it with success
Who likes to learn this sort of gear,
And if anyone should ask him who made it, he may say that it was one who
can do whatever he wishes, once he puts his mind to it.

MAURICE VALENCY

BEATRITZ DE DIA

I Dwell in Deep Anxiety

Estat ai en greu cossirier

I dwell in deep anxiety
for a knight who gave himself to me;
it would have done him ease to see
I loved him clear to piety.
I know now I myself deceived
when I did not give myself to him
and now indeed my days are dim:
my grief will not be soon relieved.

I wish my knight might share my bed
and hold me naked in his arms,
that now he might win joys for harms,
with me the pillow for his head.
I am more enamoured of this man
than any famous lovers cast apart.
I make him master of my love and heart,
my senses, life and all I can.

My good and goodly well-loved friend,
when will I hold you in my power?
That I might lie with you one hour
and kiss you 'til my life would end!
How I feel the lovers' fire
to hold you in my husband's place,
if only you would swear with grace
to do whatever I desire.

HARVEY BIRENBAUM

RAIMBAUT DE VAQUEIRAS

Watchman on the Tower, Watch with Care

Gaita ben, gaiteta del chastel

Watchman on the tower, watch with care,
For she who is my truest and most fair
Lies with me till the dawn.
The day approaches, uninvited,
And the new joy in which I have delighted
Is stolen by the dawn, yes, the dawn.

Watch us well; do not forget to warn
My dearest love and me, when it is morn.
How I resent the dawn!
And when the sun has risen high,
I curse the day that made me bid goodbye
More keenly than at dawn, yes, the dawn.

Watchman on the tower, do not tire.
Preserve us from my lady's jealous sire,
More dreadful than the dawn;
Keep him from us while we sigh
Of love's sweet tenderness, for she and I
Are fearful of the dawn, yes, the dawn.

God above! No longer may I stay;
Despite myself I must be on my way.
I cannot face the dawn
Whom I see rising at his leisure.
For none delights at cheating lovers' pleasure
More than perfidious dawn, yes, the dawn.

NORMAN R. SHAPIRO

⚜

High Waves That Ride the Sea

Altas undas que venez suz la mar

High waves that ride the sea
That makes the wind shift to and fro
Do you bring me news how my lover
Passed you by? I don't see him return.
And oh, God of love,
Now he gives me joy and now it's pain.

Oh sweet breeze that rides from where
My lover dwells and sleeps and fares,
Bring me a wisp of his sweet breath:
My mouth I open, great desire have I,
And oh, God of love,
Now he gives me joy and now it's pain.

Bad love comes from foreign soldiers
Turning bliss and smiles to tears;
I never thought mine would desert me
For I gave him all in love he wished,
And oh, God of love,
Now he gives me joy and now it's pain.

WILLIAM M. DAVIS

GIRAUT DE BORNELH

Heavenly King, Glorious God of Light

Reis glorios, verais lums e clartatz

"Heavenly King, glorious God of light,
Look down with kindly favor, if you will,
Upon my friend who, with his lady, still
Reposes. There has he been all the night,
And soon it will be dawn.

"Good friend, if you are sleeping or awake,
Gently arise and sleep no more. Afar,
The East is brightened by the morning-star,
Bringing the day, unless I much mistake;
And soon it will be dawn.

"Good friend, I sing to you this eager warning;
I fear your lady's lord will soon appear.
Already in the forest I can hear
A song-bird's love-call to his mistress morning,
And soon it will be dawn.

"Good friend, look out and let the signs of day—
The fading stars—prove I have not been lying.
Heed to my word, the night is quickly dying,
For yours will be the grief if you delay
And soon it will be dawn.

"Good friend, since first you left to undertake
Your amorous night, I have not slept, but stay
Upon my knees, and reverently pray
Our Lord protect you for my friendship's sake;
And soon it will be dawn.

"Good friend, why did you earnestly implore me,
Upon the terrace, not to yield to sleeping?
Throughout this night gladly have I been keeping
A faithful watch. Why do you now ignore me?
And soon it will be dawn.

"Good friend and true, now taste I such delight
That nevermore wish I to see the morn.
The fairest creature e'er of mother born
Lies in my arms. Thus care I not a mite
For jealous sire nor dawn."

NORMAN R. SHAPIRO

PEIRE VIDAL

When I Breathe This Air

Ab l'alen tir vas me l'aire

When I breathe this air,
It is the scent of Provence that I bring to my nostrils:
All that comes from there delights me,
And when I hear good things said of it,
I stop and smile with pleasure,
And for each word I ask a hundred,
Such pleasure it gives me to hear of it.

For there is no land more lovely
Than the land which stretches from Vence to the Rhone,
Whose borders are washed by the Durance and the sea,
Nor is there any land which sparkles with such true joy.
And that is why I have left my heart to rejoice
Among those joyful people,
With her who brings laughter even to the afflicted.

For no one can be sad on the day
When her face comes to his mind,
And in her alone joy is born and has its beginning.
And whoever speaks of her worth,
No matter how high his praise, he does not lie,
For without doubt, she is the best
And most beautiful of all who live on this earth.

And if I am able to say or do anything well,
It is thanks to her, for it was she
Who gave me the knowledge and the understanding
That makes me a poet of love.
And when I consider carefully,

Whatever I do that is beautiful
Is but a reflection of her charm and her beauty.

MAURICE VALENCY

⚜

My Lord Dragoman, If I Had a Good Steed

Dragoman senher, s'agues bon destrier

My lord Dragoman, if I had a good steed
My enemies would be in a desperate plight,
For the instant they hear me mentioned
They fear me worse than the quail the hawk,
And they value their lives at not a denier
So proud and savage and fierce they know me.

When I lace up my strong double hauberk
And buckle on the brand that Don Guy just gave me,
The earth trembles where I tread,
And there is no enemy so haughty
Who does not at once clear the way for me,
So much they fear me when they hear my step.

In courage I equal Roland and Oliver
And in courtesy Bérard de Montdidier,
And my prowess is such and I have such praise
That often messengers come to me
With a gold ring, with a black and white cordon,
With greetings such that they fill my heart with joy.

In all things I show myself a knight,
And so I am, and know all the mastery of love,
And all that belongs to courtship,
For never in a chamber have you seen such a delightful man,
Nor with arms in his hand one so terrible and fierce,
Wherefore those love me and fear me who have never seen me
nor heard me speak.

And if I had a good courser,
Tranquil the King should lie beyond Balaguer,
And he should sleep long and sweetly,
For I would keep the peace at Montpellier and in Provence
So that neither brigands nor savage riders
Should waste his lands at Autavès nor Crau.

And if the King comes to the gates of Toulouse along the river sands,
And the Count issues forth with his wretched archers
Who all day long shout "Aspa!" and "Orsau!"
I dare boast that I shall strike the first,
And I will do so much that they will run back in twice as many as they came out,
And I with them, unless they shut the gates against me.

And if I come upon a Jealous One or a *lauzenjador*,
Those who with false tales seek to ruin those better than themselves,
And in every way lessen the joy of life,
In truth they shall see what blows I strike,
For even if they have bodies of steel and iron,
It will avail them no more than a peacock's feather.

Lady Vierna, Mercy of Montpellier,
Don Rainier, now you shall love your knight;
And since through you my joy has grown, I praise God.

MAURICE VALENCY

Well Pleased Am I with the Gentle Season

Be m'agrada la convinens sazos

Well pleased am I with the gentle season,
And pleased with the glorious summertime
And pleased with all sweetly singing birds,
And pleased with the flowerets in thickets,

And with all which delights the gentle people,
And pleasant above all, all noble talk:
Soon will good fortune grant me enjoyment,
Where I willingly lay my heart and soul

For love keeps me joyful and delighted,
Love cradles me in her tender embrace,
Love renders me both brave and valiant,
For love am I pensive and reflective;
For love am I so strongly enamored
That all my desires are fashioned of love,
For love I admire courtesy and youth,
Love dictates all my deeds, all my words.

Joyful, fair lady, when I think on you,
Joyful am I under your dominion,
Joyful with your noble virtues praised,
Joyful with your handsome bearing.
Joyful to behold your perfect beauty
And joyful when I am wholly your slave,
Joyful that my thoughts are only of you
And joyful that I love no one but you.

May God protect you, fair and noble one,
But damn the vicious and the envious,
God protect me, whom you have made humble,
But confound the slanderous and jealous.
God save the valiant, courteous, esteemed,
But confound the wicked and importunate,
May God save all who love with perfect love,
But confound all the allies of ennui.

Fair dame, I long to see you again,
Fair dame, that I can think on nothing else,
Fair dame, you can make me feel so wretched,
And it please you, richer than King Alfonse.
Noble lady, you hold me so in thrall,
Lady, that all will has forsaken me;

Oh bear these feelings gently if you please,
And thus, Oh fairest dame, please pity me.

With you is love's sovereign and perfect joy,
Joy which revives all good and gracious things,
No other joy can equal the delight,
Of your joy which makes all the world joyous.
Near you is joy born, from you radiates,
It is joy which rejuvenates the world,
And I am filled with great joy to recall
The joy of you and your beautiful self.

DAISY ALDAN

I Put an End to Singing
De chantar m'era laissatz

I put an end to singing
Out of my grief and sadness
My lord, the count, bequeathed,
But since the king desires it
I'll quickly make a song
For William and Sir Blascol
To take to Aragon
If they deem the music worthy.

And if I sing like one obliged
Because my lord desires it
Don't despise my song
For my heart has turned away
From her who won't reward me
And robs me of my hope:
And how the parting hurts me
God alone can know.

I've been tricked and duped
The way good servants are

For I am thought a fool
—An honor, I suppose—
And similar reward
I wait, for if I'm hers
Then I'll count myself
More lowly than a Jew.

I gave myself to one
Who lives on joy and love
On merit and great valor
Whence beauty is refined
Like gold, in searing flame:
For it seems the world is mine
And kings hold fiefs from me.

I'm crowned by perfect joy
Above all emperors
For I love a viscount's daughter
So much, that just a ribbon
My lady might bestow,
I'd count as worlds more precious
Than King Richard would three towns.

And though some call me wolf
I don't feel it's a slur
Nor if the shepherds hunt me
Or chase me with their shouts;
For I'll take woods or bushes
To palace or to home
And joyously I'll meet her
Mid ice or wind or snow.

The She-Wolf says I'm hers
And has good grounds and cause
For, on my faith, I'm hers
More than others' or my own.
Fair Sambelin, for you
I love Saut and Uisson
And Alion, as well,

But gazed on you so briefly
That now I'm sad and grieved.

WILLIAM M. DAVIS

It'll Be a Long Time Again before My Friends

Tart mi vieran mei amic en Tolosa

It'll be a long time again before my friends
In Toulouse see me, and long also
Before I see Montreal or Puy,
For I'm staying here with en Barral,
Mon Bel Rainier: here's ambience
And security.
But Loba!
Because my eyes
Cannot contain you in their compassing,
They are blurred and wet—my heart
Sighs after you, remembering
The slender body on you,
The soft stroke of your voice,
A smile
Your face wore once—

Your name is such the best are envious, and
You can afford to let their bitchery run.
Your welcomes are so greatly prized, men come
Only to hear and see. Beauty's dress
Is your soft speech and youth, your insolent
Vigor, and your balanced mind.

Na Raimbauda, at Biolh I'm fixing to
Take a garden and a house for hire.
To be near
Her I most desire. Among
Such mountains, who can recall the plain?
Lady, lovely lady, how I love you! Life

's nothing without you, death more than life.
May clemency and mercy come upon you,
For my heart's in you, and all my desire.

Lady, when I was within your hall,
It seemed St. Julian must have been my host.
God never made such a perfect day
As you formed of that day with your hand.
In your making He made no mistake;
Such arms were cast only to kill me, sure.
I trust your excellence is too good a thing,
But even if you killed me,
It'd be my honor,
And if I died,
I could only die praising, and rejoicing.

PAUL BLACKBURN

BERTRAN DE BORN

I Have Made a Sirventes in Which No Word Is Missing

Un sirventes cui motz no falh

Bertran de Born, as I have said to you in other razos, had a brother who was called Constantine de Born, who was a good knight-at-arms, but not a man to concern himself overmuch with honor and valor. Indeed, he always hated Bertran and loved all those who wished en Bertran ill. Once he seized the castle of Altafort, which belonged to them both in common, and en Bertran recovered it, likewise by force of arms, and chased him out.

Then Constantine went to the viscount of Limoges and asked that he be upheld against his brother. And he upheld him. King Richard also upheld him against en Bertran. Now Richard was, at that time, warring with Aimar, the viscount of Limoges. But Richard and Aimar turned their wars against Bertran, ravaging and burning his fields.

Bertran had made swear together the viscount of Limoges

with the count of Périgord who was called Talairan from whom Richard had taken the city of Périgord without having put himself in any danger since Talairan was soft and lazy. Richard had also seized Gourdon from Guilhem de Gourdon, who had promised to swear with the viscount and with Bertran de Born and other barons of Périgord, Limousin, and Quercy; all of whom Richard had despoiled, for which reason Bertran blamed him exceedingly; and for all these reasons (razos), made the sirventes:

I have made a sirventes in which no word is missing
and it never cost me a garlic.
And I have learned such cunning, that if I have
a brother, say,
or a cousin
or a second cousin,
I'll split the last egg and the half-denier.
But then if he wants my portion
I'll run him out of the county!

I hold my wits under lock and key these days,
they've gotten me into such scrapes with both
Aimar and Richard.
For a long while those two have kept me worried,
but now,
they've got such a scrap going between them that
if the king doesn't separate them,
they'll have the profit from it—
each with a knife in his guts.

William of Gourdon, you've put a hard
clapper in your bell
and I must say
you ring it hard, which is crazy.
But God keep me, I am fond of you.
And the two viscounts hold you a fool
and laughing-stock
on account of the treaty: yet they long
you were in their brotherhood.

Day long I dispute and contend with myself,
defend and attack and struggle within:
while men destroy
my lands and my stratagems
make deserts of my orchards,
mixing
the grain with straw.
There is neither bold enemy nor cowardly foe of mine
who does not assault me.

Day long I re-sole and re-shape the barons,
recast and unite them,
thinking to get them into the field.
I'm a fool to bother with 'em—
badly made, the most meager workmanship,
as split as the chain of Saint Leonard—
a man would be mad to concern himself.
Talairan does not leap nor trot
nor stirs him out of his district.
He hurls neither lance nor dart
and lives the life of a Lombard.
He is so stuffed with sloth that
when alliances break up
he yawns, and stretches himself.

At Périgord, near to the wall,
close enough for a man to throw a mace,
astride Bayart, I shall come
armed.
And if I find fat Poitevins, they
shall see how my steel cuts!
brains mixed with armor, a red mud smearing their heads!

God save you and keep you baron,
and aid you and prosper you.
May it be granted you tell Richard
what the peacock tells the jackdaw.

PAUL BLACKBURN

⚜

If All the Grief and Sorrow, the Strife

Si tuit li dol e'lh plor e'lh marrimen

If all the grief and sorrow, the strife,
The suffering, the pains, the many ills
That men heard tell of in this woeful life
Assembled, they would count as nil
Compared to the death of the young English king
Who leaves behind youth and worth in tears
In this dark world beset with shadowy fears,
Lacking all joy, abounding in doleful spite.

Grievous and sad, sensing the bitter wrong,
Stand his noble soldiers, left behind;
His troubadours, his jongleurs sing no song,
For death's bereft the warrior from mankind.
Still they salute their young English king,
Who makes the generous seem steeped in greed.
He never did, nor will he now, take heed
To repay this wicked world its tearful spite.

O boundless death, abounding yet in pain,
Brag, brag that you've got the finest cavalier
Who ever stalked upon this broad terrain,
Who, needing nothing, never knew his peer,
For peer there never was to that English king.
God, it's more just, if ever you would grant:
Let *him* live, instead of all those tyrants
Who never pay with worth—just doleful spite.

Since love now flees this jaded age, down-weighed
By grief, I consider all its joys a lie,
For nothing lasts that doesn't soon decay,
The way tomorrow feels today slip by.
Let everyone admire the young English king!
Who in all the world of valiant men was best
And bore his noble body lovingest:
He's gone. What's left? Grief, discord, spite.

You, who desired to enter all this pain,
To rid our world of its many waiting snares,
To suffer death that we might live again—
We cry out in your just and humble name:
Show mercy upon our young English king!
Pardon, if pardon pleases, toward this end:
That he may stand among his honored friends
There where grief never goes—nor spite.

JAMES J. WILHELM

⚜

Rassa Rises, Thrives, and Prospers

Rassa, tan creis e monta e poia

Rassa rises, thrives, and prospers,
She's void of all deceit
And her merit troubles others
Though none alone can harm her.
The radiance of her beauty
Wins champions to her cause
(Though some may burn with pain)
The best and those most prudent
E'er maintain her praise
And consider her most gentle,
For her honor, she makes plain,
Allows but one adorer.

Rassa, fine, fresh lady,
Young, spirited, and gay,
Ruby, auburn tresses,
Flesh, white hawthorn spray,
Hard nipples, dimpled elbows,
Her back, hot rabbit swayed;
By her fine, fresh color,
Her merit and her fame,
And easy best they'll deem her
(Those who know and claim)
How madly I adore her.

Rassa, proud before rich lords
Like some young haughty thing
Who won't take Poitou or Tolosa
Or Brittany, or Saragossa,
Is so covetous of merit
She's partial to poor knights,
And since she made me counselor,
I beg you, prize her love,
And may she take a gentle vavassor
To some mocking count or duke
Who'd hold her in dishonor.

Rassa, a stingy lord
Who won't protect, confide, or spend,
Who accuses guiltless men
And, for mercy, won't forgive,
Vexes me, and every person
Who serves without reward.
And rich nobles on the hunt
Vex me, and the buzzards
That boast of falcon flights
(Among themselves, they never
Speak a word of arms or love).

Rassa, here's who you should like:
A rich noble, not tired by war
Who won't retreat when threatened
Or till the battle's won.
Better than hunters of birds or beasts
Who can't win repute or lands
Maurin made war on Sir Aigar, his lord,[1]
And won great fame and valor.
The viscount defended his honor;
The count tried to wrest it by force,
And we'll see him at Easter, full of glory.

Marinier, you're a man of honor,[2]

---

1 *Aigar and Maurin = heroes of a Provençal* chanson de geste.
2 *Marinier = King Henry II*

And we've changed our good
Warlike lord for a jouster
So I beg Golfier de la Tor[3]
Not to let my singing scare him.

Papiol, take my song
To the court of my bad Fair-Lord.[4]

WILLIAM M. DAVIS

⚜

About Two Kings I'll Write Half-a-Poem

Miei sirventes vuolh far dels reis amdos

About two kings I'll write half-a-poem
For shortly we'll see which one has more knights;
Brave Alfonso of the Castilian throne
Is on the look for soldiers, if I hear right.
Richard will let his gold and silver fight
By the bushel and peck; to him's no great fuss
To lavish and spend; who cares about trust?
Why, war's more to him than a quail to a kite!

If both these kings prove strong and hale
Soon we'll see strewn on the grassy plain
Helmets, swords, shields and mail,
And bodies, spear-split from belt to brain,
And stallions running unmounted, unreined,
And many a lance through thigh and chest
With tears and joy, sorrow and happiness.
The loss'll be great; greater still the gain.

Trumpets and drums, banners and flags,
Standards and stallions of every hue
Soon we'll see, as our great age drags
The holdings from every usurious Jew.

---

[3] *Golfier de la Tor = the troubador's nephew*
[4] *Fair-Lord = pseudonym for an unknown woman.*

Down no highway will go no laden mule
Trusting the day, no burgher unaskance,
Nor any merchant heading out from France.
No, he'll be rich who grabs as he chooses.

If Richard comes, I'll put my faith in God:
Either I'll live or lie hacked on the sod.

And if I live, great will be my bliss;
And if I die, thank God for what I'll miss!

JAMES J. WILHELM

I Apologize, My Lady, Though Guiltless

Ieu m'escondisc, domna, que mal no mier

I apologize, my lady, though guiltless
Of what slanderers accuse
And pray no lies or discord
Will move you, faithful, loyal, and true,
Frank and humble, courteous and pleasing,
From me, lady, nor let such things ensue.

May one jess[1] destroy my sparrowhawk
And my lanner be killed in my fist
Torn and plucked before my eyes
If I do not prefer sad thoughts of you
To desire for any other
And love they'd grant, or dalliance in bed.

I plead guiltless, and more deeply
For no crueler loss is borne,
If ever I should fail you, although in thought alone,
When alone with you in bedroom or in orchard
May I be powerless in love
And find I cannot serve.

---

[1] *Jess = wrist thong*

When I sit down to play at tables[2]
May I never win a fig
May I never score a point
And throw snake-eyes evermore
If I have ever courted or pursued
My lady, anyone but you.

May my castle be divided
With four owners to one tower
May they never live in friendship
And always need their bowmen
Doctors, soldiers, gatemen, guards,
If I ever longed to love another lady.

May my lady leave me for another knight
And I never know to whom to turn for help
May the wind grow slack when I put out to sea
And porters beat me up when I'm at court
May I campaign, and be the first to run
If he's not lied, who spread his rotten slander!

With my shield aloft, I'll ride the storm
Wearing hood and helmet backwards,
With reins too short, not made to stretch,
Long stirrups on a low-cut horse
And at the inn, find a taverner:
If he's not lied, who spread his rotten slander!

If I had a high-flying duckhawk
Fine and moulted and tame
And able to seize any prey:
Swans and cranes, and black and silver herons,
Would I trade it for one badly moulted,
A fat, queasy hen that can't fly?

---

[2] *tables = backgammon*

False, envious, perjured slanderers,
Since you perturbed my lady
I'd like it best if you'd just left me alone!

WILLIAM M. DAVIS

Ah How I Like to See Great Power Pass

Bel m'es quan vei chamjar lo senhoratge

Ah how I like to see great power pass
As young men gather in the estates of old
And everyone—with babies by the mass—
Bequeaths hope for a leader brave and bold.
Then I think the age will soon renew
Better than any flower or bird's refrain,
For lords and ladies, knowing they are through,
Allow the young to take up hope again.

You can tell a lady's old by her balding hair.
She's old, I say, when she hasn't any knight,
Or if she takes her lovers by the pair,
Old if she takes a lover full of spite.
Old she is if she loves in her estate
Or if she uses magic as a crutch.
I call her old when jongleurs irritate,
And certainly she's old if she talks too much!

A lady's young when she values noble rank
And likes good deeds whenever good's been done;
I call her young if her heart's fine and frank
And she casts no evil eye on valor won.
She's young if she keeps her body well looked after,
Young if she knows exactly how to behave.
I call her young if gossip brings her laughter
And if she knows how to keep her lover safe.

A man is young if he'll risk his hard-won hoard,
Young if he's ever suffered need or want.

I call him young if he spreads an expensive board
Or if his gifts approach the extravagant.
He's young when he burns all his chests of treasure
And wars and jousts and hunts and rambles.
He's young if he knows every woman's pleasure
And young he is if he yearns to gamble.

A man is old when he's scared to take a dare
And stores away his bacon, wine and wheat.
I call him old if he serves eggs and Bruyère
On days when he and his friends are allowed meat.
He's old if he shivers under a cape—and cloak—
Old if he rides a horse he hasn't tamed,
Old if a day of peace doesn't seem a joke
Or if he runs away from a gory game.

Arnold, jongleur, take my song "Young-Old"
To Richard, let him watch it, see it's sung:
I never cared a damn for gold that's old.
I only prize my treasures when they're young!

JAMES J. WILHELM

I'm Pleased When Gaudy Eastertime

Be'm platz lo gais temps de pascor

I'm pleased when gaudy Eastertime
Makes leaves and flowers sprout
And pleased with all the happiness
Of birds, who make their shout
        Resound throughout the grove
And pleased when on the meadows
I see tents and banners rise
        And much rejoice
When on the plain I see
Armed knights and horses camp.

And I'm pleased when scouts
Make men and treasure flee
And pleased when I see after them
Great armored legions fend
        And I'm pleased within my heart
When strong castles fight a siege
And walls are torn and breached
        And I see the host ashore
Fenced in by palisaded moats
With fierce, close-driven stakes.

And likewise I'm pleased by a lord
Who's first in the attack
And fearless, with armored horse
Makes his vassals bold
        By dint of manly courage
And when the fight's begun
They follow and are brave,
For no man wins his merit
Till he's traded many blows.

With maces, swords, with colored helms
With crippled, broken shields
We'll see the battle start
With many vassals wounded
        Whose horses wander off
From masters cut or dead.
And when he joins the fight
        A man of noble peers
Will only hack at head or arms
For death's preferred to capture.

I assure you, I have less liking
For eating, drink, or bed
Than I have for cries of "At 'em!"
From either side, or neighing
        Empty horses in the shade
Or cries of "Help me! Help!"
When great and small in moats

Or pastures I see fall
With agonizing flanks
Pierced through by jagged shafts.

Barons, pawn away
Your castles, fields, and towns
But never give up war!
Now, Papiol, go quickly
And tell Sir Yes-and-No
We've had too much of peace![1]

WILLIAM M. DAVIS

RICHART DE BERBEZILH

You See Me Like the Elephant

Atressi com l'olifanz

You see me like the elephant,
who, when fallen, cannot rise
'till his companions sound their cries
to lift him with their voices' force
and I must hope for like recourse,
for my offenses are of such extent,
that, if the court with its accoutrement
and loyal lovers with true worth gifted,
will not raise me, I shall not be uplifted,
though they might pity me and beg for mercy
there were prayers nor reason has not yet helped me.

If I cannot my joy acquire
through the help they deign to bring,
I nevermore my songs shall sing,
for songs will no more be of use,
and I shall live a life recluse,
uncomforted, for so shall I desire.
My life is now all agony and fire.

---

[1] *Papiol is a jongleur; Sir Yes-and-No = King Richard the Lion-Hearted.*

For me all joy is grief and faith despair,
and I am sadly nothing like the bear,
who, beaten and treated without mercy,
revives, grows fat and thrives more happily.

Love has power on its side
to pardon what I'm guilty of
if I have sinned by too much love.
Like Simon Magus when he claimed
that he was Christ and stood unshamed,
I too all sense of rightfulness defied.
God humbled his audacity and pride,
but love is that audacity I dared,
so that for mercy's sake I should be spared;
for there are times when justice must rule mercy,
and times when reason means but cruelty.

A sad complaint I must express
against myself and restless prating.
If I could take to imitating
the phoenix bird, which burns to death
and then arises with renewed breath,
then I would burn, for I have such distress
from all my lies and my deceitfulness.
I would arise again in sighs and weeping
there where youth and worth and beauty have their keeping
and where, except for just a little mercy,
dwells every charm and virtue there might be.

I send my song to seek your ears.
I may not come (nor am so bold)
nor with straight eyes your face behold;
I am so humbled and overcome
with no excuse in Christendom.
Better than Woman, whom I fled two years,
I turn to you in misery and tears
as turns the stag, when his strength gives out,
to die at the sound of the huntsman's shout.

Lady, thus I turn and beg your mercy,
but you can know none, if love has left you free.

HARVEY BIRENBAUM

THE MONK OF MONTAUDUN

I Like Gayety and Horsing Around
Molt mi platz deportz e gaieza

I like gayety and horsing around, good
food, fine gifts, good tilting fields:
I like a comely and courteous woman,
one who's not too embarrassed to answer.
And I like a rich and generous man
who keeps his malice for his enemies.

I like a man who calls me affably
and unfastens his purse without having
to be asked first, and a rich man who
doesn't feel it's compulsory to dress me down,
like to hear a man speaking up for me, like
to fall asleep when it's thundering hard
and to eat a fat salmon in mid-afternoon.

And it relaxes me in summer to
stretch out by a brook or fountain when
the meadows are green and the flowers new
and the birds all chirm and twitter: and then
if my girl finds out where I'm holing up
I turn her over and have a quick one.

Bless them who give me a hearty welcome
and don't go scrummaging for excuses.
I enjoy the time I spend with my girl
necking, and more if she wants to make it.
Like to see my enemy lose a good thing
and better if it's me who took it off him.

And good companions please me fine
when I'm surrounded by enemies,
and I hear someone else speak my piece—
and the buggers listened without budging.

PAUL BLACKBURN

I Much Dislike, I Dare Avow It

Fort m'enoia, so auzes dire

I much dislike, I dare avow it,
The man who talks much and does little;
And the man who thinks only of slaughter
I dislike, and the horse who leans on his bit;
And I dislike, may God help me,
The young man who bears too long
A shield that has never felt a blow,
And a bearded monk, and a chaplain,
And the gossip with the filed tongue.

And I hold that woman to be a bore
Who is both poor and haughty,
And the husband who dotes on his wife,
Though she be heiress of Toulouse;
And I dislike the knight
Who is a braggart in a foreign land
But without employment in his own
Save to grind pepper in a mortar,
Or to warm his feet by the fire.

And I dislike profoundly
The coward who bears a proud standard,
And a wretched falcon chasing ducks on a river bank,
And a little meat cooking in a great cauldron;
And I dislike, by Saint Martin,
Much water in a little wine;
And when I meet a cripple on the road,

I dislike him, or a blind man in the morning,
For I take little pleasure in their company.

I dislike the fiddler who takes forever to tune his instrument,
And meat which is cooked till it is tough,
And a priest who lies and swears falsely,
And an aged whore who survives her usefulness,
And I dislike, by Saint Dalmatius,
Men whose lot is above their merit;
And to run on foot when the road is icy
Or to flee on horseback, fully armed,
I much dislike, and to hear people swearing at dice.

And I dislike, by the eternal life,
To dine without a fire in midwinter,
And to stand a vigil when the north wind blows,
And bears to my nose the smells of a tavern;
And it mislikes me to the very heart
When one who washes a chamber pot investigates the contents,
And I dislike it greatly when I see an ugly man
Who has a lovely wife
And who neither offers nor gives me anything.

And I dislike, by Saint Savior,
To hear bad fiddling in a fine court,
And to see too many heirs living on a narrow fief,
And to see a bad lender lucky at dice.
And I dislike, by Saint Marcel,
A double lining in a single gown,
And too many masters in one castle,
And a rich man who has little joy,
And in a tournament when they use darts and quarrels.

And I dislike, so help me God,
To see a long table with a short table cloth,
And one who carves meat with scabby hands,
And a heavy hauberk of untrustworthy mail,
And I dislike waiting in a seaport
When the weather is bad and it rains hard,

And to see friends quarrel,
I dislike it, and worse than death
When I know it is all about nothing.

And I will tell you what annoys me greatly:
An old hen who struts about overdressed,
Giving offense to poor wenches,
And a young squire admiring his own legs;
And I dislike, by Saint Aon,
A broad woman with a narrow cleft,
And a bad lord who shaves his serfs too closely:
But in all the world I dislike nothing more
Than to be sleepy when I cannot sleep.

And there is another thing that I dislike:
To ride in the rain without a mantle,
And when I find a sow next to my horse
Emptying his manger for him,
And I am annoyed out of all measure
By a saddle with a shaky tree,
And a buckle without a prong,
And a man who is mean in his own house,
Who does nothing but make himself unpleasant.

MAURICE VALENCY

PEIROL AND DALFIN D'ALVERNHE

Dalfin, a Target for Your Bow

Dalfi, sabriatz me vos

"Dalfin, a target for your bow:
Granted a lover fair and true
Whose lady's wise and gentle too;
Can you decide and fairly show
If he loves more
After he's had her or before?

Master, disclose to me your thought:
I know in love's lore you're well taught."

"Peirol, I'll give you swift reply:
    I know as each true lover knows
    That love with sweet possession grows;
Here is a truth none may deny;
            And it is right
That sharing love be love's delight;
Indeed love must the act await
Before it can grow strong and great."

"Dalfin, this only I know well:
    A lover's longing has no end
    Until he lies with his sweet friend;
Her favors his dark fears dispel
            But after—then,
Such is the law of love with men,
Desire accomplished, slaked at last,
The finest hour of love is past."

"Nay, nay, Peirol, mark you well this:
    A lover grows more ardent still
    And fixed more firmly in his will
With the fruition of love's bliss,
            For after joy
Love is a man, no more a boy;
Bethink you of Lord Tristram dead
With Iseult's love ne'er surfeited."

"Dalfin, I hold Tristram's desire
    Was born of Brangwain's poisoned drink,
    That magic potion was, I think,
His passion's sources, not love's true fire.
            I'll be much blamed,
I know, by lovers who feel shamed
By what I say in this debate
But my opinions I must state."

"Peirol, let's end our argument.
You cannot doubt you're in the wrong
Since in the burden of your song
Defense of falsehood's evident.
I'll not concede
That playing on a lover's need
Is like to whet his amorous thirst;
Nay rather, love will weary first."

"Dalfin, this far
I'll yield to you: if love's gifts are
A check to love, the lover wise
Will surely such effect disguise."

"Peirol, so well
I know your story I can tell
You but reveal your own false heart
In here defending the worse part."

THOMAS G. BERGIN

GUILHEM DE CABESTANH

The Sweet Softness with Which Love Serves Me Often

Lo dous cossire que'm don' amors soven

The sweet softness with which love serves me often
Makes me write much vers of you, my lady.
I gaze imagining on your bright body,
Desiring it more than I can let you know.
Although I seem to swerve and stand aside
It is for your sake, not to deny one whit
That I supple and bend toward you in all love's ways.
Too often, lady, I forget, and so
Implore mercy and am forced to praise
When beauty finds itself mere ornament.

May the love you deny me hate me always
If my heart ever turns to love another.
Yet you've left me sadness, taken all my laughter,
Stiffer suffering than I, no man can say
He's felt, for, you, whom I most want
Of anything on earth, I have to
Disavow, deny, pretend
I've fallen out of love, and all
For fear,
Which you must take wholly on good faith,
Even those days when I do not see you.

Your face and smile I keep in memory's place,
Your valor, your body smooth and white.
If my Faith were as faithful as that image there,
I'd walk living into Paradise.
I am rendered so utterly
Yours, without reservation,
That not one who wears ribbon
Could bring me any joy,
Nor I prize the compensation
Even if she made me lover
And had me sleeping with her,
Taken against your simple straightest greeting.

The charm of how you are gives me such joy
That my desire pleasures me every day.
Now totally and in full you mistress me,
How overmastered I am, I can scarce say,
But even before I saw you
I'd determine to serve and love you.
And so I have remained,
Alone and without aid
At your side: and lost by
Doing so many gifts.
Let who desires them have them.
I'd rather wait for you, even
With no understanding between us,
For my joy can come from you alone.

May mercy and love descend upon you, lady,
Before the sickness inflames,
May joy burn us, tears and sighs banished,
May neither rank nor riches separate us.
All good's forgot
If I do not obtain
Some mercy, beautiful thing.
It would give some relief at least
If you answered what I've asked.
Either love me, or not at all, for now
I don't know how it is.

Because I find no defense against your valor,
May you have pity, so it end in honor.
May God never hear prayer of mine if I
Would take the rents of the four richest kings there are,
Put together,
Against the chance of finding mercy with you.
For I cannot
Stir one jot
Away from you where my love is set.
And if you found you could
Accept it
With a kiss
I'd never want to be dissolved from this.

Frank and courteous lady,
Come hell or high water,
Anything that pleased you
No matter how forbid,
I would set me to it.

Ray, the good and beauty
Residing in my fair lady
Has enlaced me softly
Taken me completely.
How can I deny it?

PAUL BLACKBURN

GAUCELM FAIDIT

A Knight Was with His Lady Fondly Lying

Us cavaliers si iazia

A knight was with his lady fondly lying—
The one he cherished most—and gently sighing
As he kissed her, complained: My love, the day
Soon will arrive, chasing this night away.
Alas!
Already I can hear the watchman crying:
Begone!
Quickly, begone! You may no longer stay,
For it is dawn.

My love, if there were but some wile or way
To banish hostile morn and prying day—
At least from where we two are fondly lying—
Then filled with thanks would be my gentle sighing.
Alas!
Already I can hear the watchman crying:
Begone!
Quickly, begone! You may no longer stay,
For it is dawn.

My love, I know that he is surely lying
Who tells you there is any sadder sighing
Than of two lovers who bemoan the day
That comes too soon to chase their night away.
Alas!
Already I can hear the watchman crying:
Begone!
Quickly, begone! You may no longer stay,
For it is dawn.

My love, forget me never, for today—
Although I now must rise and go my way—

I leave my heart there, where we two were lying,
To pledge unending love in endless sighing.
Alas!
Already I can hear the watchman crying:
Begone!
Quickly, begone! You may no longer stay,
For it is dawn.

My love, if you were not close by me lying,
Then death would echo in my doleful sighing.
I will return. So does my torment weigh,
That without you I cannot live the day.
Alas!
Already I can hear the watchman crying:
Begone!
Quickly, begone! You may no longer stay,
For it is dawn.

NORMAN R. SHAPIRO

UC DE LA BACALARIA

To Praise the Gift of Love That Binds My Heart

Per grazir la bona estrena

To praise the gift of love that binds my heart,
And to appease its pain, I wish to write
An "alba" of a different sort. The night
Is clear and calm; a songbird's supple art
Echoes my plight.
God! bring the day and let a lover's sorrow
Fade with the morrow.

By all the Holy books, gladly I swear
That Tristan, Flore, and all their amorous kin
Were not so true to love as I have been.
Let her but start to speak and I am there
Ere she begin.

God! bring the day and let a lover's sorrow
Fade with the morrow.

I shall not trust the fools who think that I
Should leave my love; I know there is no flight.
She wounds my heart; I cannot sleep the night.
Were I afar, I should return to die
Within her sight.
God! bring the day and let a lover's sorrow
Fade with the morrow.

To trap a bear or leopard I possess
The art; or to besiege a fort, the might.
With Love my foe, however, I am quite
Unskilled, and wish to be more powerless
In such a fight.
God! bring the day and let a lover's sorrow
Fade with the morrow.

NORMAN R. SHAPIRO

GAUCELM FAIDIT, UC DE LA BACALARIA AND SAVARIC DE MAULEON

A Debate
Partimens

SAVARIC DE MAULEON:

Gaucelm, three plays of love
I'll divide with you and Hugo.
Each of you take whatever pleases
And leave me whichever one you care to.
A lady has three gallant lovers
And with their loves they press her hard:
And when all three are there before her
To each she makes love's semblance.
At one she casts an amorous glance,
Squeezes the second's hand, the third,

She presses his foot and smiles. Now,
Since one is so, tell me in which
Move she shows the greatest love.

GAUCELM FAIDIT:

Savaric, you know too well, which
Friend received the kindest gift.
No lies, frankly it was the one
Who from her eyes took loving glance.
It's from the heart such softness moves,
Her love's a hundred times better shown.
For, as far as holding hands goes,
I say she meant neither good nor harm
From a mutual pleasure that's so common.
Why, a lady would do as much in greeting.
As for the foot, don't think it's proof
That the lady was making love to him.
If you took it for love you'd be mistaken.

UC DE LA BACALARIA:

Say what you will, Gaucelm, you're
Crazy man, you're so far off,
For in a glance I know no gain
To a lover—as you claim,
And if he thinks so, he's mad.
The eye regards others—and him,
It has no other power than this.
How much more when, ungloved, the white
Hand squeezed her lover's softly! Then
Love moved both from the heart and sense.
Since I'm maintaining the noblest part
En Savaric, the polite pressure
Of a foot I can scarcely credit.

SAVARIC DE MAULEON:

Uc, you've left the best to me, so
I'll uphold it and not say no.
I say the gentle pressure given
By her foot was the surest proof:

She hid her fine love from gossiping.
And best, while she gave such heaven
To her lover, she smiled, rejoicing.
Now *that* is love, and undisguised!
Whoever thinks the hand's caress
Shows greater love just makes no sense.
Gaucelm, it doesn't seem to me that
You can equate a glance with it if
You know love as well as you claim.

GAUCELM FAIDIT:

Whoever demeans the glances of eye
And the pleasure that may be made thereby,
Doesn't recognize the messengers of the heart
That sends them. They are, assuredly,
For the eyes discover to the lover
What timid hearts keep under cover;
Thus they show *all* of love's pleasure.
But in jest and laughing, a lady often
Will nudge the feet of many men
Without any other understanding.
Uc maintains a fallacy when
He claims the hand is such a treasure.
I say it is not worth a glove.
I bet he's never been moved by love.

UC DE LA BACALARIA:

Gaucelm, against Love you've been
Outspoken, the lord of Mauleon too,
And does it ever show in the argument!
For, the eyes, which you have chosen,
Have fooled many a faithful lover.
As for a lady with faithless heart
If she stepped on my foot for a year
My heart would have no rejoicing. But
The hand is beyond contention, for that
Moment of tension is better than either.
If it had not been Love that moved her
Heart, she'd not have put her hand there.

SAVARIC DE MAULEON:

Gaucelm, you've lost the argument,
You and Uc both, indisputably.
And I would have make judgment
Mos-Garda-Cors who's conquered me,
and lady Marie where price frequents.

GAUCELM FAIDIT:

Vanquished? I sir? By no means,
And the judge shall make it all too plain.
And I wish might be that same
The lady Guillema de Benauges
With her courteous, loving words.

UC DE LA BACALARIA:

Gaucelm, I've argued in such degree
That both of you are outside, and I
Sustained. I know a heart so good
In which the judgment may be put,
I've more gain there than any three.

PAUL BLACKBURN

PEIRE CARDENAL

I Am an Enemy to Trickery and Pride

Tostemps azir falsetat et enian

I am an enemy to trickery and pride
and try to live avoiding moral taint,
for when I know that I have virtue on my side,
then all is well and I have no complaint.
Some men we see who know not right
and put the truth and faithfulness to flight,
but he who rises using such deceit
will fall from his ascent in hard defeat.

The rich man shows the others such regard
as Cain showed Abel when he left him dead;

they rob like wolves robbing a farmer's yard
and tell more lies than prostitutes in bed.
If you would pierce them here and there, no doubt
you would not find the truth come pouring out,
but lies, which in their hearts such flood tides bring,
they overflow like water from a spring.

Many barons make the world believe
their merit, though they're as false as glass rings,
and those who call them noble men deceive
you like the man who sells an ass that sings.
They are not genuine by law nor weight.
Like false coins they hold their rate:
although they carry cross and crown,
they'd show no gold if they were melted down.

I have a bargain, if everyone will grant
it, from the Orient to the end of the sun's trail:
to every faithful man I'll give one bezant,
if every traitor lets me have a nail.
I'll hand out golden coins among the brave,
if I may have one copper from every knave.
I'll give a pile of gold to every honest man,
if every liar puts an egg in my pan.

All the law that most men ever heard of
I can write upon a piece of parchment big
enough to fit in half a finger of my glove.
I could feed all men of merit with one fig:
food for the worthy will never be in need,
although it may be so when villains feed.
If you would call, "You honest men, come eat,"
I do not think a man could leave his seat.

He who calls himself a noble knight
and lives ignobly, should never hear the name.
He is no Justice who doesn't care for right;
he is not honest who tells no truth. A shame
to reason is that men of wicked ways

gather gratitude and fame and praise.
On palace walls this saw we should engrave:
Who flayed you once, the next time will not shave.

My verses and I warn you in palace and city
that, if with righteousness and truth and pity
man does not rule himself in earth's domain,
not here nor later will courage hide his pain.

HARVEY BIRENBAUM

Once on a Certain Nameless Town
Una ciutatz fo, no sai cals

Once on a certain nameless town
A heavy rain came pelting down,
A very special kind of rain
For all it touched became insane.
Save for one man they all went crazy
But he, tired out or maybe lazy,
Was in his house serenely snoring
What time the magic rain was pouring.

The shower had ceased when he awoke;
He went forth and beheld the folk
Behaving in the maddest fashion
And giving vent to every passion.
Some wore their winter underwear,
Some waltzed about completely bare;
Some tore their clothes as he went by,
Others were spitting at the sky.
Some were hitting, punching, stabbing
Their dearest friends and others grabbing
Sticks and stones which then they'd fling
Not aiming them at anything.
One hurdles benches, one assumes
A regal stance, another fumes

And mutters incoherent speech:
Some curse, some blaspheme and some preach.

Now he whose wits are whole and sound
In fear and wonder looks around
Hoping to find one friend still sane,
But hope and anxious search are vain.
He looks on them with troubled gaze
But greater still is their amaze.
They mark his sober attitude,
His modest manner, and conclude,
Since he is different from the rest,
He must be mad. And so with zest
They fall upon him, rip his coat
And try to seize him by the throat.
They shove and slap and pummel him,
Threaten to tear him limb from limb.
He struggles, falls, gets up, breaks free
And strains his aching legs to flee;
With tattered garments, bloody head,
At last he staggers home, nigh dead.

'Tis of this world my tale is telling
And of the people therein dwelling:
Our world, with which we're so contented,
Is the town of the demented,
For mark, the truly wise 'tis clear
Will honor God and so revere
His holy law, but to our cost
That wholesome simple wit is lost.
A rain of greed and avarice
Has nourished pride and wickedness
And led the whole wide world astray
And none will follow on God's way.

If one should cling to our Lord's school
His neighbors would dub him a fool,
Deride him, scoff at him, mistreat him,
Persecute him, starve him, beat him.

Because, not being like the rest,
They'd judge he must be mad, at best.
God's wisdom's folly, they well know,
And his liegemen in madness go,
Wherefore they must be hunted down
And taught the wisdom of the town.
A world deranged cannot permit
God's sanity to thrive in it.

THOMAS G. BERGIN

Priests Disguise as Shepherds

Li clerc si fan pastor

Priests disguise as shepherds
And are murderers;
And falsify great sanctity
In priestly garb
Which brings to mind
How Master Fox, one day,
Planned to raid the fold:
But fearing dogs
He wore a wooly fleece
Thanks to which he fooled them,
Then ate and swallowed
Everything he pleased.

Kings and emperors,
Dukes, counts, and lesser men,
And with them, knights,
Were rulers of the world;
Now I see their property
In priestly mastery
With theft and treason,
And with hypocrisy,
With violence and preaching;
Nor can they bear it

When all's not left to them
And so it goes, however long it takes.

The greater they are
The less their worth
The greater the folly
The less plain truth
The greater the lies
The less loyal friends,
The greater the breach
The less the priestliness.
Of false priests, I must say this:
I've never heard of any
Worse enemies of God
Since ancient times.

When I'm in a refectory
I don't think it's an honor,
For at the highest table
I see great rascals sit
And take their pottage first.
Listen to this villainy:
For still they dare to come
And none turns them away.
Yet I've never seen a beggar
Beside such wealthy hosts:
Of that much I'll excuse them.

Let chiefs or sultans
Never fear
That priors or abbots
Will assail them
Or start to grab their lands,
For that would be hard work.
But here they try to find
How to make the world their own
And how to pry
Lord Frederick from his refuge

But that attack
Did not give cause for joy!

Priests, whoever said
Your heart's no wicked traitor
Mistook his calculations
For no one's worse than you.

WILLIAM M. DAVIS

NOTES AND BIOGRAPHICAL SKETCHES

Toward the year 1100 there appeared in Provence, in Southern France, a subjective lyrical utterance which imposed its unique character on all the poetry of medieval Christian Europe. Written in a vernacular language—the Romanic Languedoc—it was a coherent, cultivated expression, from writers who revealed distinct personalities and who seemed to be no longer fettered to the world of folklore or to the storytelling tradition of an earlier period.

Provençal poetry came to its greatest fruition during a half-century (1162-1213) and derived its inspiration from courtly love and feudal manners. The poetic forms created and developed were the *canso,* for the expression of erotic sentiments; the *sirventes,* for personal and political attacks, and for moralizing; the *planh,* for lamenting the death of some personage; the *tenso,* for debating, generally about love; when more than two poets participate, the debate is called *partimen* or *joc partit.* The *alba* (the same as the *aube* of Northern France and the *Tagelied* of Germany) was a dawn-song depicting the unhappiness of lovers who, after spending the night together, must separate at dawn. Finally, the *pastorela,* so ubiquitous during the Middle Ages—it was variously called *serranilla* in Spain, *serrana* in Galicia-Portugal, and *pastourelle* in Northern France—charmingly presented a gentleman, generally the poet himself, wooing a shepherdess who, after a lively dialogue, either accepted his advances or sent him away.

BEATRITZ DE DIA (fl. 1160), la Comtessa de Dia, is the most significant *trobairitz,* or lady-troubadour. The object of her love is supposed to have been the arrogant lady-killer Raimbaut d'Aurenga (q.v.), a maker of intricate verse, and among her works is a *tenso,* or debate-song, with him. Her few songs, about five, are striking in their utter frankness and the devotion they express to the passion of love—whether the passion is biographical or literary fiction.

BERNART DE VENTADORN (fl. 1150-1180), the son of an ovener in the castle of Ebles II of Ventadour, was one of the first poets to formulate the convention of courtly love. His satire, "Friend Bernard de Ventadorn" presents a cynical attitude toward love that is contradicted by his delicate lyrics. After quarreling with Ebles III, Bernart sojourned in the court of King Henry II of England and Eleanor of Aquitaine. Later he was protected by Count Raimon V of Toulouse and entered the monastery of Dalon after Raimon's death. The number of his surviving poems, about forty-five, attests to his popularity.

BERTRAN DE BORN (fl. 1180), a turbulent Baron born at the castle of Hautefort, loved schism and warfare, fighting as savagely against his own brother and neighbors as against Henry II of England and Richard the Lion-Hearted. Bertran's quarrelsome nature is reflected in fiery *sirventes*, but he also wrote an elegiac *planh* or lament, "If All the Grief and Sorrow, the Strife," on the death of the young Henry "del Curt Mantel," and a few love lyrics—some forty poems in all which prove him to be one of the outstanding and most original poets of medieval Europe.

CERCAMON (c. 1100-1152) was a native of Gascony but apparently traveled widely as a jongleur or minstrel. He is said to have received his name from the fact that "he sought out the whole world [*e cerquet tot lo mon*] wherever he could go." "With Mournful Tones My Verses Start," a lament on *planh* for the death of William X (April 9, 1137) has a rhyme repetition with a dirge-like effect, suggesting the chanting of mourners or the tolling of bells. Cercamon has left us eight poems, mostly love lyrics, written c. 1135-1145 at Limousin and Poitevin courts.

DALFIN (d. 1234). Although the anonymous *Vida* regularly uses the article with "Dalfin," this was the name and not the title of the Count of Clermont and Montferrand, a patron of many troubadours and a poet himself. Some ten poems are attributed to him.

GAUCELM FAIDIT (fl. 1185-1215), a native of Urzèche, lived as a professional troubadour in the courts of Marie de Ventadour and other nobles, including Boniface II of Monferrat, Raimbaut de Vaqueiras' protector, whom he followed on the Fourth Crusade (1202). Addicted to good eating and heavy drinking, he competed with his mistress in stoutness, sang in a disconcertingly shrill voice, and constantly lost at dice. Among his seventy poems the most memorable are a *planh* on the death of Richard the Lion-Hearted and the tender *alba* "A Knight Was with His Lady Fondly Lying."

GIRAUT DE BORNELH (c. 1165-1200) came from humble parents in the Excideul region of Dordogne, and his poems —some eighty of them—show a wide range in subject matter. His prosody, favoring precious complexity and artificiality, seems to have won him the title of "*maistre des troubadours,*" although, strangely enough, in a *tenso* or debate with Raimbaut d'Aurenga held probably at Christmas, 1170, Girault defended simplicity of expression. His *alba,* "Heavenly King, Glorious God of Light," is one of the finest medieval poems. The first six stanzas are recited by the watchman, a friend of the lover, and in the last stanza (of questionable authenticity) the lover replies.

GUILHEM DE CABESTANH (c. 1190-1212) is remembered for the legend of the *coeur mangé* rather than for his nine or ten lyrics. "Guilhem de Cabestanh," reads his *Vida,* "was a knight from the country of Roussillon which borders on Catalonia and Narbonne. He was quite as handsome as he was renowned in arms and chivalry. And there lived in his country a lady named Soremonda, wife of Raimon of Castel Roussillon, a rich and noble knight who was cruel and fierce and base. Guilhem de Cabestanh fell madly in love with Soremonda and made songs for her and she was young and beautiful and gay and loved him better than anything on earth. And so

Raimon was told by gossips and he, jealous and wrathful, looked into the matter and finding it was true, set watch upon his wife. And one day Raimon found Guilhem a-hawking and killed him and ripped his heart out of his body and had it carried to be roasted and seasoned with pepper and set before his wife to eat. And when the lady had eaten it, Raimon told her what she had eaten. When she heard, she fell into a swoon and on recovering, she said: 'My lord, you have given me such good meal that I shall never touch any other.' On hearing this, he ran upon her with his sword and would have split open her head, but she ran to a balcony and cast herself down, and so died." Among Guilhem de Cabestanh's admirers are to be counted Petrarch and Stendhal.

JAUFRÉ RUDEL (fl. 1148), Prince of Blave, in Saintonge, on the Garonne, is best known for the legend that probably was fabricated from his references to a far-away love. He is said to have fallen in love with a countess of Tripoli merely from reports of her. In order to see her, he joined a crusade, but he fell ill on the way. His countess came to him, he died in her arms, and she, in her grief, became a nun. Jaufré's charming song, "When Days Grow Long in May," so sweetly melancholy and so suggestive of a far-away love (the word *lonh* recurs several times in each stanza), helped to inspire the legend, so dear to Petrarch, Heine, Browning and the Edmond Rostand of *The Far-Away Princess.*

MARCABRU (fl. 1129-1150), a foundling from Gascony, was brought up by Sir Aldric d'Auvillars and trained in the art of poetry by Cercamon. He was hostile to women and love, and "much feared for his tongue," and was murdered by the castellans of Guienne "of whom he had spoken great ill." Among the forty-five pieces he has left us are to be found sprightly *pastourelles,* a charming romance relating to the crusade of 1147—introducing for the first time the theme of a maid forsaken by her lover for the Cross—and, above all, mordant poems exposing the moral turpitude of his age. In *Marcabrun,* Raymond Guthrie had dramatized the poet's life.

THE MONK OF MONTAUDUN (c. 1180-1215). Because he became the Prior of Vic, although rarely to be found in that village, this vagrant monk enjoyed the patronage of Richard I of England and Alfonso II of Aragon, and was known as Peire de Vic and Lo Monge de Montaudun (The Monk of Montaudun). His colorful work comprises slanderous sketches of contemporary troubadours, *tensos* with God or between Saints —one of these debates is on whether women should use make-up—and, finally, enumerations of *enuegs,* i.e., pet aversions or annoyances, and *plazers,* i.e., delights, which reveal the manners and intimate customs of his period.

PEIRE CARDENAL (c. 1225-1272) was the best of the troubadours who in the thirteenth century expressed the political and religious tensions that led to the Albigensian crusade. His *sirventes,* or satiric songs, are witty, earthy, and vigorous, especially in attacks against venal clergy and generally unscrupulous nobility. However, he sometimes combines racy satire with an eloquent sense of piety in a manner similar to that of Villon. One of his best songs is a simple prayer to the Virgin. Texts of about seventy of his songs are extant.

PEIRE VIDAL (1175-1205), son of a furrier of Toulouse, served Raimon V, Alfonso II of Aragon, Alfonso VIII of Castile and several Italian lords. Dressed in a wolf-skin to court his lady love, his Loba de Paugnautier, he was attacked by dogs. Later he married in Cyprus the granddaughter of the Emperor of Constantinople and traveled with an imperial throne among his baggage, calling himself Emperor—in short, he led a life filled with picturesque and not-too-credible happenings, quite proper for a romantic novel. (See Cronin's *The Fool of Venus.*) Peire Vidal's fifty odd poems evidence extraordinary verve and originality, a felicitous fusion of realism and fantasy. From his song "When I Breathe This Air" emanates a genuine feeling for Provence; his "I Put an End to Singing" is also unique as a love song: it praises *three* ladies and complains of a *fourth.*

PEIROL (1160-1225) was an impoverished knight of Auvergne, taking his name from a castle called Peirol in the country of the Dauphin, at the foot of Roquefort. He was a courteous man whom the Dauphin of Auvergne kept in his household, clothed, and gave him horses and arms. The Dauphin had a sister called Sail de Claustra (Out of a Cloister), fair, kind, and highly esteemed; she was the wife of a great baron of Auvergne, Lord Beraut of Mercoeur. Peirol loved her with true love and the Dauphin interceded for him; he was pleased with the songs that Peirol made for his sister and persuaded her to be pleased with them likewise; so much so, that the lady, to her brother's knowledge, reciprocated the poet's affection and yielded him the pleasures of love. But this love reached such a height that the Dauphin became jealous on his sister's behalf, thinking that she was conceding more than was becoming to her, and so he dismissed Peirol and sent him into exile and ceased to provide him with clothing and arms. Peirol could no longer maintain himself as a knight and went forth among the courts as a jongleur; the barons rewarded him with clothing and money and horses—thus goes the Provençal *Vida*. We may add that Peirol was born about 1160 and died about 1225; that his wanderings included a trip to the Holy Land (1221) and some residence in Italy. S. C. Aston's edition of Peirol's works (Cambridge, 1953) contains thirty-four poems, two of doubtful attribution.

RAIMBAUT D'AURENGA (c. 1150-1173), was the Count of Orange, object of Beatritz de Dia's love and poetic inspiration. He cultivated the *trobar ric,* full of subtleness and hermetic preciosity: the forty poems he has left us are shot through with recondite imagery and ambiguity and show him to be a virtuoso, rather artificial and cold.

RAIMBAUT DE VAQUEIRAS (c. 1155-1205), son of an impoverished Provençal knight, spent much of his time in Italy, mostly in the court of Boniface II of Monferrand, whom he accompanied on the Fourth Crusade (1202). From the forty poems extant can be seen his wide range: the technical ability in the *estampida* "Kalenda maya"; the charming *tenso* or debate in which the Italian girl replies to him in Genoese; the *planh* "High Waves That Ride the Sea," a Provençal adaptation of the delightful Galician-Portuguese *cantiga do amigo*

"Oy, aura dolza, qui vens deves lai," which has been attributed to him, for it is assumed that his wanderings took him as far as Galicia.

RICHART DE BERBEZILH (c. 1180-1207), a native of Saintonge, enjoyed the patronage of Marie of Champagne and Diego López de Haro, Lord of Vizcay. His ten extant poems are distinguished for their lucid expressions of courtly love motifs, colored by witty animal metaphors drawn from medieval bestiaries. As for his song "You See Me like the Elephant," the poet, tired by long, unrequited love service, is said to have succumbed to an invitation from a neighboring lady, who promised to grant all his desires. He took leave of his first mistress, but when he addressed himself to the second, she upbraided him for his faithlessness to the first. He then returned to the first lady, "the saddest man in the world." After much begging for mercy, partly with the song, but then only on the strength of a stipulated appeal from one hundred knights and one hundred ladies, he was pardoned.

SAVARIC DE MAULEON (c. 1200-1232), a powerful baron of Poitiers, handsome and generous, took part in tournaments, courted the ladies, and composed songs. He waged war against the King of France and was rewarded by John, King of England, with an English peerage. The *partimen*, or debate, here included, a fine piece of medieval casuistry, concerns a lady who had three suitors: she gives one an amorous glance; another, a squeeze of the hand; and presses the foot of the third—Savaric calls his friends Gaucelm Faidit [q.v.] and asks them to decide who is the most favored of the lady's suitors.

UC DE LA BACALARIA (c. 1200-1232), jongleur from Bacalaria or Bachélerie, near Urzèche, "of little worth and little travel," according to his contemporaries, left us at least six pieces which indicate a great deal of refinement and good taste.

WILLIAM IX, COUNT OF POITIERS (1071-1127), the earliest Provençal troubadour, was the seventh Count of

Poitou and ninth Duke of Aquitaine. Owning more land than the King of France, he waged constant wars to enlarge his possessions, attacked Church property, undertook a disastrous crusade in 1101, helped to defeat the Spanish Moors, and was several times excommunicated for his riotous living. At the end of his life, he left his domains in a precarious position. Bearing the stamp of his personality, his poems combine delicacy with sensuality.

NORTHERN FRANCE

ANONYMOUS

The Sequence of Saint Eulalia
La Cantilène de Sainte Eulalie

Good was the girl Eulalia,
　　Fair-formed, of soul far fairer.
God's foemen strove to vanquish her
　　And make her serve the Devil.
She would not heed their wicked rede,
　　Forswear Him Heaven-dwelling
For silver, finery or gold,
　　For royal threats or pleading;
No earthly thing could swerve the girl
　　From loving aye God's service.
Hence, brought before Maximian,
　　Who then was king o'er pagans,
She, never warmed to heed, was urged
　　To flee the name of Christian.
She gathered up her spirit's might,
　　Liefer would writhe in torture
Than lose her maiden innocence;
　　For this she died in honor.
They threw her in the fire to blaze;
　　She burned not, being sinless.
The heathen king was unconvinced;
　　He bade the sword behead her.
The maid did not gainsay this doom,
　　To Christ she prayed, world-weary.
In shape of dove to Heaven she flew.
　　Let us beseech her succor
That Christ have mercy when we die
And deign to let us come Him nigh
　　Through gracious loving-kindness.

CHARLES MAXWELL LANCASTER

ANONYMOUS

Malady, Death and Resurrection of Saint Lazarus

Maladie, mort et resurrection de Saint Lazare

Marthe:
Death execrable!
Death detestable!
Death deplorable!
    Weary, grieved!
Since my brother is dead
    Why do I live?

My brother's burial
cruel and sudden
is cause for lamenting
    Weary, grieved!
Since my brother is dead
    Why do I live?

Since my brother is dead
I deny not death
nor fear I death
    Weary, grieved!
Since my brother is dead
    Why do I live?

For my brother's dying
I renounce living
Woe! Misery is mine!
    Weary, grieved!
Since my brother is dead
    Why do I live?

DAISY ALDAN

SPINNING SONGS (ANONYMOUS)

When It Is May, and the Darkness Is Short
Quant vient en mai que l'on dit as lons jors

When it is May, and the darkness is short,
The Frenchmen of France return from the court.
Passing in front of Erembor's door,
Raymond is with them, well in the lead,
but to the lady he pays no heed.
O Raymond, ami!

At the tower window sat fair Erembor;
On her lap silk thread of all colors lay.
Frenchmen of France were returning from court;
When she saw Raymond not looking her way,
Well knew the lady what she should say.
O Raymond, ami!

"Raymond, my friend, on many a day
I've seen you stand at my father's door
Grieving if I sent no message your way."
"Emperor's daughter, the vows we swore
You've broken; our love I'll remember no more."
O Raymond, ami!

"Raymond, my lord, I'll tell you this:
On the relics of a hundred maids
I'll swear that I never our love betrayed,
And a hundred ladies will serve me for witness.
Take it for true, and I'll give you a kiss!"
O Raymond, ami!

Then Count Raymond climbed up the stair;
Broad are his shoulders, narrow his waist,
Curly and bright blond is his hair.

Never was there so handsome a knight!
He saw Erembor, and wept at the sight.
O Raymond, ami!

Then Count Raymond climbed up to the tower.
There he sat down on a bed trimmed with flowers.
Next to him sat the fair Erembor;
And they went on with their love as before.
O Raymond, ami!

PATRICIA TERRY

Fair Aye Sits at Her Cruel Lady's Feet

Siet soi bele Aye as piez sa male maistre

Fair Aye sits at her cruel lady's feet,
Upon her knees an English damascene
Whereon she sews in lovely filigree—
Ho! Ho! Love from a stranger realm
Did trap my heart and I am overwhelmed.

Adown her cheeks the tears course hot. She grieves
For that she is whipped every morn and eve
Because she loves a foreign knight. Ah me!
Ho! Ho! Love from a stranger realm
Did trap my heart and I am overwhelmed.

JACQUES LECLERCQ

On Saturday Evening, the Week at an End

Lou samedi a soir falt la semaine

On Saturday evening, the week at an end,
two sisters, Gaiette and Oriour, went
hand in hand to bathe at the fountain.

Wind blows and the branches sweep;
those who love will softly sleep.

On his way from the quintain, young Gerard
saw Gaiette as he passed the fountain,
kissed her and held her tight in his arms.
Wind blows and the branches sweep;
those who love will softly sleep.

"When you have drawn enough water, you may
go home, Oriour—you remember the way;
Gerard loves me, and with him I'll stay."
Wind blows and the branches sweep;
those who love will softly sleep.

Now Oriour, pale and sad, must go;
she sighs from the heart, and her tears flow
because her sister will not follow.
Wind blows and the branches sweep;
those who love will softly sleep.

"Alas that I was born to sorrow!
My sister remains in the valley below;
Gerard will take her away to his home."
Wind blows and the branches sweep;
those who love will softly sleep.

Gerard and Gaiette had already left
on the road which straight to the city led;
as soon as they arrived, they were wed.
Wind blows and the branches sweep;
those who love will softly sleep.

PATRICIA TERRY

⚜

By Water's Edge Sing Sisters Three

Trois sereurs seur rive mer

By water's edge sing sisters three,
Full earnestly.
The youngest is a darksome lass:
"I would a tawny love," quoth she,
"For dark am I,
And fain would have a lad like me."

By water's edge sing sisters three,
Full earnestly.
The second to her Robin calls:
"Ah! you have ta'en
My heart in yonder wooded grove,—
Let's back again!"

By water's edge sing sisters three,
Full earnestly.
At length the third:
"Ye amorous swains, hark to my word:
Love none but tender damosel,
And love her well."

NORMAN R. SHAPIRO

SONG OF THE ILL-MARRIED (ANONYMOUS)

In an Orchard a Little Fountain Flows

En un vergier lez une fontenele

In an orchard a little fountain flows,
Shadowless ripples over white stones,
There a king's daughter, her head bowed low,
Remembers her sweet love and her sorrows.
Alas, Count Guy, my friend!
Without you I'll never know joy again.

Count Guy, my love, how cruel is my fate!
The old man my father gave me for a mate
Keeps me in his house and locks every gate,
Nor can I leave it early or late;
Alas, Count Guy, my friend!
Without you I'll never know joy again.

The cruel husband hears her, and soon
Appears in the orchard, his belt removes,
And belts her until she is so badly bruised
She falls at his feet in a deathlike swoon.
Alas, Count Guy, my friend!
Without you I'll never know joy again.

The lady arose from her faint to pray
That God in pity her grief allay,
"Let me not be forgotten! Oh, may
I see my love before vespers today."
Alas, Count Guy, my friend!
Without you I'll never know joy again.

And Our Lord listened to her lament;
Her lover consoled the chatelaine.
Beneath a great tree whose branches bend,
Many tears for their love have fallen.
Alas, Count Guy, my friend!
Without you I'll never know joy again.

PATRICIA TERRY

WORKERS' SONGS (ANONYMOUS)

Poem of a Glass Blower

Poeme du souffleur de verre

Were you not enchanted evenings
When you watched me blowing glass
Sounding like the roar of thunder?

I believe you surely were.
You imagined imps and Demons
Helped me fashion all these baubles,
Especially these huge vials
Formed by the breathing of my lungs.

This object so round and clear
Seemed to shoot forth gleaming sparks
Bursting suddenly in the air
Shattering in a million shards;

I'm sure that I amazed you
And the same happened to me;
I was struck dumb with surprise
When the glass bottle exploded.

DAISY ALDAN

Sounds of the Trades
Bruits de métiers

When the miller starts to grind,
Trique, traque, goes the millstone,
Trique, traque, goes the millstone,
Good wheat, fine wheat,
He puts a fourth aside.

When the tailor shapes his robe,
Rique, raque, on the table,
Rique, raque, on the table,
Good cloth, fine cloth,
He puts an ell aside.

When the weaver is in a rush,
Zigue, zagu', to warp his patch,
Zigue, zagu', to warp his patch,
Good yarn, fine yarn,
He puts a ball aside.

When the cartwright forms his wheel,
Tique, tac, with his mallet,
Tique, tac, with his mallet,
From the rim to the knob
He notes if the lathe is round.

DAISY ALDAN

Why Do We Let Them Oppress Us?

Pourquoi nous laisser faire dommage?

Why do we let them oppress us?
We are men as they are,
Limbs we possess even as they,
And our hearts are just as noble;
And as deeply can we suffer . . .

DAISY ALDAN

By the Sweat of My Brow I Toiled

A la sueur de mon visage

By the sweat of my brow I toiled
And I am dying of hunger,
Three days and no morsel of bread
Has been tasted in my household,
Where none is.

I planted, harvested, and pressed
The grapes; smoked the fields and pastures,
To sustain life in our children,
But I see where all is laid waste
Otherwise.

My Lord God, surely Thou knowest
How my days were made days of fear,

By royal bailiffs, by gendarmes
Along with others, one knows well
Who.

For to cleave the heads of my calves,
Ready to devour my sheep
Are they with beards on their chins
But try to get their protection
Some job!

Alas! We must simply struggle
Together, we poor laborers,
When a lot of wicked scoundrels
Use force and don't reinforce us.

DAISY ALDAN

CHRÉTIEN DE TROYES

Complaint of the Weavers

Complainte des tisseuses de soie

Yarn of gold and silk spun
They, giving their best, each one,
But so wretched and so poor
Were they, that at elbows and breasts
Their gowns hung like lacey shreds.
Stained were their shirts with dirt,
Necks scrawny, faces pale and hurt.
Hunger and ills they reaped.
He looks at them and they at him,
All bow their heads and weep;
We weave forever silk and cloth
Yet never will be better clothed;
With want and nakedness accursed;
Always hunger, always thirst.
We will never master the feat
Of learning to earn enough to eat;

Only bread and nothing else,
Little at morn, and at even' less;
For with all our handiwork
Each is given for his living
But four deniers[1] of the livre[1]
And surely this is not enough
To buy our meat, to buy our cloth.
Who earns a week but twenty sous
Cannot be free from pain and woes.
So let all the world know this:
There is not even one of us
Who gets more than twenty sous.
A duke could grow rich on such fare!
Great indeed is our despair;
But growing fat on our labor
Is he for whom we work and slave.
We wake to work most of the night
And through the day we toil and sweat
And are tormented by the threat
Of beating when we stop to rest
So we dare neither stop nor rest.

DAISY ALDAN

MARIE DE FRANCE

The Laustic

Le Laustic

Now I will tell you an adventure
Of which the Bretons made a lai.
Its name is *Laustic*, I heard,
And so they call it in their country.
That is *rossignol* in French
And *nightingale* in good plain English.
In the country of Saint-Malo
There was a city much renowned.

---

[1] *Old French money.*

Two knights had residences there
As owners of two fortress mansions.
The excellence of these two barons
Gained them a good name in the town.
The one was married to a lady
Wise, courteous, and well adorned;
Wondrously well she kept herself
According to the use and fashion.
The other was a bachelor
Reputed well among his peers
For prowess and great valor and
For generous hospitality.
He tourneyed much and freely spent
And gave away what he possessed.
He was in love with his neighbor's wife.
So long he asked, so long he begged,
And had so much good virtue in him,
That she loved him above all else,
Both for the virtue she had heard
And because he lived so near her.
Wisely and well they loved each other.
Much they dissembled and took care
That people should not notice them
Nor yet disturb them or suspect them,
And this they could well do because
Their place of meeting was so near;
Their houses were right next each other,
As were their halls and tower-keeps.
There was neither bar nor division
Except a high wall of gray stone.
From chambers where the lady slept,
When she stood at the window there
She could converse with her friend on
The other side, and he with her.
They could exchange their messages
By throwing them or tossing them.
There was but little to displease them
And both of them were well content
Except that they could never come

Together for their pleasure, for
The lady was most straitly guarded
As long as he was in the land.
But still they had the satisfaction
Whether by night or whether by day
Of being able to converse,
And there was no one to prevent
Their coming to their windows there
To have a look at one another.
A long time they loved one another
Until it came to summer time
When field and wood grew green again
And all the orchards were in flower.
The little birds in their great sweetness
Sang their delight atop the blossoms.
It is no wonder, if one loves,
That he should yield himself to it.
About the knight I tell you truly
He yielded himself utterly,
And from the other side the lady
Likewise longed with look and glance.
At night time when the moon was shining
And when her lord was in his bed,
From by his side she often rose
And wrapped her mantle close around her
And went to stand before her window
For her friend's sake, who she well knew
Was likewise there and who was likewise
Watching most of the night through.
Theirs was delight in simply gazing
As long as they could have no more.
So often she would leave her bed
That her lord finally grew angry
And questioned her repeatedly
Why she got up and where she went.
"My Lord," the lady answered him,
"No one has had joy in this world
Who has not heard the laustic;
It is for that that I am here.

He sings so sweetly through the night
It seems to me a great delight.
I take such pleasure in his song
I cannot shut my eyes in sleep."
But when her lord heard what she said
He laughed in anger savagely,
And one thing he decided then:
That he would trap the laustic.
There was no servant in his house
But who could rig a net or snare.
They put them all around the orchard;
No hazel tree or chestnut tree
But they had coated it with glue
Till they had caught and held the bird.
And when they had the laustic
They took it to their lord alive,
And he was happy when he held it.
He went then to the lady's chambers:
"Lady," said he, "Lady, where are you?
Come from your room and talk to us.
I have the laustic stuck fast
That kept you up so many times.
From now on you can sleep in peace,
It will not wake you any more."
But when the lady heard those words
She was all sorrowful and sad.
She asked her lord to have the bird,
But he from malice killed it there:
With his two hands he wrung its neck,
And then did something viler still:
He threw the body at the lady
So that it stained her dress with blood
In front and just above her breast.
And then at once he left her chamber.
The lady picked the tiny body up.
Bitterly she wept and cursed
All who betrayed the laustic
And made the engines and the nets,
For they had robbed her of great joy.

"Alas!" she said, "An evil chance.
I can no longer rise at night
Nor go and stand before the window
To watch for sight of my beloved.
One thing I know for certain though:
He will think I pretended merely.
I must devise some other plan.
I'll send the laustic to him
And give him word of the adventure."
Then in a piece of samite worked
With gold and covered with her writing
She wrapped the body of the bird.
Then she sent for a page of hers
And charged him well to take the message
To be delivered to her friend.
He went directly to the knight
And gave him greeting from his lady,
Recounted to him all her message,
And gave the laustic to him.
When he had shown and told him all
And when the knight had heard him out,
He was downcast at the adventure,
Yet he was neither vile nor slow.
He had a little coffret made,
No part of it was iron or steel,
But only gold and costly gems
Very precious and very dear,
And with a lid that fitted closely.
He placed the laustic within,
Then had the tiny casket sealed,
And always had it carried with him.
This adventure was recounted:
It could not long remain concealed.
A lay the Bretons made of it,
Which people call *The Laustic.*

CHARLES E. PASSAGE

RICHARD THE LION-HEARTED

In No Way Can a Prisoner Reveal

Ja nus hons pris ne dira sa reson

In no way can a prisoner reveal
His true thoughts unless he tells his grief;
But sorrow in a song may find relief.
I'm strong in friends, but their support is weak;
Their shame if I, unransomed, cannot leave
Prison two winters long.

They know well, my barons and liege-men,
English, Norman, Gascon, Poitevin,
I would not suffer any one of them
For money's sake to come to such an end.
Nor do I say this to reprove the men
Who leave me here so long.

The dead and prisoners have neither friend
Nor family, no doubt that's what it meant
When neither gold nor silver would they send.
Misfortune more than to me, to all my men:
When I die they will have cause to repent
Leaving me here so long.

It is no wonder my heart breaks to see
My lands invaded by that enemy
Who, if he remembered now that we
Once pledged each other our security,
Would surely turn instead to have me free
From prison before long.

In Anjou and in Tours they're well aware,
Those young lords, so rich and without care,
That far away a captive's bonds I wear.

They loved me once, but now they do not care.
The fields which rang with gallant deeds are bare
Since I've been here so long.

To those I loved and still love, to the men
Of Cayeux, to Geoffroy the Percherain,
Say, my song, that faithless they have been
To one whose heart was never false to them.
Vile is the deed if they attack me when
I'm kept away so long.

PATRICIA TERRY

LE CHASTELAIN DE COUCY

The Sweet Voice of the Woodland Nightingale

La dolce voix del rosignol sauvage

The sweet voice of the woodland nightingale
All day and all night long enchants my ear
And from my heart draws grief and care away
So that I want to sing out joyfully.
Let my song be worthy, then, to please
The lady whom I in all things obey,
For joy rules in my heart while I can stay
In her service, never to be free.

Never has my heart been false or strayed,
Happier by far though it might be,
Yet in her presence I dare not betray
How I have loved and serve her faithfully;
For all her beauty so bewilders me
That with her I can't find the words to say,
Nor can I even look into her face
My eyes would leave her so unwillingly.

I think of nothing else all night and day
But that God grant me joy of my sweet lady!

And never did Tristan by the drink betrayed
Yield to love with such sincerity.
I've given all to her, though it be folly,
My heart and body, will and mind as gage
Of love, yet my whole life will pass away
Before I've served my lady worthily.

Even if I with life itself must pay
For loving her, I would not call it folly;
No one will ever find her like again,
And nothing in the world so pleased me.
I bless my eyes which placed my heart in fief
To her at the first moment; I've remained
Long her hostage, nor shall I complain
At any time to have her set me free.

My song, now carry all that I would say
Where I myself dare not trespass for fear
That evil scandal-mongers lie in wait;
Anticipating lovers, they foresee
Love's pleasures, may God show them no mercy!
And thus have brought so many to dismay
That I must from my lady keep away,
For love has no defense but secrecy.

PATRICIA TERRY

CONON DE BÉTHUNE

If This Insensate Rage

La rage et derverie

If this insensate rage
And the distress of love
Have brought me to complain
As fools speak ill of love,
Let no one this reprove;
If love my faith betrays,

I who have been love's slave,
What can I hold true?

My grievance, love, shall tell
And demonstrate your guilt;
You claimed me as chattel,
Nor challenged me, but killed.
You have compelled my will
Where my cold joy lies still,
Now she whose love was all
Drives me toward hopes fulfilled.

Lovely as an idol
Is she of whom I speak,
But vileness in her soul,
Petulant and weak,
Makes her appear to me
Like the wild she-wolf
Who from within the wood
Only the worst will seek.

Why should she be proud
Of so disdaining me?
For this no wisdom bows
To her, for what is she?
And yet, if her folly
My banishment allows,
I give her back her vows
And take my leave.

Now has the earth grown hard,
Nowhere do waters flow;
My heart would set its mark
Where I can never know
Fruit nor leaf nor flower.
It's time; now serve, my heart,
Justice and reason's part;
Give back her love and go.

PATRICIA TERRY

ANONYMOUS

The Circumcision of Our Lord
La Circoncision du Seigneur

At the entrance to the church
Light this day, light of joy! I say he who is sad
Must be turned away from this celebration.
This way let all hatred, all sorrow be allayed;
They desire gaiety, those who celebrate the festivity of the ass.

Singing, the procession moves toward the tableau. (This designates to each his role during the service.)

From the Orient
The ass has come,
Fair and valiant,
Ready for his burden.
Ho, my Sire Ass, ho!

On the hills of Sichem
Fed by Ruben
He crossed the Jordan,
He climbed toward Bethlehem.
Ho, my Sire Ass, ho!

Galloping, he outran mules
Deer and mountain goats,
Fleeter than the Madianites'
Swift dromedaries.
Ho, my Sire Ass, ho!

Gold from Arabia
Incense and myrrh from Sheba
Brings to the Church
The strength of the ass.
Ho, my Sire Ass, ho!

While he draws the carts
Piled up high
His jaw
Grinds his tough fodder.
    Ho, my Sire Ass, ho!

Bearded barley
And thistles he eats.
Wheat from the chaff
He winnows in the air.
    Ho, my Sire Ass, ho!

Then say, Amen, Ass,
Now sated with grain
Amen, repeat amen;
Let the old make way,
    Ho, my Sire Ass, ho!

The notice having been read, the Priest begins:

God, come to the aid
Of those who are hurt,

Quickly to help them
Efface their pains.

Pity all those
Who believe in you, Christ,
You are God of the centuries
Eternal in your glory.

So that our choir may
Sing and say your praises
To you, Christ, king of glory,
Glory to you, Oh Lord!

Prose

Alle . . . Let all churches sing
The sweet sound of the symphony.

Son of Mary,
Holy Mother,
Overwhelm us with your gifts
Of grace sevenfold, and of glory.
Thus we say to God: luya!

Four or five Priests sing in falsetto behind the altar:
This is a day of clarity, light among days of clarity,
This is a holy day, holy among holy days
Deserving the diadem of noblesse among other noble days.

Two or three Priests sing before the altar, in full voice: (Pastiche du *Salve, festa dies,* Paschal hymn of Fortunat.)

Salutations, holy day, venerable in all ages,
When God came from the womb of the Virgin.

Small verses sung by two or three Priests:

Trinity
Deity
Unity
eternal;
Majesty
Holy Might
Piety
supreme.

Sun, light
Divine
And summit
Path,
Rock mountain,
Rock, spring,
River, bridge
and life.

You who sow,
Creator,
Loving,
Redeemer,

Saviour,
    Light eternal;

You, splendor,
And beauty,
Brilliance,
And splendor
And fragrance
    Waking life in all that is mortal.

You the pole
The summit
King of Kings,
Law of Laws
And avenger
    Angelic light,
Are proclaimed
And adored
Praised
And acclaimed
And loved
    by celestial legions.

You God
The hero,
Radiant flower,
Dew of life,
Reign over us,
Save us,
Lead us
To the supreme
Thrones
    and to true joys.

You honor
And virtue,
You are the just
And the true,
You the holy

And the good,
The righteous
And the sovereign
Our Lord,
Glory be unto you!

DAISY ALDAN

May I Sing to You?
Voulez-vous que je vous chante?

May I sing to you
A song of charming love?
Not of any knave,
But of a gentle knight
Under an olive's shade,
Holding his love.

A blouse of fine linen,
A cloak of white ermine,
And a silk bodice she had;
Her hose were of irises,
In shoes of mayflowers neatly
Her feet were clad.

Her girdle was of leaves
That grew green in the rain;
Its clasp was wrought of gold;
Her purse was made of love,
Tasseled all with flowers
Given by love to hold.

She rode upon a mule
Shod with silver shoes,
The saddle of gold was made;
Behind, upon the crupper,
Three rose trees had she planted
To give her shade.

So she went along the lea,
Knights did meet with her,
And greeted courteously:
"Fair maid, where were you born?"
"All France sings my praise,
I am of high degree.

"My father is the nightingale
Who sings upon the bough
Of the highest tree;
The mermaid is my mother
Who sings on the farthest shore
Of the salty sea."

"How well are you born, fair maid!
Of noble parentage,
You come of high degree.
May it please God, our Father,
That as my wedded wife
You may be given me."

MURIEL KITTEL

GUIOT DE DIJON

I Will Sing and So Relieve

Chanterai por mon corage

I will sing and so relieve
the sorrow in my heart, for I
fear that left alone to grieve
I'll go mad or else will die.
From that barbarous land where he
went a pilgrim, none arrive
home again, and I receive
no promise that he is alive.
God, the warcry sounding clear,
Lord, help the crusader then

for whom I so greatly fear;
evil is the Saracen.

As I am I shall remain
till my love returns to me.
May God bring him home again
from pilgrimage across the sea!
Be it known that I disdain
every other chance to marry;
though my family complain,
there is no one else for me.
God, the warcry sounding clear,
Lord, help the crusader then
for whom I so greatly fear;
evil is the Saracen.

He is lost to me out there;
that is what so grieves my heart.
Now surrender to despair
pleasures from my life depart.
He is handsome, I am fair.
God, why did you let it start?
When we for one another care
why have you forced us to part?
God, the warcry sounding clear,
Lord, help the crusader then
for whom I so greatly fear;
evil is the Saracen.

Because he pledged me fealty
I am well content to wait.
When the wind blows from the sea,
from that sweet land far away
where he is who longs for me,
toward the wind I turn my face:
it seems to be my love I feel
underneath my cloak of gray.
God, the warcry sounding clear,
Lord, help the crusader then

for whom I so greatly fear;
evil is the Saracen.

It grieved me that I was deprived
of going to the parting place.
His crusader's robe arrived,
sent me as a last embrace.
When love tortures me at night,
I invoke its healing grace,
around my body wrap it tight
as if it took my sorrow's place.
God, the warcry sounding clear,
Lord, help the crusader then
for whom I so greatly fear;
evil is the Saracen.

PATRICIA TERRY

GACE BRULÉ

Most Hateful Is It to My Eyes

Cant voi l'aube dou jor venir

Most hateful is it to my eyes
when the dawn comes to the skies
telling my true love to arise
and with me no longer stay;
nothing I hate so much as day
which keeps me away, love, from you.

By daylight you cannot appear
for I have good cause to fear
the jealous ones who hover near
to spy on us—you know it's true.
Nothing I hate so much as day
which keeps me away, love, from you.

When I am lying in my bed
and toward my lover turn my head

to find your empty place instead,
thus I lament as lovers do:
nothing I hate so much as day
which keeps me away, love, from you.

You must go now, my sweet friend,
your body I to God commend,
that you forget me not I pray;
my love for you can have no end.
Nothing I hate so much as day
which keeps me away, love, from you.

To all who truly love I bring
this my song, and may they sing
in despite of gossiping
and of jealous husbands too:
nothing I hate so much as day
which keeps me away, love, from you.

PATRICIA TERRY

GUILLAUME DE LORRIS

Romance of the Rose
Le Roman de la Rose

I was aware that it was May,
Five years or more ago; I dreamed
That I was filled with joy in May,
The amorous month, when everything
Rejoices, when one sees no bush or hedge
That does not wish to adorn itself
With new leaves. The woods, dry in winter,
Recover their greenery, and the very earth
Glories in the roses which water it and forgets
The poverty in which the winter was passed.
Then the earth becomes so proud
That it wants a new robe; and it knows

How to make a robe so intricate
That it has a hundred pairs of colors,
This robe of grass and flowers, blue,
White, and many others, by which
The earth enriches itself. The birds,
Silent while they were cold and the weather
Hard and bitter, become so gay
In May, in serene weather, that their hearts
Are filled with joy until they must sing
Or burst. It is then that the nightingale
Is constrained to sing his sound, then
That both parrot and lark take their pleasure,
And then that young men must become gay
And amorous in the sweet, lovely weather.
He who does not love in May
Has a very hard heart, when he hears
The birds on the branches, singing their heart-sweet
Songs. And so I dreamed one night
That I was in that delicious season
When everything is stirred by love,
And as I slept I became aware
That it was full morning. I got up
From bed straightway, put on my shoes
And washed my hands. Then I drew
A silver needle from a dainty little
Needle-case and threaded it.
I had a longing to go out of town
To hear the sound of birds that sang,
In that new season, among the trees.
I stitched my sleeves in zigzag lacing
And set out, quite alone, to enjoy myself
Listening to the birds who strained
Themselves to sing of the gardens bursting
Into bloom.
Happy, light-hearted, full
Of joy, I turned toward a river
That I heard murmuring nearby,
For I knew no place to go for pleasure
More beautiful than by that river,

Whose water gushed deep and swift
From a nearby hill, as clear and cold
As that from a well or fountain. It was
But little smaller than the Seine,
But spread out wider. I had never seen
A stream so charmingly placed; it pleased
And delighted me to look on it.
As I washed my face and refreshed myself
With the clear, shining water, I saw
That the bottom of the stream was all covered
And paved with gravel. The wide, beautiful
Meadow came right to the edge of the water.
The mild morning air was clear,
Pure, and beautiful. Then I walked
Out away through the meadow, full
Of joy as I kept to the river bank
In descending the stream.

CHARLES DAHLBERG

JEAN DE MEUN

Romance of the Rose
Le Roman de la Rose

In short, all men betray us women.
All are sensualists, taking their pleasure
Anywhere. Therefore we women should deceive them
In turn, not fix our hearts on one.
A woman who does so is a fool. She should have
Several friends and, if possible, try
To delight them so that they are driven to distraction.
If she has no graces, let her learn them:
Let her be haughtier toward those who, because
Of her hauteur, will take more trouble to serve her
So as to deserve her love, but let her
Scheme to take from those who make light
Of her love. She should know games and songs

And flee from quarrels and disputes.
If she's not beautiful, she should pretty herself.
The ugliest should wear the most coquettish
Adornments.
Now if, to her great sorrow,
She should see her beautiful brown hair
Falling, or if, because of a serious illness,
She has to have it cut off
And her beauty spoiled, or if it happens
That some vulgar fellow has cut it off
In anger, so that she is unable to recover
Her long locks, she should have someone
Bring her a dead woman's hair, or pads
Of light silk, stuffed into shapes.
Over her ears she should wear such horns
That they could not be surpassed by stag,
Billy goat or unicorn, even if he
Had to burst his forehead; if they need color,
She should tint them with plant extracts,
For fruits, woods, leaves, bark,
And roots have strong medicinal properties.
Lest she should suffer loss of color,
A heart-rending experience, she
Must make sure always to have pots of moistening
Skin-creams in her rooms so that she
May hide away to put on her paint;
But she must be very careful
Not to let any of her guests notice
Or see her, or she would be in trouble.
If she has a lovely neck
And white chest, she should see
That her dress-cutter lower her neckline
So that it reveals a half-foot, in front
And in back, of her fine white flesh;
Thus she may deceive more easily.
And if her shoulders are too large
To be pleasing at dances and balls
She should wear a dress of fine cloth
And thus appear less ungainly. And if,

Because of insect bites or pimples,
She doesn't have beautiful, well-kept hands,
She should be careful not to neglect them
But should lift the pimples with a needle
Or wear gloves so that the scabs
And pimples will not show.
If her breasts
Are too heavy she should take a scarf
Or towel to bind them against her chest
And wrap it tight round her ribs, securing it
With needle and thread by a knot;
Thus she can be active in her play.
And like a good little girl she should keep
Her chamber of Venus tidy. If she
Is intelligent and well brought-up, she will leave
No cobwebs around, but will burn or destroy them,
Tear them down and sweep them up,
So that no grime can collect anywhere.
If her feet are ugly, she should keep them covered
And wear fine stockings if her legs are large.
In short, unless she's very stupid
She should hide any defect that she knows of.
For example, if she knows that her breath
Is foul she should spare no amount of trouble
Never to fast, never to speak
To others on an empty stomach, and,
If possible, to keep her mouth away
From people's noses.
When she has
The impulse to laugh, she should laugh discreetly
And prettily, so that she shows little dimples
At the corners of her mouth. She should avoid puffing
Her cheeks and screwing her face up in grimaces.
Her lips should be kept closed and her teeth
Covered; a woman should always laugh
With her mouth closed, for the sight of a mouth
Stretched like a gash across the face
Is not a pretty sight. If her teeth
Are not even, but ugly and crooked,

She will be thought little of if she shows them
When she laughs.
There is also a proper way
To cry. But every woman is adept
Enough to cry well on any occasion,
For, even though the tears are not caused
By grief or shame or hurt, they are always
Ready. All women cry; they are used
To crying in whatever way they want.
But no man should be disturbed when he sees
Such tears flowing as fast as rain,
For these tears, these sorrows and lamentations
Flow only to trick him. A woman's weeping
Is nothing but a ruse; she will overlook
No source of grief. But she must be careful
Not to reveal, in word or deed,
What she is thinking of.
It is also proper to behave suitably
At table. Before sitting down she should look
Around the house and let everyone understand
That she herself knows how to run a house.
Let her come and go, in the front rooms and in back,
And be the last to sit down, being sure
To wait a little before she finally
Takes her seat. Then, when she's seated
At table, she should serve everyone as well
As possible. She should slice the bread
In front of the others and pass it to those
Around her. To deserve praise, let her serve
The food in front of the one who shares
Her plate. She should put a thigh or wing
Before him, in his presence, carve
The beef or pork, meat or fish,
Depending upon what food there happens
To be. She should never be niggardly
In her servings as long as there is anyone
Unsatisfied. Let her guard against getting
Her fingers wet up to the joint
In the sauce, against smearing lips with soup,

Garlic, or fat meat, against piling up
Too large morsels and stuffing her mouth.
When she has to moisten a piece in any
Sauce, either *verte, cameline,* or *jauce,*
She should hold the bit with her fingertips
And bring it carefully up to her mouth,
So that no drop of soup, sauce, or pepper
Falls on her breast. She must drink so neatly
That she doesn't spill a single thing on herself,
For anyone who happened to see her spill
Would think her either very clumsy
Or very greedy. Again, she must take care
Not to touch her drinking cup
While she has food in her mouth. She should wipe
Her mouth so clean that grease will not stick
To the cup, and should be particularly careful
About her upper lip, for, when
There's grease on it, untidy drops
Of it will show in her wine. She should drink
Only a little at a time, however great
Her appetite, and never empty
A cup, large or small, in one
Breath, but rather drink little and often,
So that she doesn't go around
Causing others to say that she gorges
Or drinks too much while her mouth is full.
She should avoid swallowing the rim of her cup,
As do many greedy nurses, who are so foolish
That they pour wine down their hollow throats
As if they were casks, who pour it down
In such huge gulps that they become
Fuddled and dazed. Now a lady
Must be careful not to get drunk, for a drunk,
Man or woman, cannot keep anything
Secret; and when a woman gets drunk,
She has no defenses at all in her,
She blurts out everything whenever she thinks it
And abandons herself to anyone
When she gives herself over to such bad conduct.

She must also beware of falling asleep
At table, for she would be much less pleasant;
Many disagreeable things can happen
To those who take such naps. There is no
Sense in napping in places where one
Should remain awake, and many have been
Deceived in this way, have many times fallen,
Either forwards or backwards or sideways, and broken
An arm or head or ribs. Let a woman
Beware lest such a nap overtake her;
Let her recall Palinurus, the helmsman
Of Aeneas's ship; while awake he steered it
Well, but when sleep overcame him,
He fell from the rudder into the sea and drowned
Within sight of his companions, who afterward
Greatly mourned for him.

Further,
A lady must be careful not to be too
Reluctant to play, for she might wait around
So long that no one would want to offer
His hand to her. She should seek the seduction
Of love while youth leads her in that
Direction, for, when old age assails
A woman, she loses both the joy
And the assault of Love. A wise woman
Will gather the fruit of love in the flower
Of her age. The unhappy woman loses
Her time who passes it without
Enjoying love. And if she disbelieves
This advice of mine, which I give
For the profit of all, be sure that she
Will be sorry when age withers her. But I know
That women will believe me, particularly those
Who are sensible, and will stick to our rules and will say
Many paternosters for my soul
When I am dead, who now teach
And comfort them. I know that this lesson
Will be read in many schools.

O fair sweet

Son, if you live—for I see well that you
Are writing down in the book of your heart
The whole of my teaching, and that, when you depart
From me, you will read more, if pleasing
To God, and will become a master
Like me—if you live I confer on you
The license to teach, in spite of all
Chancellors, in chambers or in cellars, in meadow,
Garden, or thicket, under a tent
Or behind the tapestries, and to instruct the students
In wardrobes, storerooms, pantries, and stables,
If you find no pleasanter places.
And may my lesson be well taught
When you have learned it well.

A woman
Should be careful not to stay too much
Shut up, for while she remains indoors
She is less seen by everybody, her beauty
Is less well-known, less desired and in demand
Less. She should go often to the principal
Church and go visiting, to weddings, on trips,
At games, feasts, and round dances, for in such places
The god and goddess of love keep their schools
And sing mass to their disciples.

But of course,
If she is to be admired above others,
She has to be well dressed. When she is well
Turned out and goes through the streets,
She should carry herself well, not too stiffly
Nor too loosely, neither too upright
Nor too inclined, but easily and graciously
In any crowd. She should move her shoulders
And sides so elegantly that no one might find
Any movements more beautiful. And she should walk
Daintily in her pretty little shoes, so well made
That they fit her feet without any wrinkles
Whatever. If her dress drags or hangs down near the pavement,
She should raise it on the sides or in front as if
To have a little ventilation

Or as if she had the habit of tucking up
Her gown in order to step more freely.
Then she must be careful to let all the passers-by
See the fine shape of her exposed foot.
And if she is the sort to wear a coat
She should wear it so that it will not
Hinder too much the view of the beautiful body
It covers. She will want to display
Her body and the cloth in which she is dressed;
The stuff should be neither too heavy nor light,
With threads of silver and seed pearls. She will want
Particularly to show off her purse, which should be
Exposed for all to see; therefore
She should take the coat in both hands and widen
And extend her arms, whether she's on
A clean street or a muddy one. Remembering
The wheel which the peacock makes with his tail,
She should do the same with her coat, to display
Openly both her body and the fur linings
Of her clothing, squirrel or other costly fur,
To all she might see staring at her.
Now if her face is not handsome,
She must be clever and show to people
Her beautiful priceless blond tresses
And her well-coiffed neck. A lovely head
Of hair is a very pleasant thing.
A woman should always take care
To imitate the she-wolf when she wants
To steal lambs, for, in order not to fail
Completely, she has to attack a thousand
To capture one; she doesn't know which
She will take before she has taken it.
Thus a woman ought to spread her nets
Everywhere in order to catch all men:
Since she cannot know which of them she may have
The grace to catch, at least she ought
To hook on to all of them in order to be sure
Of having one for herself. If she does so,
It should never happen that she will have

No catch at all from among the thousands
Of fools who will rub up against her flanks.
Indeed she may catch several, for art
Is a great aid to nature.
But if she does
Hook several of those who want to skewer
Her, let her be careful, however things run,
Not to make appointments at the same hour
With two of them. If several were to appear
Together they would think themselves deceived
And they might even leave her. An event like this
Could set her back a long way, for at the least
She would lose what each had brought her.
She should never leave them anything
On which they might grow fat, but plunge them
Into poverty so great that they may die
Miserable and in debt; in this way she
Will be rich, for what remains theirs
Is lost to her.
She should not love a poor man,
For a pauper is good for nothing. Even if he
Were Ovid or Homer, he wouldn't be worth
Two drinking mugs. Nor should she love
A foreign traveler, for his heart is as flighty
As his body, which lodges in many places;
No, I advise her not to love a traveler.
However, if during his stay he offers
Money or jewels, she should take them all
And put them in her coffer; then he
May do as he pleases, in haste or at his leisure.
She must be very careful not to love or value
Any man who is too elegant or haughty
About his beauty, for it is pride which tempts him.
The man who pleases himself, never doubt it,
Incurs the wrath of God; so says Ptolemy,
The great lover of knowledge. Such a man
Has so evil and bitter a heart that he cannot
Love well. What he says to one woman he says
To all. He tricks many to despoil and rob them.

I have seen many complaints of maidens
Thus deceived.
And if anyone,
Honest man or swindler, makes promises,
Hoping to beg for her love and bind her
To him by vows, she may exchange vows,
But she must be careful not to put
Herself at his mercy unless she gets hold
Of the money as well. If he makes any promise
In writings, she must see if there is any
Deception or if his good intentions
Are those of a true heart. She may then write
An early reply, but not without some delay.
Delay excites lovers as long
As it's not too great.
Again, when she hears
A lover's request, she should be reluctant
To grant all her love, yet shouldn't refuse
Everything, but try to keep him in a state
Of balance between fear and hope. When he makes
His demands more pressing and she doesn't yield
To him her love, which has bound him so strongly,
She must arrange things, through her strength and craft,
So that hope grows constantly, little by little
While fear diminishes, until peace and concord
Bring the two together. In giving in to him, she,
Who knows so many wily ruses,
Should swear by God and by the saints
That she has never wished to give herself
To anyone, no matter how well he may have plead;
Then she should say, "My lord, this
Is my all; by the faith which I owe to St. Peter
Of Rome, I give myself to you
Out of pure love, not because of your gifts.
The man isn't born for whom I would do this
For any gift, however greatly he desired it.
I have refused many a worthy man, for many
Have gazed adoringly at me. I think
You must have cast a spell over me;

You have sung me a wicked song."
Then she should embrace him closely
And kiss him so that he'll be better deluded.
But if she wants my advice, she should think
Only of what she can get. She's a fool
Who doesn't pluck her lover down
To the last feather, for the better she can pluck
The more she'll have, and she'll be more highly
Valued when she sells herself more dearly.
Men scorn what they can get for nothing;
They value it at not a single husk.
If they lose it, they care little, certainly
Not as much as does one who has bought it
At a high price.
Here, then, are proper ways
To pluck men: Get your servants, the chambermaid,
The nurse, your sister, even your mother,
If she's not too particular, to help on the task
And do all they can to get the lover
To give them coats, jackets, gloves,
Or mittens; like kites, they will plunder
Whatever they can seize from him,
So that he may in no way escape from their hands
Before he has spent his last penny.
Let him give them money and jewels
As though he were playing with buttons instead
Of money. The prey is captured much sooner
When it is taken by several hands.

CHARLES DAHLBERG

COLIN MUSET

My Lord, Although I Strum and Sing

Sire cuens, j'ai vielé

My Lord, although I strum and sing
For you and all your company,

Not so much as a ha'penny
Has yet repaid my offering.
        My Lord, for shame!
Thus, by the Virgin shall I swear
To quit your hire. My purse is bare;
Alas, alack, my sack's the same!

My loyalty no bounds would know,
If only my obedience
Were crowned with worthy recompense,
Would you, My Lord, some boon bestow,
        And handsomely!
For when I venture home, unpaid,
I cannot pass the ambuscade:
My wife is there to welcome me!

"Well, Master Dolt! (Thus she descends
Upon me!) So! You dare come in
With empty hands! Where have you been?
Carousing with your scurvy friends
        All round about!
See how your sack hangs airily!
Oh, fie on the society
That suffers such a knavish lout!"

But when I have a better day
And homeward come, she sees the sack
Heavily hanging on my back,
Well filled, and me in garments gray,
        Splendidly dressed;
Then does she lay her spinning staff
Aside, and with a hearty laugh
Presses me warmly to her breast.

My sack she empties in a trice.
My kitchen-wench, the while, makes haste
To cook two capons to my taste,
Served up with garlic-sauce and spice.
Scarce have I from my horse alit

Than comes my groom to water it.
My daughter, then,
(A comely lass) brings me my comb.
And so I reign within my home,
Indeed the lordliest of men!

NORMAN R. SHAPIRO

RUTEBEUF

His Poverty
La Pauvreté

I do not know where to begin,
Except to boldly ask, and in
God's name, frank king of France, you see
How you may treat me as your kin,
In gracious charity, and win
Grace for thus ending misery.
One act of kindness cannot sate
The donor, and my debt is great:
No one will credit poverty.
You have been far away of late;
My earnest pleas were forced to wait;
And I need help most desperately.

The home I had I cannot claim,
For sickness and hunger came
And banished me to beggary.
My former friends are friends in name:
I asked for alms; they dispensed blame
And bad advice too lavishly.
Each husbands wisely lest his own
Possessions die. Good king, my moan
Must reach, through Afric savagery
And heathendom, your absent throne.
Absence has harmed me, left me alone,
And death has robbed me willfully.

If it should be, great king, you lack
All that I need—even a sack
On which to rest a weary head
(The straw I lie on breaks my back
And ribs; a straw bed is a rack)—
Then I might just as well be dead.
If I may your attention hold,
Sire, I am dying of the cold;
Hungry and frozen, I must tread
The road from here to Senlis—old,
Forgotten, homeless, without gold;
No one so poor; my cloak a shred.

In Paris, sire, riches surround
A misery that knows no bound;
I lack a coin for daily bread.
With poverty my head is crowned:
This is the largesse that I found
In St. Paul's words, which once I read.
These are the times that almost shake
Man's faith, his emptied spirit break;
I beg a father with that dread
I pray Our Father not forsake
My trust. *Credo;* no credit take.—
Now I lack paper, as my plaint is sped.

JAMES EDWARD TOBIN

His Repentance
La Repentance

Now must I disown poesy,
For I confess full wretchedly
That I have practiced it too long;
And sorely does it grieve my heart
That never have I turned my art
To praise the Lord in sacred song.

But rather have I tuned my voice
To accents of a different choice,
For naught but worldly mirth outspun
My rhymes. Oh! Virgin Mother mild,
Thou who hast borne the Holy Child,
Pray for me, else I am undone.

Alas! Too late do I repent
The folly of a life ill spent
In idleness, iniquity,
And earthly joys. Yet if I dare
Confess my sins, my soul lay bare,
Even the just will shrink from me.
I filled my belly well, but not
With what my labors had begot.
Worldly success is falsehood's kin!
And if I claim that ignorance
Alone kept me from penitence,
I see no hope of Heaven therein.

No hope of Heaven! Alas! Yet why
Lament? The wrong is mine. Did I
Not take God's priceless offering,
Intelligence? Was I not wrought
In His own image? Did He not
(Most precious gift!) suffer the sting
Of death, to save my soul? Did He
Not grant me the ability
To outwit the Malevolent,
Accursèd jailor who would fain
Add my soul to his dark domain
Of ransomless imprisonment?

In fleshly joys I spent my time,
Singing my song, rhyming my rhyme,
To please some with my calumny
Of others. Thus the King of Sin
Has chosen me to dwell within
His realm for all Eternity.

And if the Maid of Innocence
Ignores my suppliant penitence,
Then has my evil heart a wealth
Of grief bestowed upon me, nor
Shall any human art restore
My sickly soul to holy health.

There is a Doctoress whose skills
In healing mankind's mortal ills
Surpass the cures of Lyons' sage
Physicians, and those of Vienne.
Her art is infinite; for when
She would your suffering assuage,
No wound resists her surgery.
She cleansed the sainted Mary, she
In Egypt born, and to the King
Of Heaven rendered her free from stain.
Oh! could my wretched soul but gain
The solace of her comforting!

Alike, the stout and weak must die.
What consolation, then, can I
Expect? What bulwark can I raise
Against this enemy? I see
No one so sound and strong that he
Can long endure; Death lays
Him sharply down. No age is spared:
The young are with the old ensnared
In Death's unyielding grasp. And when
Our bodies are to dust restored,
Then stand our souls before the Lord
To answer for our flaws as men.

Now I have reached the end, outworn
With all the sins my soul has borne.
God grant I be not yet without
Salvation! For, unceasingly
Did I compound my infamy;
And I have heard it said about:

"Long-smold'ring fires burn hot!" I thought
I could deceive Deceit; I sought
To vanquish him. Nay, not a whit!
He reigns supreme, and I retreat,
Leaving this life, in dark defeat,
To anyone who prizes it.

NORMAN R. SHAPIRO

The Dispute of Charlot and the Barber
La Desputoison de Charlot et du Barbier

One day as I was going
To St. Martin of Auxerre
Early in the morning
Before I like to rise
I came upon Charlot
Half-way up the road
Holding the barber's hand
Yet it was plain as day
That they were not first cousins.
Their jokes about each other
Were coarse, and very true:
"Charlot, you're up to mischief
To make some Christian rue
Your perfidy and treason
For everyone's aware
You only curse to swear
And have no shame at all."
"Barber, by the suburb
Where you ply your hairy trade,
Your gout is on the rampage,
It never stops a day;
St. Lazarus got after you
And lepered up your face.
If you want the plague to spare you,
Don't scorn his holy place."
"Charlot, by good St. James,

I'd swear you found a wife.
Is she some poor defective
The rabbi gave away?
You believe as much in Our Lady
Whose virginity's astray
As I believe a she-ass has a soul;
You don't love God or Holy Church."
"Razorless, scissorless Barber,
You can't cut hair or shave.
You have no towels or basins
Or water-heater paid.
You're simply good for nothing
But chewing off my ear.
If you were overseas, or started off, I'd say
Maybe he'll do well on the crusades."
"Charlot, you know all laws,
You're Jew and Christian both,
Strutting knight and townsman,
Or grizzly priest of old.
You're mackerel and fishing,
That's what the old folks say:
By your jokes, you often couple
Young blood that needs a fling."
"Barber, the time has come
To call a spade a spade:
Your hair will turn snow-white
Before you quit that trade.
But you'll die poor and naked
You're slipping down the stream:
If people say I'm pimping,
They'll say you go between."
"Charlot, Charlot, my handsome friend,
You condescend to children of the king.
If you're in the palace, who put you there?
You're there as much as I.
You've learned to act half-crazy
You've greased your palms with gold
And money's even crazier for you."
"Barber, now the currants
And bushes are in thorn:

And here's some news you'll relish:
Your forehead's sprouting horns.
It looks as if scarlet berries
Have ripened on your face:
They'll turn a pretty crimson
Before you're dragged away."
"It's not a touch of leprosy,
Charlot, it's just pink gout,
I swear by St. Marie;
You don't love her for anything;
You have more faith in Jewry
Than in him who by his power
Unbolts the gates of hell."
"Yet nonetheless if Rutebeuf
Who's known us these ten years
Would like to make new ditties,
Providing we can get him
To judge the matter fairly
And only tell the truth,
Then, if you like, he'll choose
The better of us two."
"Lord, by the faith I owe you,
I can't choose which is best
But only who's less evil
From him who's really worst.
Charlot's not worth a sneeze,
If you insist on truth,
He has no more belief or faith
Than a dog that drags a corpse.
The barber knows good people
He serves and honors well
And splurges heart and money
To please from here to hell.
He knows his job so wholly
That should the need arise
With flaming cheeks and phallus
He'll serve you for a price."

WILLIAM M. DAVIS

⚜

To the Virgin
De la Chanson de Nostre Dame

As the fair sun touches the earth each day,
Probing each pane
And warming every room,
And undimmed brightnesses in every ray
Fall yet remain,
So in the Virgin's womb
She carried God, and fed
Him whom she nourished:
Sun, Son; His life, and hers,
Gives and is given, confers
The light and warmth of Him
Which never dim.

JAMES EDWARD TOBIN

ADAM DE LA HALLE

So Much the More as I Draw near My Land
De tant com plus approime mon pais

So much the more as I draw near my land
does love renew, and all its bonds invoke;
and things appear more fair as I approach
and sweeter air blows upon gentler folk.

Having been exiled long—
yet never in thought—
for old-times' sake I sought
converse with honored ladies, here;
and found in one of them a grace
recalling my old Lady's face;
and this had charm to make me find
delight in her fair countenance.

Thus does the tigress when her cub is seized,
gulled by her own reflection in a glass,

think she has found the very thing she sought,
and from her lets its captor freely pass.

Do not pass thus from me,
Oh Lady dear,
nor put me from your mind
for my long tarrying here.
It is through memory of you
that in a likeness I forget
myself; for all in you are set
my heart and my hope's sustenance.

IRMA BRANDEIS

To All My Dainty Loves, Goodbye

A Dieu comant amourettes

To all my dainty loves, goodbye,
for I depart
against my will into a foreign land.

Sweet things, I leave with bitter sigh
and heavy heart
to all my dainty loves, goodbye.

You should be little queens if I
played the king's part
and could command.

To all my dainty loves, goodbye,
for I depart
against my will into a foreign land.

IRMA BRANDEIS

All Too Much I Long to See

Trop désir a voir

All too much I long to see
her I prize.
I cannot change or turn away:
all too much I long to see;

both by night and by day
poor heart cries:
all too much I long to see
her I prize.

IRMA BRANDEIS

Love and My Lady, Too

Amours et ma Dame aussi

Love and my Lady, too,
hands-joined, for favor's grace I sue;
from your great beauty springs my rue,
Love and my Lady, too.

Hands-joined, for favor's grace I sue.
if prayer can no pity woo,
from your great beauty springs my rue,
Love and my Lady, too.

IRMA BRANDEIS

JACOB BAR JUDA, HAZAK

Sorely Tried Is Israel, the Hapless Folk

Mont sont a mecchief Isr[ael], l'eegaree gent

Sorely tried is Israel, the hapless folk,
And not to blame if overcome by rage,

For many a valiant, wise, and gentle man
Was burned, who could not buy his life with silver.

Our joy has fled, and with it our delight
In those who studied Scripture night and day
And pursued their task without respite:
Now they are burnt and dead: each acknowledged God.

From the wicked people this outrage came:
Well may we change our color pale or bright:
Lord! Take pity and hear our cries, our tears!
For naught have we lost many an upright man.

To the stake was led Rab Isaac of Chatillon
Who for God left flush with rents and houses.
He returns to God. Rich was he in properties,
Good author of comments on the Talmud and the Bible.

When his noble wife saw her husband burn,
The loss hit her hard: she screamed with all her might:
"I will die the death my lover died!"
She was great with child; her suffering was great.

Then her sons were burned, one big, one small.
The younger, startled by the rising flames,
Cried, "Haro, I'm burning up!" And the elder:
"You'll go to Paradise, I promise that."

The daughter-in-law was so fair, they sent for a priest:
"We'll give you a squire who'll hold you very dear."
Then she started spitting in their face:
"I won't leave God—you can flay me alive!"

With one voice all together their song rose loud and clear
Like celebrants performing at a feast;
Their hands were tied; they could not dance;
Never did men leave life so well.

A bridegroom was dragged swiftly to the fire
And sang the prayer of sanctity on high:
He gave the others courage; well born was he,
Samson by name, son-in-law of the Scribe.

After him came Solomon; a victim highly prized
Who, thrown into the fire now ablaze,
Did not deny his body to the Lord,
But suffered death for love of Him, prepared.

The wicked hangman frowned and burned them all
One after the other. Then spoke a saint:
"Stoke it higher, wicked man!" And the hangman dared
to curse him.
It was beautiful, the death of Baruch d'Avirey.

A noble man there was, who then began to weep,
And said: "I weep for my poor children,
Not myself." They burned him on the spot.
It was Simon, the Scribe, who always prayed so well.

. . . .

Preachers came and fetched Rab Isaac Cohen:
"Let him abjure, or he will perish, too."
He said: "What are you asking? I want to die for God.
I am a Cohen.[1] I give my body unto God."

"You can't escape. We've got you.
Become a Christian." And he answered, "No!
For dogs I won't forsake His Holy Name."
He was called Haiim,[2] the master of Brinon.

Another saint[3] was now brought to the pyre:
They stirred slow flames until they flickered high
With all his heart he called to God and prayed
And suffered torture sweetly in His Name.

---

[1] Cohen = *priest, in Hebrew.* [2] Haiim = *Living, in Hebrew.*
[3] Kadosh = *saint, usually in the sense of* martyr.

Vengeful God, jealous God, avenge us on the wicked!
Waiting for Thy vengeance, day ne'er seems to end!
When we sit in our houses and walk by the way
We are prepared and ready
To pray with all our hearts.
Answer us, Lord, we beseech Thee!

WILLIAM M. DAVIS

GUILLAUME DE MACHAUT

As Lilies White, More Crimson Than the Rose

Blanche com lys, plus que rose vermeille

As lilies white, more crimson than the rose,
Resplendent as a ruby from the East,
Your beauty is; now as I gaze it glows
As lilies white, more crimson than the rose;
My senses are ravished and my spirit knows
Her it must serve, by love's law unreleased:
As lilies white, more crimson than the rose,
Resplendent as a ruby from the East.

DWIGHT DURLING

If I Must Feel Your Wrath Eternally

Se vos courrous me dure longuement

If I must feel your wrath eternally,
I fear my days their waning measure spend.

Thus will you see me perish wretchedly
If I must feel your wrath eternally.

So grows my passion, unrelentingly,
That life itself is yours, to add or end.

If I must feel your wrath eternally,
I fear my days their waning measure spend.

NORMAN R. SHAPIRO

Rich in Love and Beggar to My Heart

Riches d'amour et mendians d'amie

Rich in love and beggar to my heart
Poor in hope and surging with desire
Full of grief and destitute of help
Far from pity, greedy for renown,
Love makes me so, and I fear death
When my lady hates and I adore her.

I feel no balm is curative
However far I seek it:
For love so blossoms here within
That I can't revel or repent it.
I can't find death or happiness
Or treasure, short of grief,
When my lady hates and I adore her.

But the wish for my sweet enemy
Will gladly, humbly suffer,
For great's the honor done to me
Despite her, when I love her.
And if love wills my mortal end
For cherishing, naught better,
When my lady hates and I adore her.

WILLIAM M. DAVIS

I Curse the Hour, the Moment and the Day

Je maudis l'eure et le temps et le jour

I curse the hour, the moment and the day,
The week, the place, the month, the tide, the year,
And the twin eyes which fell a willing prey
To that fair lady who hath killed my cheer.
I curse my heart, too, and my thought, my sheer
Loyalty and desire and love whose sway
Abandons to its perilous dismay
My grieving heart in this strange country here.

I curse the welcome, the allure, the gay
Grace of the glance mine heart hath grown to fear,
Which love and passion now do burn and flay,
I curse her hour of birth, her insincere
Mock semblance and her falsity made clear,
Her monstrous pride and harshness which betray
No wraith of tenderness that might allay
My grieving heart in this strange country here.

And I curse Fortune and her traitorous way,
The planet and the lore and the career
Which led my foolish heart so far astray
That, loving her, I held her service dear.
Yet pray I God maintain her fame austere,
To guard her goods and land and honor aye,
To grant her His forgiveness who did slay
My grieving heart in this strange country here.

JACQUES LECLERCQ

Strike Down My Heart with But a Single Blow

Faites mon cuer tout a un coup morir

Strike down my heart with but a single blow;
Milady, let this be my recompense,

Since you have naught of pleasure to bestow.
Strike down my heart with but a single blow,

For better thus, than to endure my woe,
Hopeless of cure, bereft of my defense.
Strike down my heart with but a single blow;
Milady, let this be my recompense.

NORMAN R. SHAPIRO

Milady, Comely, Candid, Worldly-Wise

Douce dame, cointe, apperte et jolie

Milady, comely, candid, worldly-wise,
With all my soul I wish to serve you well.

Fie, fie on arrant fool who "folly" cries—
Milady, comely, candid, worldly-wise—

When thus your sweet enchantments tyrannize
My heart, happy in servitude to dwell.
Milady, comely, candid, worldly-wise,
With all my soul I wish to serve you well.

NORMAN R. SHAPIRO

Open Your Eyes, Milady, Run Me Through

Partués moy a l'ouvrir de vos yeux

Open your eyes, Milady, run me through,
You who feel no compassion for my pain!

If I can earn no kinder fate from you,
Open your eyes, Milady, run me through.

Alas, I fear you can naught better do
For hopeless love. Give ear to my refrain:

"Open your eyes, Milady, run me through,
You who feel no compassion for my pain!"

NORMAN R. SHAPIRO

⚜

Ah! How I Fear, Milady, Lest I Die

De morir sui pour vous en grant paour

Ah! how I fear, Milady, lest I die
For love of you and for my eagerness;

Your willing subject, nay, your slave am I.
Ah! how I fear, Milady, lest I die.

For when I may not cast my anxious eye
Upon your all-alluring comeliness,
Ah! how I fear, Milady, lest I die
For love of you and for my eagerness.

NORMAN R. SHAPIRO

JEAN FROISSART

Be Gallant, Mannerlie and Pure of Heart

Aies le coer courtois et honnourable

Be gallant, mannerlie and pure of heart,
Meek and discreet, tacit and fraught with glee,
Sincere and moderate; for thine high part
Be gallant, mannerlie and pure of heart.
Do as may be, indifferent of art,
Then love and ladys fair shall pity thee.
Be gallant, mannerlie and pure of heart.

JACQUES LECLERCQ

⚜

O Love, O Love, What Wouldst Thou Make of Me?

Amours, Amours, que volés de moi faire?

O Love, O Love, what wouldst thou make of me
Who in thee find naught save extravagance?
I know thee not nor what thy traffick be.
O Love, O Love, what wouldst thou make of me?
Silence, speech, prayer—which choose I of these three?
Make answer, thou, whose ways are of fair chance!
O Love, O Love, what wouldst thou make of me?

JACQUES LECLERCQ

Of All Known Flowers, Men Hold the Rose Most Rare

Sus toutes fleurs tient on la rose à belle

Of all known flowers, men hold the rose most rare,
And, after it, I think, the violet;
Lilies are proud, corncockles debonair,
The lofty gladiol is comelier yet;
Many a wight treasures the columbine
Or deems the lily-of-the-valley fine,
Or prizeth peonies, since all are sweet;
But for mine heart, one choice alone is mine:
Of all known flowers, I love the Marguerite.

Let rain or hail or hoarfrost fill the air,
And be the season dry or harsh or wet,
This flower is ever gracile, fresh and fair,
All dainty, pink-and-white, earth's amoret,
Perfect in bud, in blossoming divine,
Never to pale, to perish, or to pine;
For him who reads the writ upon its sheet,
Kindness and beauty rise from every line.
Of all known flowers, I love the Marguerite.

As I recall this flower, excess of care
Burdens my soul, for how shall I forget
Its heart, a stronghold, with that turret where
Rise obstacles I ceaselessly beset?
Daylong, nightlong, I seek to countermine,
Yet will her love not forward my design
Nor yield one sconce or fort though I repeat
Attack upon attack to storm this shrine . . .
Of all known flowers, I love the Marguerite.

JACQUES LECLERCQ

AGNES DE NAVARRE-CHAMPAGNE

Lover, as God May Comfort Me

Amy si Dieu me confort

Lover, Lover, as God may comfort me,
So shalt thou boast my heart and soul,
In that I love thee mightily.
Lover, as God may comfort me,
Lay care by and anxiety
Since thine I am, entire and whole—
Lover, as God may comfort me,
So shalt thou boast my heart and soul.

JACQUES LECLERCQ

Without My Heart, Love, Thou Shalt Not Depart

Sans coeur de my pas vous ne partirez

Without my heart, love, thou shalt not depart,
Nay but thy leman's heart shall go with thee
To lie deep in thee wheresoe'er thou art—
Without my heart, love, thou shalt not depart.
Well shalt thou harbor it from duel or smart
And dearly prize thine own for company . . .

Without my heart, love, thou shalt not depart,
Nay but thy leman's heart shall go with thee.

JACQUES LECLERCQ

EUSTACHE DESCHAMPS

One Day the Rats of All Degrees

Je treuve qu'entre les souris

One day the rats of all degree
Convened in wondrous parliament
Against the cats, their foe, to see
How to contrive, as matters went,
To live securely. This intent
Inspired much speech of this and that,
Till one remarked in argument:
"Which one of us shall bell the cat?"

Since none was found to disagree,
They voted to adjourn, content,
Then met a lowland mouse. As he
Asked news of what was imminent,
They vaunted their accomplishment:
Their foe, beguiled and vanquished, at
His neck a bell, was impotent!
Which one of us shall bell the cat?

A gray rat ventured: "As for me,
I find this hard of management!"
"Who shall our gallant savior be?"
The mouse inquired. Incontinent,
Each one begged off with eloquent
Excuses, and the plan fell flat,
Though all joined in the sentiment:
Which one of us shall bell the cat?

Envoi

Prince, counsel may be excellent,

But very often, like the rat,
We had best look to the event:
"Which one of us shall bell the cat?"

JACQUES LECLERCQ

But Is There No Flower, Perfume or Violet?

Or, n'est-il fleur, odeur ne violete?

But is there no flower, perfume or violet,
Tree or eglantine, however sweet within,
Beauty or kindness, however perfect a thing,
Man or woman, however fair or gentle,
Curly or blond, strong, frank or lovely,
Wise or foolish, that by Nature has been made,
Which in its time will not be old or stale,
Which in the end death will not pursue,
And when old, will not lose its fame?
Old age is final, youth is the time of grace.

The perfumed flower of May delights all men
Who smell it, but for little more than a day,
For in a moment comes the waiting wind
And makes it fall, or cuts it into two;
The lives of trees and people pass like this,
Nothing stable by Nature is decreed:
All things must die that have been born;
A poor access of fever snuffs out man,
Or old age, whose limits have been set.
Old age is final, youth is the time of grace.

How then can any maid or mistress do
So great a harm unto her lover's love
When they will wither all, as grass beneath
Our feet? It is pure madness. Why don't we then
Have pity on each other? When all are rotten—
Both those who never loved and those who did—

Those who refused will be proclaimèd weak,
And those who gave will have rosy faces,
And their fame will spread throughout the world.
Old age is final, youth is the time of grace.

Envoi

Prince, each man in his youthful age
Should grasp the time that is allotted it.
When old he should do the contrary things.
So both ages will be dear to him,
Nor will he be too proud when he's in love.
Old age is final, youth is the time of grace.

MURIEL KITTEL

Am I, Am I, Am I Fair?
Suis-je, suis-je, suis-je belle?

Am I, am I, am I fair?
It seems as far as I can tell
My brow is fair, my face is sweet.
And my mouth is red and neat;
Tell me if I'm fair.

I have green eyes and small eyebrows,
My nose is delicate and blond my hair,
My chin is round, my throat is white;
Am I, am I, am I fair?

My breasts are firm and carried high,
My arms are long, my fingers slim,
And my waist is small and trim;
Tell me if I'm fair.

I have tiny rounded feet,
Good shoes and pretty clothes I wear,
I am gay and full of mirth;
Tell me if I'm fair.

I have cloaks fur-lined in gray,
I have hats and trimmings fine,
I have many a silver pin;
Am I, am I, am I fair?

I've silken sheets and tapestry,
I've sheets of white and beige and gold,
Many a dainty thing I hold;
Tell me if I'm fair.

I'm fifteen only, I tell you;
Many my pretty treasures are
If I keep the key with care;
Am I, am I, am I fair?

Those who would be my friends
Must indeed be brave
If such a maid they'd have;
Tell me if I'm fair.

Before God, I promise too,
That if I live I'll be most true
To him—if I don't falter;
Am I, am I, am I fair?

If he be courteous and kind,
Valiant, well read and gay,
He shall always have his way;
Tell me if I'm fair.

It is an earthly paradise
To have a woman always near
Who is so blossoming and fresh;
Am I, am I, am I fair?

Among yourselves, faint-hearts,
Think on what I say;

Here ends my virelay:
Am I, am I, am I fair?

MURIEL KITTEL

CHRISTINE DE PISAN

Ye Gods! of Time I Am Weary
He Dieux! que le temps m'anuye!

Ye gods! of time I am weary,
A day seems like a week;
Than the winter's rain more dreary
This season weighs on me.
Alas, I have an ague,
With dizziness it fills me,
And loads with sorrow too:
This, sickness does to me.

More bitter than sweat is my taste,
My color's unhealthy and pale;
I need support when I cough,
And my breath does often fail.
And when the fever takes me,
So little strength I feel,
I can only drink herb tea:
This, sickness does to me.

To escape I've no intent,
For when I walk, 'tis little,
And not a league's extent;
But in a crowded room
They still must make me stay;
And: "Support me, I am weak,"
I often need to say.
This, sickness does to me.

Doctors, I'm full of ills,
Cure me, I'm bereft

Of health, which is far from me.
This, sickness does to me.

MURIEL KITTEL

⚜

You Have Done So Much by Your Great Gentleness

Tant avez fait par votre grant doulçor

You have done so much by your great gentleness,
Most gentle friend, that you have conquered me,
No longer may I cry out or protest,
Nor will there be defenses set by me,
For love commands by gentle mastery,
And I too wish it; for, so God help me,
'Tis madness, after all, should I consider
Refusing one who loves so graciously.
And I have hope that there is so much worth
In you, that my love shall well seated be;
As for beauty, grace and all honor,
There is so much that there should rightly be
Enough, if it be right to choose you above
All, when you deserve to have much more;
So were I wrong, when so much does persuade me,
Refusing one who loves so graciously.

If my subtle gentle heart can hold
You and give to you my love, it begs
That no deceit or falsehood in you be,
For everything subdues me utterly:
Your gentle bearing, your calm behavior,
And your most gentle, loving, lovely eyes;
So far would I be wrong, in any wise
Refusing one who loves so graciously.

My gentle love, whom I love best, and prize,
I have such pleasure telling you alway

That by Reason I reproved should be
For refusing one who loves so graciously.

MURIEL KITTEL

Alone Am I, Alone I Wish to Be

Seulette suis, et seulette veuil estre

Alone am I, alone I wish to be,
Alone my gentle love has left me,
Alone am I without friend or master,
Alone am I, in sorrow and in anger,
Alone am I, ill at ease, in languor,
Alone am I, more lost than anyone,
Alone am I, left without a lover.

Alone am I standing at door or window,
Alone am I in a corner creeping,
Alone am I to feed myself with weeping,
Alone am I suffering or at rest,
Alone am I, and this pleases me the best,
Alone am I imprisoned in my chamber,
Alone am I, left without a lover.

Alone am I everywhere, by every hearth,
Alone am I, wherever I go or be,
Alone am I more than anything on earth,
Alone am I, by all men left alone,
Alone am I, most cruelly cast down,
Alone am I often full of weeping,
Alone am I, left without a lover.

Princes, now has my pain begun,
Alone am I, to deepest mourning nigh,
Alone am I, gloomier than the darkest dye,
Alone am I, left without a lover.

MURIEL KITTEL

Now Has Come the Gracious Month of May

Or est venu le très gracieux mois

Now has come the gracious month of May
The gay, who brings such bountiful delights
That these meadows, bushes and these woods
Are laden all with greenery and flowers,
　　And each thing does rejoice.
Among these fields all blossoms and turns green,
And nothing there but does forget its grief,
For delight in the lovely month of May.

The little birds sing on their way for joy,
With one heart all things do rejoice,
Except for me, alas! My grief is great
Because I am far distant from my love;
　　And I can feel no joy;
With the season's mirth my sorrow grows;
As you will know if you have ever loved,
For delight in the lovely month of May.

And so with frequent weeping I must mourn
For him, from whom I have no help;
The grievous hurts of love I now more deeply
Feel: the stings, th'attacks, the tricks and turns,
　　In this sweet time than ever
I have before; for all conspires to change
The great desire I once too strongly felt,
For delight in the lovely month of May.

MURIEL KITTEL

Ah Moon, You Shine Too Long

He, lune trop luis longuement

Ah moon, you shine too long,
You do the honeyed joys remove,
Given true lovers by Love.

Your brightness does much wrong
My heart, desiring love;
Ah moon, you shine too long.

For you are too revealing
Of me and the sweets of love;
Neither of us grateful prove.
Ah moon, you shine too long.

MURIEL KITTEL

Sweet Lady Fair
Plaisant et belle

Sweet lady fair,
Wherein does rest
My heart, and where
As in a nest
Lie tightly pressed
Kindness and grace,
Grant me thy grace.

More fresh and clear
Than the rose is blest,
To plaintive tear
From me expressed,
Do not molest
Pity's grace;
Grant me thy grace

Ah, turtle dear,
Shy in thy nest,
I beg thee fair,
In heart's distress,
I dare express
My love, no less;
Grant me thy grace.

So now unless
Thy heart repress
The desire I trace,
Grant me thy grace.

MURIEL KITTEL

Alone in Martyrdom I Have Been Left

Seulete m'a laissié en grant martyre

Alone in martyrdom I have been left
In the desert of this world, that's full of sadness,
By my sweet love, who held my heart
In sorrowless joy and in perfect gladness;
But he is dead, and such deep griefs oppress
Me, my weary heart such sorrows gnaw,
I shall bewail his death for evermore.

What can I ever do but weep and sigh for
My departed love, what wonder is this?
For when my heart profoundly ponders how
I lived secure and without bitterness,
Since childhood and early youthfulness
With him—at me such sufferings gnaw
I shall bewail his death for evermore.

As the turtledove without her mate does turn
To dry things only, nor cares more for greenness;
As the ewe that the wolf seeks to kill
Is terrified, by her shepherd left defenseless;
So am I left in great distress
By my dear love whose loss to me is sore;
I shall bewail his death for evermore.

MURIEL KITTEL

⚜

To Sing with Joy from out a Sorrowing Heart

De triste cuer chanter joyeusement

To sing with joy from out a sorrowing heart
And laugh while mourning, hard it is to bear,
To show the opposite of all one's care,
Nor betray a hint of any painful smart,

This must I do, nor keep myself apart,
But needs must—to hide my sad affair—
Sing with joy from out a sorrowing heart.

For secretly I carry in my heart
That grief that brings me most despair,
Therefore must I, to keep men's silence fair,
Laugh while I weep and with bitterest art
Sing with joy from out a sorrowing heart.

MURIEL KITTEL

I Will No Longer Serve You

Je ne te veuil plus servir

I will no longer serve you,
Love, to God I leave you.
You would too much subject me
And pay me scurvily;
Torment for hire you give me.
It is a hard thing to bear:
I will not stand it more.

To win favor from you
I served you faithfully,
But now cannot continue
Service, for you grievously
Torment me, so briefly

Prefer I to withdraw:
I will not stand it more.

Who binds himself to you
And gives himself completely,
Then down and up does go
If bid accordingly,
Must do so painfully
If my memory is sure.
I will not stand it more.

MURIEL KITTEL

The Gods and Goddesses, Those Great

Jadis par amours amoient

The gods and goddesses, those great
Servants of Love, were diligent,
As Ovid tells, to celebrate
Love's rites—and suffered discontent
And woes of love. But true intent
And faith they kept, left none aggrieved,
If ancient fables be believed.

They left Olympus for some mate
Of lowly earth, in their descent
Impetuous to participate
In earthly joys, with quick consent
Embracing them, indifferent
To costs of all such zeal achieved
If ancient fables be believed.

Delights of love could subjugate
Enchantress and nymph; immortals spent
Time, strength, and wealth immoderate
On maids and shepherds, earthward went
Bestowing boons munificent

On those whose favor they received
If ancient fables be believed.

So, ladies, lords, submit, assent
To love, nor seek to be reprieved
From service proved so excellent
If ancient fables be believed.

DWIGHT DURLING

If I'm in Church More Often Now

Se souvent vais au moustier

If I'm in church more often now
It's just that I can see her there
Fresh as new-opened roses are.

Why gossip of it, why endow
It with such consequence? Why stare
If I'm in church more often now?

Where I may go—or when—or how
It is to come more near to her.
Fools call me fool! It's whose affair
If I'm in church more often now?

DWIGHT DURLING

My Heart Is Captive to Gray, Laughing Eyes

Rians vairs yeulx qui mon cuer aves pris

My heart is captive to gray, laughing eyes,
To the entrapment of your boldest stare;
The happy victim of your sweetest snare,
I give myself to you, in willing wise.

What is the ransom price for such a prize?
One cannot tot its worth, yet does not care;
My heart is captive to gray, laughing eyes.

You are so sweet, so pleasant a surprise,
That no man lives, however weighed by care,
In all the world, but by your glance so rare
Recaptures peace, gains calmness as reprise:
My heart is captive to gray, laughing eyes.

JAMES EDWARD TOBIN

ALAIN CHARTIER

Most Foolish Fools, Oh Foolish Mortal Men

O folz des folz, et les folz mortels hommes

Most foolish fools, oh foolish mortal men
Who put such trust in Fortune's merchandise
On this earth, in this land where we live,
Can you call a single thing your own?
There is nothing here belongs to you,
Except the fair gifts of grace and nature.
If Fortune then, through some happenstance
Deprives you of the things you think are yours,
She does no wrong, but acts with simple justice,
For you had nothing the day that you were born.

No longer leave your naps of deepest slumber
In your own bed, by dark and shadowy night,
To gather riches, great and deep in number,
Nor covet anything beneath the moon,
Nothing between Paris and Pampelune,
But only that which every creature needs
To gain his livelihood, just that, no more.
Let it be enough to win renown,

And carry a good name to the tomb:
For you had nothing the day that you were born.

The joyous fruit of trees, the apples too,
In the age when everything was held in common,
The fine honey, the acorns and the gums
Were enough and more for every man and woman:
For no dispute or rancor was among them.
Be happy in the heat and in the frost,
And accept Fortune, gentle and secure.
As for your losses, wear not deep mourning for them,
Except in reason, justly and in moderation,
For you had nothing the day that you were born.

If fortune does any wrong to you,
It is her right, indeed, you must not blame her,
Even though she strip you of your shirt:
For you had nothing the day that you were born.

MURIEL KITTEL

Almighty God, Who Made the Noble State

Dieu tout puissant, de qui noblesse vient

Almighty God, who made the noble state,
Whose hands have molded all perfection,
Sustained and nourished all He did create
With providential, kind protection,
Ordained for everyone's direction
To keep in peace a land worth such endeavor—
For one, mastery; others, subjection—
Maintaining faith, respecting justice ever.

He who has highest honor by dictate
Of heaven and thus holds domination
Is also most severely bound to hate
Lack in himself of true affection,

Respectful awe, and deep devotion,
Shame for all sinful acts which might grace sever;
To act always with good intention,
Maintaining faith, respecting justice ever.

He thus is noble who commends his fate—
With no false boast, no self-deception—
To God: obedience a willing trait
And ways divine his firm confession.
He who gives variant attention
Betrays his noble name, wounds God, and never
Holds to a clear-defined profession,
Maintaining faith, respecting justice ever.

Lord, serf, rich, poor fall the possession
Of death at last, having served God; but never
May lord neglect his highest station,
Maintaining faith, respecting justice ever.

JAMES EDWARD TOBIN

CHARLES D'ORLÉANS

News Has Been Spread in France Concerning Me

Nouvelles ont couru en France

News has been spread in France concerning me
In various regions how that I was dead
Which filled some men with no uncertain glee,
Those wrongly hating me; and it is said
That others were truly discomforted,
Who loved me with a loyal inclination,
As real and honest friends do without fail,
Wherefore I now make public proclamation
That this mouse here, at least, is live and hale.

From hurt and harm I have, thank God! been free,
Healthy of limb and unimpaired of head,

I spend my time hoping that I may see
Long-slumbering peace at last awakened.
So may it flourish everywhere and spread
Its happiness to each and every nation,
Therefore may Heaven curse all who bewail
That great and happy news with desolation:
That this mouse here, at least, is live and hale.

Youth still governs my being puissantly
Though age makes efforts with accustomed dread
To grasp me in its cruel mastery,
But, for the while, its witchery is sped;
Too far removed I, from an oldster's bed
To give my heirs due cause for lamentation.
Praise God who gave me power to prevail
In strength, in fortitude and in such station
That this mouse here, at least, is live and hale.

Envoi

None need mourn me or pray for my salvation,
Gray cloth was ever cheaper by the bale,
So let all men know without hesitation
That this mouse here, at least, is live and hale.

JACQUES LECLERCQ

Pray for Peace, Oh Gentle Virgin Mary

Pries pour paix, doulce Vierge Marie

Pray for peace, oh gentle Virgin Mary,
Queen of heaven and the world's mistress,
Set to praying through your courtesy
The company of Saints—then turn your skillfulness
Towards your Son, beseeching his greatness
To look with pleasure on his people
Whom with his blood so willingly he bought,
And outlaw war which brings all things to naught;

Cease not your prayer, leave not for weariness,
But pray for peace that joy's own treasure is.

Pray, all bishops and holy men of God,
You monks and friars, sleep not in idleness,
Pray, all clerks who follow the priesthood,
For power of war will make all learning cease;
Your churches will be all destroyed—unless
You help. God's service you must leave
When you can dwell in it in peace no more;
Pray so earnestly that God may quickly hear,
The Church's will is to command you this;
Pray for peace that joy's own treasure is.

Pray, all princes who have sovereign rights,
Kings, dukes, counts, lords full of nobleness,
Gentlemen and company of knights;
For evil men are trampling greatness,
And holding in their hands your wealthiness,
Your quarrels let them rise to high degree,
This, every day, is seen with clarity;
They are rich with gold and property
Which you should hold and for your people use;
So pray for peace that joy's own treasure is.

Pray, all people suffering tyranny,
Your overlords are showing such weakness
They can no longer keep their sovereignty
O'er you; nor help your great distress;
Loyal merchants, the saddle hard does press
Upon your backs, each man does threaten you
So that your usual trade you may not ply,
For you have neither passage safe nor way
Through which to pass: your path in peril is;
So pray for peace that joy's own treasure is.

Pray, all gallants in joyful company,
Wishing to spend your money with largesse;

War keeps your purses empty constantly.
Pray, all lovers who wish in mirthfulness
To serve your loves; for war with its harshness
Hinders your visits to your mistresses,
And oftentimes will make them change their mind:
And when you think you have the rein, you'll find
A stranger comes and takes it to be his.
So pray for peace, that joy's own treasure is.

Envoi

That God Almighty may our comfort be,
Let all that lives on earth, in sky, or sea,
Pray to him, for each thing His care is;
Only through Him can evil's ending be;
So pray for peace that joy's own treasure is.

MURIEL KITTEL

Summer Has Sent His Minions on

Les fourriers d'Esté sont venus

Summer has sent his minions on
His spacious mansion to prepare
With arras woven everywhere
Of leaves and flowers, to spread upon

The earth green carpetry of lawn
And mead; to courts once cold and bare
Summer has sent his minions on.

Those folk but lately sad and wan
Have health, praise God, are freed from care.
Then go your way, plague of the year,
Winter; your time is past. Begone!

Summer has sent his minions on
His spacious mansion to prepare.

DWIGHT DURLING

Away with You! Begone! Begone!

Ales vous ant, ales, ales

Away with you! Begone! Begone,
Gray Melancholy, Grief, Despair!
How could you dream you could ensnare
Me always as you once have done?

Your stern dominion I disown;
Reason shall master it, I swear.
Away with you! Begone! Begone,
Gray Melancholy, Grief, Despair!

If with your retinue anon
You would revisit me, forbear!
I pray God curse you and declare
Your claims all void from this day on.
Away with you! Begone! Begone,
Gray Melancholy, Grief, Despair!

DWIGHT DURLING

Lovers, Beware the Dart That Flies

Gardez le trait de la fenestre

Lovers, beware the dart that flies
From windows as through streets you go,
For more swift to wound it is
Than arrow from arbalest or bow.
Look neither to your right nor left
As you pass by, but keep eyes low;

Lovers, beware the dart that flies
From windows as through streets you go.
If you have no doctor, sir,
When you feel the piercing blow,
God alone can help you now,
Send for the priest, you are Death's prize;
Lovers, beware the dart that flies.

MURIEL KITTEL

The Weather Has Laid Aside His Cloak

Le temps a laissié son manteau

The weather has laid aside his cloak
Of wind and frost and rain,
And has clothed himself with embroidery
Of sunshine clear and fine.
Every beast and bird
In his own tongue shouts and sings.
The weather has laid aside his cloak
Of wind and frost and rain.
River, stream and spring
Are wearing for gay livery
Silver and golden jewelry,
All wear new clothes again.
The weather has laid aside his cloak.

MURIEL KITTEL

While We Watch These Flowers Fair

En regardant ces belles fleurs

While we watch these flowers fair,
With whom the Springtime is in love,
Each of them makes gay her face,
Painting it with charming hues.

When flowers are embalmed with scent,
All our hearts with new life move,
While we watch these flowers fair,
With whom the Springtime is in love.

Birds turn into dancers now
Under many a flowering bough,
And form a joyful choir
With descant voices and with tenors,
While we watch these flowers fair.

MURIEL KITTEL

In the Book of My Thought
Dedens mon livre de pensée

In the book of my thought
I found my heart writing
Sorrow's true story
Illumined with tears.

Destroying the well-loved
Image of sweet delight;
In the book of my thought
I found my heart writing.

Ah! where had my heart found it?
Pain and toil stained him
With great drops of sweat
As he toiled day and night
In the book of my thought.

MURIEL KITTEL

Come, Let Us Taste Delight
Alons nous esbatre

Come, let us taste delight,
My heart, just you and I,
Leave Care alone
To carry on his fight.

He always will feel spite,
Quarrel, and know not why:
Come, let us taste delight,
My heart, just you and I.

Men should turn to smite
And point at you,
If you should let yourself
Fall under his might:
Come, let us taste delight.

MURIEL KITTEL

I Love Him Who Loves Me, Otherwise None
J'ayme qui m'ayme, autrement non

I love him who loves me, otherwise none;
And nonetheless, I hate no one,
But do wish that all went well
According to good Reason's rule.

I talk too much, alas! 'tis true!
But still, I hold unto this rule:
I love him who loves me, otherwise none,
And nonetheless I hate no one.

Pansies, for thought, upon his hood
My poor heart has strewn:

Directly from his side I come,
He has given me this tune:
I love him who loves me, otherwise none.

MURIEL KITTEL

Who's There, My Heart?—It Is We, Your Eyes

Cueur, qu'est-ce la?—Ce sommes-nous voz yeux

Who's there, my heart?— It is we, your eyes.
What do you bring?— A goodly crop of news.
What sort of news?— Fair news, and of love.
None for me, indeed, God help me, no!

Whence do you come?— From many a pleasant place.
What happens there?— Bargains in cheap strife.
Who's there, my heart?— It is we, your eyes.
What do you bring?— A goodly crop of news.

News for young men?— But it's for old men too?
Your news is all stale.— It's long since there were such.
But I know it, I know it.— Listen to it, at least.
Peace, I would sleep.— You act not for the best.
Who's there, my heart?— It is we, your eyes.

MURIEL KITTEL

Ah, God, Who Made Her Good to See

Dieu, qu'l la fait bon regarder

Ah, God, who made her good to see,
So gracious, beautiful, and sweet;
With the great gifts she has, how meet
That all in highest praise agree.

How could one tire of her, lovely
And ever-fresh from head to feet?
Ah, God, who made her good to see,
So gracious, beautiful, and sweet!

To think of her is melody!
Here or afar we cannot greet
A maid or matron half so sweet,
Or half so perfect as is she.
Ah, God, who made her good to see!

JAMES EDWARD TOBIN

Winter, You Are Merely a Churl

Yver, vous n'estes qu'un vilain

Winter, you are merely a churl;
Summer is kind, charming and gay,
As bear witness from dawn until dark
Her companions, April and May.

Summer decks the fields and flowers
And woods with new livery
Of green and many colors more,
Following Nature's own decree.

But you, Winter, overflow
With snow, wind, rain and hail;
We should send you into exile.
Without flattery I tell you so:
Winter, you are merely a churl.

MURIEL KITTEL

FRANÇOIS VILLON

I Am François, to My Dismay
Je suis François, dont il me poise

I am François, to my dismay,
Parisian born, out Pontoise way,
And through the lesson ropes convey
My neck'll learn what my arse may weigh.

HARVEY BIRENBAUM

The Belle Heaulmiere to the Daughters of Joy
La belle Heaulmière aux filles de joie

So think things over, pretty Glover
Who used to be my pupil,
And you, Blanche the Cobbler,
It's time you thought about yourself.
Take them right and left—spare no man
I pray you; for when you're old
You'll have less currency or place
Than coins they've taken out of circulation.

And you, sweet Sausage-vendor,
Who's such a graceful dancer;
Guillemette the Tapestry-maker,
Don't do your master in, for soon
You'll have to close your shop.
When you're old and faded
You'll be serving some old priest,
Like coins they've taken out of circulation.

Jeanneton the Bonnet-maker,
Don't let your lover hobble you;

And Catherine, Purse-vendor,
Stop putting men to pasture;
For even if those girls who aren't
So pretty, make no sour face, but smile,
Old-age's ugliness will frighten love away,
Like coins they've taken out of circulation.

Girls, for your own good
Listen to why I cry and weep:
I can no longer get around—I am
Like coins they've taken out of circulation.

ANTHONY BONNER

⚜

The Old Woman Laments the Days of Her Youth

Les regrets de la belle Heaulmière

I seem to hear lamenting
The Armoress who once was fair,
Wishing she were a girl again
And speaking after this manner:
"Ha! old age, villainous and fierce,
Why so soon have you laid me low?
If I strike myself, what shall hinder
My killing myself with such a blow?

You have taken the great dominion
That Beauty did ordain for me
Over scholars, merchants, churchmen,
For then no man born could be
Who wouldn't give everything to me—
Even if later he might regret—
If only I would yield him freely
What the beggars now reject.

Many a man I have refused—
Which wasn't behaving sensibly—

For the sake of a crafty lad I used
To give myself too generously.
Others I treated treacherously,
But loved him well, upon my soul!
But he only repaid abusively,
And loved me only for my gold.

However much he bullied me,
Trampled me, I loved him still;
And had he even crippled me,
He need only ask me for a kiss
To blot out all my ill.
The scoundrel, marked with evil stain,
Embraced me . . . hardly profitable!
For what is left? Sin and shame.

But he is dead these thirty years,
And old and gray-haired I remain.
When I think of the good years,
What I was, what I became!
When I look at my naked frame,
And see how much I have changed,
Wretched, wizened, shrunken, lean,
My mind is nearly deranged.

What has become of my smooth brow,
My blond hair, my eyebrows' span,
My well-spaced eyes, that glance now,
That used to trap the cleverest men?
My fine straight nose, then
Not big nor small, each dainty ear,
The clear, curved cheeks and dimpled chin,
And those red lips so fair?

Those shoulders, slender and fine,
Those long arms and shapely hands,
The tiny breasts, hips round and high,
Shaped perfectly—a land
Made for love's tournaments;

The wide loins; and pleasure's seat
Set in the firm thighs' extent,
Inside its little garden sweet?

The wrinkled brow, the hair turned gray,
Eyebrows fallen out, dimmed eyes
That once attacked with looks and gay
Smiles, winning many a merchant prize;
Nose bent, as beauty far off flies.
Ears drooping, full of hair,
Wan cheeks, dead and colorless,
Puckered chin, lips like leather.

This is human beauty's end!
The short arms, gnarled fists,
Shoulders quite humped and bent;
What of the breasts? mere shriveled tits;
Hips and dugs have called it quits;
And pleasure's seat? Ugh! And as
For thighs, they're no thighs now but bits
Of things, all flecked like sausages.

And so we lament the good old days
Among ourselves—poor old fools,
Squatting low here on our haunches,
Bunched up like woolen balls
Around a fire of hempen straw,
Quickly lit and quickly gone.
And once we were cute and fair!
—But so it goes with many a one.

MURIEL KITTEL

Ballad for Fat Margot
Ballade de la Grosse Margot

If I love and serve my beauty with good heart,
Must you think me common and a mug?

She has in her all that a man could want.
For love of her, both sword and shield I lug;
When people come, I run and fetch a jug,
And get some wine, as quiet as I can do't
I offer water, cheese and bread and fruit.
If they pay well, I say to them: "Good Sport!
Come again, when you feel in rut
Here to this brothel where we hold our court!"

But then disharmony its reign does start
When Margot comes to bed and brings no cash;
I cannot bear her, but feel a deathly hate.
I snatch her dress and petticoat and sash,
And swear I'll keep them all instead of cash.
She, arms akimbo, cries: "You Antichrist,"
And swears to me by death of Jesus Christ
It shall not be. And so I grab a stout
Stick, and on her nose my message write,
Here in this brothel where we hold our court.

Then we make up, and she lets out a fart,
Since she's more bloated than a venomous bug.
Then laughing, claps her fist upon my pate,
Calls me cute, and hits me in the leg.
Completely drunk, we both sleep like a log.
And when we wake, her belly shows its might,
She mounts me, so as not to spoil her fruit.
I groan beneath her, squashed flat like a board;
By lechery she has me ruined quite,
Here in this brothel where we hold our court.

Come wind, hail, or frost, my bread is won.
I'm a lecher, she's a lecherous one.
Which is better? We are both as one.
Bad cat, bad rat: each a no-good sort.
Garbage we love, garbage follows on.

We flee from honor, from us it flees, is gone,
Here in this brothel where we hold our court.

MURIEL KITTEL

Ballad of the Ladies of Olden Times
Ballade des Dames du Temps jadis

Tell me where, in what foreign place
Is Flora, who wore Roman dress,
Archipiades, and Thais,
Her first cousin in loveliness;
Echo, whose voice was a caress
Over the river or mere,
Fairer than human heart may guess—
Where are the snows of yesteryear?

Where is the love of Abelard,
The prudent Heloise, for whom
He bore the pain of manhood scarred
And lived in monastery gloom?
Where is the queen decreed the doom
Of Buridan, that he must wear
Sack for shroud in the Seine his tomb?
Where are the snows of yesteryear?

The lily-queen who graced the palace—
Blanche, who sang in a wondrous strain,
Bertha Giant-foot, Beatrice, Alice,
Lady Haremburgis of Maine
And Joan, the good girl from Lorraine
Whose burning gave the English cheer;
O Virgin, do I ask in vain?
Where are the snows of yesteryear?

Envoi

Prince, do not ask whither they go
Or where they are, lest to your ear

The same refrain sound sad and low,
Where are the snows of yesteryear?

ELLEN WILLIS

Villon's Epitaph [The Ballad of the Hanged]
L'Epitaphe Villon [*La Ballade des pendus*]

Brother men, who after us still live,
Let not your hearts towards us turn to stone,
For if to wretched us you pity give,
God's mercy will to you be sooner shown.
You see us, five or six, strung up here now;
As for our flesh which once we overfed,
It has long since been rotted or devoured,
And we, the bones, to dust and ashes fall.
Let no one mock at our unhappy fate,
But pray to God that he absolve us all.

If we dare call you brothers, you should show
No scorn for us, although we have been slain
In justice. In any case, you know
That all men are not reasonable and sane;
So intercede for us, now we are gone,
With the Blessed Virgin Mary's Son,
That his grace may not dry up its spring,
But keep us from the thunderbolt of Hell;
We are dead, let no one hound us on;
But pray to God that he absolve us all.

The rain has washed and scoured us clean,
And the sun blackened and dried us now;
Daws and crows made holes where eyes have been,
And plucked away our beards and each eyebrow.
Never at any time have we sat down;
But here and there as the wind does blow,

It carries us at will incessantly,
Pecked by birds, more nicked than any thimble.
Seek not to join with our fraternity;
But pray to God that he absolve us all.

Prince Jesus, who over all hold sway,
Keep us from Hell's dominion; we'd not pay
There any debt, or dealings have at all,
Men, there's no intent to joke or play;
But pray to God that he absolve us all.

MURIEL KITTEL

NOTES AND BIOGRAPHICAL SKETCHES

The earliest lyrical expressions of medieval France were short poems and dramatic pieces dealing with religious subjects: lives of saints, martyrdoms, etc. The "Cantilène de Sainte Eulalie," here included, was modeled after Latin hymns sung at church, and dates back to the ninth century. Also popular were the *chansons de toile* or sewing-songs, so called because they present women at the spinning wheel or doing needlework. The songs take the form of mono-rhyme stanzas with a refrain, and relate vividly and charmingly some love episode. Among the many other types of lyrics there were the workers' songs, wherein they complain of their hard lot and expose abuses of the rich and powerful; and *chansons de mal-mariée,* wherein a disgruntled wife regrets having married the good-for-nothing who is now her husband; the *chansons à personnages,* in dialogue form, dramatizing a quarrel between husband and wife; in the *albas* or *aubes* (dawn-songs) lovers regret the coming of dawn which obliges them to part; in the *pastourelles* a knight makes love to a shepherdess; and, finally, the *reverdie* celebrates the coming of spring and frequently birds join in with their songs.

From the fourteenth century on, and particularly through the contributions of such master technicians as Guillaume de Machaut, Eustache Deschamps, Christine de Pisan, and Charles d'Orléans, a "new rhetoric" emerged. Predominantly concerned with prosodic manipulations, the new rhetoricians made a cult of technique. Such artificial forms as the rondel, the rondeau, the ballade, the triolet, the virelay, monopolized their concern —until poets of the Pléiade, who were also formalistic, rejected most of the rondeau and ballade forms in favor of the ode and the sonnet.

ADAM DE LA HALLE (c. 1240-1288), poet from Arras, nicknamed Adam the Hunchback, elevated his Picard dialect to a literary language through his witty popular poems, some of which he set to music. He served the Count of Artois and followed him to Naples. From c. 1282 to 1286 he sojourned in Sicily, having joined Charles of Anjou's suite. On his return home he died of consumption. His plays *Le Jeu de la feuillée* (c. 1276) and *Le Jeu de Robin et Marion* constitute his remarkable contribution to the early French theatre: the former shows a striking similarity with *A Midsummer Night's Dream,* and the latter is an adaptation of a *pastourelle* to a musical dramatic form. Adam's poetry, in his refined songs and rondeaux, gracefully tender and bright, points to a Provençal influence.

AGNES DE NAVARRE-CHAMPAGNE (XIVth century), Countess of Foix, was the daughter of Jeanne de France and Philippe d'Evreux. In 1349 she married the famous Count of Foix, with whom she had several children. Disagreements on money matters forced them to separate. One of their sons, Gaston, tried to bring about a reconciliation but he had become involved in a plot to kill Charles le Mauvais and soon thereafter was killed by his own father. Agnes remained at the court of Navarre, returning to France only to die.

CHARTIER, ALAIN (c. 1390-1440), born at Bayeux, in Normandy, studied in Paris, and served under Charles VI and VII, traveling widely on diplomatic missions. In addition to his prose work *Le Quadrilogue invectif* (1422), an analysis and critique of the social and political situation, his reputation rests on his ballads and rondeaux and most especially on that poem, *La Belle Dame sans merci* (1424), which has elicited such widespread echoes.

LE CHASTELAIN DE COUCY (d. 1203), a writer of melancholy lyrics, perhaps named Gui de Thurotte, was the chatelain of the town of Coucy. A legend exists which was transcribed into a metrical romance, *Le Chastelain de Couci* (c. 1205) by Jakemon or Jakemes le Vinier, that he died at sea on his way to the Holy Land at the time of the crusades and that his heart was sent to his lady love. Her jealous husband intercepted the gift and served it to her in a dish. (Cf. note on Guilhem de Cabestanh, the Provençal poet, for a variation on this *coeur-mangé* theme.)

CHRÉTIEN DE TROYES (c. 1135-1190), hailed from Troyes, capital of Champagne, and frequented the court of Marie de Champagne. He wrote romances of love and chivalric adventures: his *Lancelot, Yvain* and *Percival* were circulated widely, found their way into other European languages, and were frequently imitated.

CHRISTINE DE PISAN (1364-1430), born in Venice, the daughter of the astrologer and physician of Charles V of France, was brought up in Paris. At fifteen, she married Étienne de Castel. Widowed ten years later, she underwent many reverses and privations and had to write for money in order to support her family. Deep sincerity and natural grace characterize her verse. A staunch defender of women, she replied with singular eloquence to Jean de Meun's (q.v.) attacks and wrote a treatise on the education of women; she used Jeanne d'Arc as a female paragon. She ended her days in a convent.

COLIN MUSET (after 1234), jongleur from Lorraine, wrote about life's joys and occasionally parodied the courtly poets, making facetious remarks about courtly love and even criticizing the lords for their stinginess.

CONON [*or* QUESNES] DE BÉTHUNE (d. 1220), a crusader from Picardy, member of the high nobility, ancestor of Sully, took part in the conquest of Constantinople (1204) and became Regent of the Empire (1219). A man of action, highly praised by the historian Villehardouin, he was also a gifted imitator in French of the troubadours.

DESCHAMPS, EUSTACHE (1346-1410), born at Vertus (Marne), was brought up by his uncle(?) Guillaume de Machaut (q.v.) who taught him the art of poetry. Deschamps held various offices at the courts of Charles V and VI of France, wrote a considerable number of ballads and rondeaux in the courtly tradition, some of them satiric or patriotic. He wrote a ballad on the death of Guillaume de Machaut and another to Chaucer, whom he addresses as *"grant translateur"* because of his English version of the *Roman de la Rose.* The poem "One Day the Rats of All Degrees," included here, is the basis of La Fontaine's famous fable.

FROISSART, JEAN (1337-1410), the great historian, whose *Chronicles* made him known as the "Herodotus of a barbarous age," wrote lovely *lais,* ballades and shorter lyrics which compare favorably with those of the best poets of his times—in fact, his verses have perhaps more personality than Machaut's in whose footsteps he followed to a large extent.

GACE BRULÉ (c. 1179-1212), a knight from Champagne, probably associated with the Duke of Brittany Geoffrey Plantagenet and his sister Marie de Champagne, is remembered for some thirty love poems, in the troubadour tradition but much more tempered, even austere at times.

GUILLAUME DE LORRIS (1210-1237), was born early in the thirteenth century in Lorris, a village east of Orleans, and died, according to Jean de Meun, before he had finished his *Roman de la Rose,* begun during the 1220's. He died c. 1237, according to the evidence in Jean de Meun's continuation, which was composed c. 1277, within the limits of 1268 and 1285. JEAN DE MEUN, born at Meung-sur-Loire, about 1240, probably died in Paris, c. 1305. Guillaume de Lorris' *Roman de la Rose* and Jean de Meun's continuation, represented in the two selections here, have been claimed by some scholars to be superficially different in style but fundamentally unified in their development of the theme. However, one may argue that Jean de Meun seems to be less interested in the allegory than in expounding a Christian-naturalistic doctrine of love as the will to perpetuate the species. In the best medieval misogynistic tradition, Jean de Meun satirizes woman as the greedy deceiver of man. Both aspects—Guillaume de Lorris' and Jean de Meun's—were powerfully influential in the late Middle Ages and the Renaissance.

GUIOT DE DIJON (fl. 1220). Several lyrics and a crusading song have been attributed to him.

JACOB BAR JUDA, HAZAK (fl. 1288), a Lorraine rabbi, wrote in French the elegy (selihah) included here, transcribed in Hebrew characters. It is the first-known literary work of this type; in it he wished to commemorate the martyrdom of thirteen Jews falsely accused of ritual murder, who, when sentenced to burn at the stake in Troyes, could have saved themselves by embracing Christianity but chose instead to perish in the flames.

JEAN DE MEUN, see entry for GUILLAUME DE LORRIS

MACHAUT, GUILLAUME DE (c. 1292-1377), poet and musician born in the village of Machaut in the Ardennes, served for years as secretary of John of Luxembourg, King of Bohemia, who took him to Germany, Austria, Italy, and even Russia. After the King's death at the battle of Crécy (1346), Guillaume served the future Charles V of France, and thereafter the King of Navarre and members of the French royal family. In 1377 he was appointed canon of Reims. In literature his renown derives from his short lyrics—rondels, triolets, ballades—elaborate in prosody and form, many of which he set to music. Memorable too are his motets and his mass at the coronation of Charles V of France (1364). Because of his musical talent and his technical innovations in poetry, his name remains among those of the truly significant figures of medieval French culture, and, in fact, some of his contemporaries placed him above Petrarch and Boccaccio. One thing is certain: he did influence Gower and Chaucer.

MARIE DE FRANCE (fl. 1181-1216), the greatest poetess of medieval Europe, was perhaps the natural daughter of Geoffrey Plantagenet and, therefore, half-sister of Henry II. Though born in France, she did most, perhaps all, of her literary work in England, where she was Abbess of Shaftesbury. Marie de France is best known for her *lais,* narrative poems of love adventure and fantasy derived from the stories which the Bretons told in the Norman and French courts and which deal with King Arthur and the Round Table, Tristan and Iseult, and Celtic legends. She also wrote Aesopic fables and paraphrased in French a Latin legend about St. Patrick.

ORLÉANS, CHARLES D' (c. 1394-1465), born in Paris, the son of Louis d'Orléans (brother of Charles VI of France) and the daughter of the Duke of Milan, when barely twenty-one was taken prisoner at Agincourt and remained a captive in England for a quarter of a century: it was then that most of his poetry was written. On his release he married Marie de Clèves and settled at Blois, where he played host to artists and poets (Villon among others) and wrote many lovely lyrics. Charles d'Orléans' rondeaux and ballades manifest consummate skill, and some, notably his ballades "News Has Been Spread from France" and "Pray for Peace, Oh Gentle Virgin Mary" and his rondels "The Weather Has Laid Aside His Cloak" and "Ah, God, Who Made Her Good to See," have depth of feeling and exquisite formal beauty. His poem written in captivity refers to his first wife, Bonne d'Armagnac, whom he hopes will free him by ransom and other means.

RICHARD THE LION-HEARTED [Richard Coeur de Lion] (1157-1199), King of England (1189-1199), writer in French and Provençal and a most dramatic medieval figure, took part in the Crusades and was imprisoned by his political enemies. He and his older brother Henry and their mother, Eleanor of Aquitaine, were patrons of the Provençal poets.

Richard left us two songs; in the *sirventes* included here the sister referred to is Mary, Countess of Champagne, daughter of Louis VII and Eleanor.

RUTEBEUF (c. 1225-1280), a gifted poet from Champagne, lived a most precarious existence in Paris, endeavoring to find the humorous side of life: in short, a poverty-stricken genius and roisterer who anticipates Villon in his experiences, in his ideas, in his lyricism, and in his truculence. Rutebeuf wrote *fabliaux,* satires, saints' lives, pious legends, panegyrics and funeral laments; he attacked King and Pope, merchant and laborer with equal venom. His play *Le Miracle de Théophile* embodies the Faust theme: it tells of an ambitious priest who sold his soul to the Devil but on repenting was saved by the Virgin Mary.

VILLON, FRANÇOIS (1431-after 1463), born in Paris, was brought up by Guillaume de Villon, chaplain of Saint-Benoît-le-Bétourné. Despite his riotous life at the University of Paris, he finally obtained a Master of Arts degree in 1452. Three years later he killed a priest in a brawl and afterward broke into the College of Navarre, carrying off 500 gold pieces. His earliest poem, the *Lais* or *Petit Testament,* was written around this time. For six years he wandered throughout different parts of France—for a short while he lingered at Charles d'Orléans' court—and on two occasions at least he was in jail. In 1461, despairing of his health, he composed the 2,000-line *Testament* recapitulating his life experiences, vituperating his enemies, expressing both his anguish and *joie de vivre,* in verses which in their sincerity and depth of feeling stand above all the poetry of his contemporaries. On his return to Paris he found himself involved in a number of quarrels and murders and in 1462 was sentenced to be hanged. However the sentence was commuted and he was allowed to go into exile for a period of ten years. After this judgment nothing more is known about him, but the few poems he wrote remain the loftiest literary contribution from medieval France.

It should be noted that the "Belle Heaulmière" (seller of

armor) included here, deals with the mistress of lame and wealthy Nicolas d'Orgemont, sometime canon of Notre-Dame. The lament of the notorious courtesan for her lost beauty and her ballade to the Parisian prostitutes are outstanding moments in Villon's creative work.

ITALY

FRANCESCO PETRARCH (1304-1374)

ANONYMOUS

Ah Me Poor Wretch, Who Loved a Falcon

Tapina oi me, ch'amava uno sparviero

Ah me poor wretch, who loved a falcon:
loved and nearly died of it!
He was docile to my beck and call,
and little would he want or get.
Now he's climbed the sky and taken
like a lord to his uncommon height,
and settled in a strange garden:
another woman keeps him strait.

My falcon, I fostered you
and had you wear a bell of gold
to make your hunting flight bolder;
then rising like the sea,
you soared away and burst your bond,
when you were sure of your game and ground.

SONIA RAIZISS and ALFREDO DE PALCHI

ST. FRANCIS OF ASSISI

The Canticle of the Creatures

Cantico delle Creature

Most High, almighty, good Lord God,
Thine are the praise, the honor and the glory
And every blessing due.
Thine alone, Most High,
And no man is worthy to mention Thee.

Be praised, my Lord, with all Thy creatures,
Especially our brother, the sun,

Who brings the day and shows Thy light.
For he is fair and radiant with great splendor
And draws his meaning, O Most High, from Thee.

Be praised, my Lord, for our sister, the moon,
And the stars, set precious, clear, and fair in Heaven.

Be praised, my Lord, for our brother, the wind,
For air and clouds, and every sort of weather
By which Thou givest sustenance to all.

Be praised, my Lord, for sister water,
For she is useful, precious, humble, and most chaste.

Be praised, my Lord, for brother fire,
Thy beacon in the night,
For he is gay and fair and vigorous and strong.

Be praised, my Lord, for our sister, mother earth,
Who gives us nourishment and life
And many fruits, bright flowerlets and grass.

Be praised, my Lord, for those who loving Thee, forgive,
And bear trials and tribulations.
Blessèd are those who peacefully endure,
For by Thee, Most High, they shall be crowned.

Be praised, my Lord, for our sister, carnal death,
From whom no living man escapes:
Woe to those who die in mortal sin;
Blessèd be those who do Thy holy will,
For the second death shall spare them.

Praise and bless my Lord, and give Him thanks,
And serve Him very humbly all thy days.

WILLIAM M. DAVIS

GIACOMO DA LENTINO

I Have Set My Heart on Serving God

Io m'agio posto in core a Dio servire

I have set my heart on serving God
So that I may go to Paradise,
To the holy place where, I have heard,
There is every pleasure, sport and laughter—

I should not wish to go there without my lady,
She of the blond head and shining face,
For without her I should not enjoy myself,
Being severed from my lady.

But I say this not in the sense
That I should not wish to commit a sin
In that place— All I desire is to look

At her fine figure and her languorous eyes,
For it would give me great delight
To contemplate my lady in her glory.

MAURICE VALENCY

The Frightful Basilisk, Most Poisonous

Guardando 'l basalisco velenoso

The frightful basilisk, most poisonous,
That slays its victim with a single glance,
The slithery asp, of snakes most envious,
Whose artful fangs are keener than a lance,
The haughty drake, whose look imperious

Is direst omen of most dire mischance—
These I compare to love, most dolorous,
Oh most tormenting, dreadful circumstance!
For love, by nature, as all lovers know,
With but one look defeats the boldest knight
And artfully contrives his sorest woe,
Offending out of pride and out of spite.
Whom Love possesses has but pains to show;
Who takes Love for his lord is conquered quite!

DANIEL J. DONNO

CIELO D'ALCAMO

Thou Sweetly-Smelling Fresh Red Rose

Rosa fresca aulentissima

HE: Thou sweetly-smelling fresh red rose
That near thy summer art,
Of whom each damsel and each dame
Would fain be counterpart;
O! from this fire to draw me forth
Be it in thy good heart:
For night or day there is no rest with me,
Thinking of none, my lady, but of thee.

SHE: If thou hast set thy thoughts on me,
Thou hast done a foolish thing.
Yea, all the pine-wood of this world
Together might'st thou bring,
And make thee ships, and plow the sea
Therewith for corn-sowing,
Ere any way to win me could be found:
For I am going to shear my locks all round.

HE: Lady, before thou shear thy locks
I hope I may be dead:
For I should lose such joy thereby

And gain such grief instead.
Merely to pass and look at thee,
Rose of the garden-bed,
Has comforted me much, once and again.
Oh! if thou wouldst but love, what were it then!

SHE: Nay, though my heart were prone to love,
I would not grant it leave.
Hark! should my father or his kin
But find thee here this eve,
Thy loving body and lost breath
Our moat may well receive.
Whatever path to come here thou dost know,
By the same path I counsel thee to go.

HE: And if thy kinsfolk find me here,
Shall I be drowned then? Marry,
I'll set, for price against my head,
Two thousand agostari.
I think thy father would not do't
For all his lands in Bari.
Long life to the Emperor! Be God's praise!
Thou hear'st, my beauty, what thy servant says.

SHE: And am I then to have no peace
Morning or evening?
I have strong coffers of my own
And much good gold therein;
So that if thou couldst offer me
The wealth of Saladin,
And add to that the Soldan's money-hoard,
Thy suit would not be anything toward.

HE: I have known many women, love,
Whose thoughts were high and proud,
And yet have been made gentle by
Man's speech not over-loud.
If we but press ye long enough,
At length ye will be bow'd;

For still a woman's weaker than a man.
When the end comes, recall how this began.

SHE: God grant that I may die before
Any such end do come,—
Before the sight of a chaste maid
Seem to me troublesome!
I marked thee here all yestereve
Lurking about my home,
And now I say, Leave climbing, lest thou fall,
For these thy words delight me not at all.

HE: How many are the cunning chains
Thou hast wound round my heart!
Only to think upon thy voice
Sometimes I groan apart.
For I did never love a maid
Of this world, as thou art,
So much as I love thee, thou crimson rose.
Thou wilt be mine at last; this my soul knows.

SHE: If I could think it would be so,
Small pride it were of mine
That all my beauty should be meant
But to make thee to shine.
Sooner than stoop to that, I'd shear
These golden tresses fine,
And make one of some holy sisterhood;
Escaping so thy love, which is not good.

HE: If thou unto the cloister fly,
Thou cruel lady and cold,
Unto the cloister I will come
And by the cloister hold;
For such a conquest liketh me
Much better than much gold;
At matins and at vespers I shall be
Still where thou art. Have I not conquered thee?

SHE: Out and alack! wherefore am I
Tormented in suchwise?
Lord Jesus Christ, the Savior,
In whom my best hope lies,
O give me strength that I may hush
This vain man's blasphemies!
Let him seek through the earth; 'tis long and broad:
He will find fairer damsels, O my God!

HE: I have sought through Calabria,
Lombardy, and Tuscany,
Constantinople, Apulia,
Genoa, Pisa, Syria,
Yea, even to Babylon I went
And distant Barbary:
But not a woman found I anywhere
Equal to thee, who art indeed most fair.

SHE: If thou have all this love for me,
Thou canst no better do
Than ask me of my father dear
And my dear mother too:
They willing, to the abbey-church
We will together go,
And, before Advent, thou and I will wed;
After the which, I'll do as thou hast said.

HE: These thy conditions, lady mine,
Are together nought:
Despite of them, I'll make a net
Wherein thou shalt be caught.
What, wilt thou put on wings to fly?
Nay, but of wax they're wrought,—
They'll let thee fall to earth, not rise with thee:
So, if thou canst, then keep thyself from me.

SHE: Think not to fright me with thy nets
And suchlike childish gear;
I am safe pent within the walls

Of this strong castle here;
A boy before he is a man
Could give me as much fear.
If suddenly thou get not hence again,
It is my prayer thou mayst be found and slain.

HE: Wouldst thou in very truth that I
Were slain, and for thy sake?
Then let them hew me to such mince
As a man's limbs may make!
But meanwhile I shall not stir hence
Till of that fruit I take
Which thou hast in thy garden, ripe enough:
All day and night I thirst to think thereof.

SHE: None have partaken of that fruit,
Not Counts nor Cavaliers:
Though many have reached up for it,
Barons and great Seigneurs,
They all went hence in wrath because
They could not make it theirs.
Then how canst *thou* think to succeed alone
Who hast not a thousand ounces of thine own?

HE: How many nosegays I have sent
Unto thy house, sweet soul!
At least till I am put to proof,
This scorn of thine control.
For if the wind, so fair for thee,
Turn ever and wax foul,
Be sure that thou shalt say when all is done,
"Now is my heart heavy for him that's gone."

SHE: If by grief thou couldst be grieved,
God send me a grief soon!
I tell thee that though all my friends
Prayed me as for a boon,
Saying, "Even for the love of us,
Love thou this worthless loon,"

Thou shouldst not have the thing that thou dost hope.
No, verily: not for the realm o' the Pope.

HE: Now could I wish that I in truth
Were dead here in thy house:
My soul would get its vengeance then;
Once known, the thing would rouse
A rabble, and they'd point and say,—
"Lo! she that breaks her vows,
And, in her dainty chamber, stabs!" Love, see:
One strikes just thus: it is soon done, pardie!

SHE: If now thou do not hasten hence,
(My curse companioning,)
That my stout friends will find thee here
Is a most certain thing:
After the which, my gallant sir,
Thy points of reasoning
May chance, I think, to stand thee in small stead,
Thou hast no friend, sweet friend, to bring thee aid.

HE: Thou sayst truly, saying that
I have not any friend:
A landless stranger, lady mine,
None but his sword defend.
One year ago, my love began,
And now, is this the end?
Oh! the rich dress thou worest on that day
Since when thou art walking at my side alway!

SHE: So 'twas my dress enamored thee!
What marvel? I did wear
A cloth of samite silver-flowered,
And gems within my hair.
But one more word; if on Christ's Book
To wed me thou didst swear,
There's nothing now could win me to be thine:
I had rather make my bed in the sea-brine.

HE: And if thou make thy bed therein,
Most courteous lady and bland,
I'll follow all among the waves,
Paddling with foot and hand;
Then, when the sea hath done with thee,
I'll seek thee on the sand.
For I will not be conquered in this strife:
I'll wait, but win; or losing, lose my life.

SHE: For Father, Son, and Holy Ghost,
Three times I cross myself.
Thou art no godless heretic,
Nor Jew, whose God's his pelf:
Even as I know it then, meseems,
Thou needs must know thyself
That woman, when the breath in her doth cease,
Loseth all savor and all loveliness.

HE: Woe's me! Perforce it must be said
No craft could then avail:
So that if thou be thus resolved,
I know my suit must fail.
Then have some pity, of thy grace!
Thou may'st, love, very well;
For though thou love not me, my love is such
That 'tis enough for both—yea overmuch.

SHE: Is it even so? Learn then that I
Do love thee from my heart.
To-morrow, early in the day,
Come here, but now depart.
By thine obedience in this thing
I shall know what thou art,
And if thy love be real or nothing worth;
Do but go now, and I am thine henceforth.

HE: Nay, for such promise, my own life,
I will not stir a foot.
I've said, if thou wouldst tear away

My love even from its root,
I have a dagger at my side
Which thou mayst take to do't;
But as for going hence, it will not be.
O hate me not! my heart is burning me.

SHE: Think'st thou I know not that thy heart
Is hot and burns to death?
Of all that thou or I can say,
But one word succoreth.
Till thou upon the Holy Book
Give me thy bounden faith,
God is my witness that I will not yield:
For with thy sword 'twere better to be kill'd.

HE: Then on Christ's Book, borne with me still
To read from and to pray,
(I took it, fairest, in a church,
The priest being gone away,)
I swear that my whole self shall be
Thine always from this day.
And now at once give joy for all my grief,
Lest my soul fly, that's thinner than a leaf.

SHE: Now that this oath is sworn, sweet lord,
There is no need to speak:
My heart, that was so strong before,
Now feels itself grow weak,
If any of my words were harsh,
Thy pardon: I am meek
Now, and will give thee entrance presently.
It is best so, sith so it was to be.

DANTE GABRIEL ROSSETTI

ENZO RE

Time Comes for Those Ascending to Descend
Tempo vene che sale a chi discende

Time comes for those ascending to descend,
For those who talk to lend an ear instead,
For those who learn to pause and comprehend;
Time comes for scanted duties to be sped,
For dire revenge on those who dare offend,
For threatening deeds in place of timid dread;
Time comes to scorn what others reprehend,
Or feign forbearance of what's seen or said.
Therefore, him only call I sagely wise,
Whose actions spring from reason's plain decree,
And bides with what occasion may proclaim.
Such conduct will find praise in all men's eyes;
For where all doing keeps its due degree,
Excess, being absent, leaves no room for blame.

DANIEL J. DONNO

Love Often Agitates My Heart to Thought
Amore mi fa sovente lo meo core pensare

(The complaint of Enzo Re from his prison palace in Bologna)

Love often agitates my heart to thought
Sending me painful sighs
For while I wait, fear rules the lot
Of all future enterprise.
No, I'm not afraid my sweet hope there
May prove untrue;

Only—that while I sit here in despair
A worse fate looms in view.

Then I'm afraid till in my inner eye
I see her noble qualities.
If I'm too long delayed, I'll surely die.
O, bitterly love holds me
Tightly snared, an animal caught at chase,
With no thought of other ease.
Yet I'm prepared to see her lovely face,
Holding her long in peace.

I have no joy. So great is my torment
I know no quietness.
Hope, alone my buoy, keeps me ever bent
On quick flight from distress
Away to that most loving lady of praise
Who owns, who holds me in her might.
With no other let me live out my days
Keeping her sole lady of delight.

Still as I wait so long and never see
Her cherished face,
Her noble quality, there steals upon me
Persistent hope for grace
By doing her pleasure; ready for decreeing
I stand, far from sin's regret.
But listen! Loving without seeing
Makes even noble lovers forget.

Go, greet that lord, my little song:
Tell him the evils that I bore
From one who holds me, his ward, in wrong
So that I can live no more.
Also greet Tuscany, that supreme domain,
Where courtliness reigns in every way.
Then, to her castle in Apulia's plain:
There where my heart is, night and day.

JAMES J. WILHELM

GUIDO GUINIZELLI

The Gentle Heart
Al cor gentil

Love to the gentle heart will hasten straight
As birds that seek the foliage of the glade,
Nor Nature first did gentle heart create
Nor love, till gentle heart for love was made.
For only when the sun
Shines forth is splendor given light,
Which dies having no sun;
So love in gentleness alone finds place,
Most fittingly aright,
Like heat within the glowing flame's embrace.

Love's fire to the gentle heart intends
As special virtue to the precious stone
To which no power of starry sphere descends
Until the purging sun thereon has shone
And by its strength drawn forth
All that which it possessed of dross before.
As to the stone its worth,
So to the heart which Nature did devise
Gentle and chaste and pure
Love comes, as from a star, in woman's guise.

Love dwells in gentle hearts by that same right
By which the flame that wraps the burning brand
Dances upon the summit in delight
And, being proud, bows down to no command.
But the corrupted will
Encounters love, as fire, burning apace,
Encounters water's chill.
In gentle heart love finds its native shore,
Affinity of place,
As does the magnet in the iron's core.

If the sun shone all day upon the mud,
Mud it would stay, nor would the sun lose dignity.
The proud man says, "Gentle am I by blood."
Yet he is mud; the sun, gentility.
For men must not proclaim
Nobility resides outside their hearts
In dignity of name.
The gentle heart virtue alone may tender:
Through water starlight darts;
Heaven retains the star, the star its splendor.

On heaven's Intelligence God's light prevails
Brighter than sunlight on our earthly eyes;
And she whose understanding nothing veils,
Turning the spheres, obeying Him, replies;
And thus His high decree
Becomes fulfillment of the Primal Will.
So must fair woman be:
Within the gentle heart her glance will stir
True love and that desire instill
To seek perfection by obeying her.

"Sir," God will say to me, "what act is this?"
(When my soul stands before his judgment throne.)
"You came through all the heavens in quest of bliss,
Yet you gave love elsewhere that's Mine alone;
That praise to Me is due,
Or to the Queen who rules with that sweet grace
That can all sin undo."
Then I shall say, "She seemed an angel fair
Whose steps I could retrace.
If I gave her my love, what fault was there?"

DANIEL J. DONNO

BONAGIUNTA ORBICCIANI

To Guido Guinizelli: Now That You Have Changed the Manner

A Guido Guinizelli: Poi ch'avete mutat

Now that you have changed the manner
Of the pleasant songs of love,
Their form and essence,
So as to overgo all other poets,

You have become as a torch which shines
In the darkness, but which pales
Wherever the sun sheds its light,
Which far exceeds your own.

Indeed, you surpass all the world in subtlety,
And there is no one who can
Interpret your language properly, so dark it is!

But it is considered a strange business—
Although learning comes to us from Bologna—
To make love-songs out of science.

MAURICE VALENCY

RINALDO D'AQUINO

No More Shall I Take Comfort

Già mai non mi conforto

No more shall I take comfort,
No joy is left to me.
The ships are ready in the port
And waiting anxiously.
The many folks are leaving

For lands beyond the sea,
And I, alas, am grieving.
What cause have I for glee?

He sails to far-off countries
And sends to me no word.
Alone, deceived, I have no ease;
My sighs cannot be heard.
They strive and war within me;
Ah, night and day they strive!
Lost, while all earth and heaven flee,
I scarcely seem alive.

Oh God of our salvation,
Born of the Virgin pure,
Who willed our separation,
Now keep my love secure.
Oh Lord supreme in power,
Oh wisest and most fair,
My love at every hour
I yield unto your care.

The cross of our salvation
Is cause of my despair;
The cross, my deprivation,
And God heeds not my prayer.
Oh cross that pilgrims carry
Why do you harm me so?
Alas, a wretch, I tarry
From fever all aglow.

The emperor by stern decree
Keeps peace where he holds sway;
And yet he wages war on me
And steals my hope away.
Oh Lord supreme in power,
Oh wisest and most fair,
My love at every hour
I yield unto your care.

When he became crusader
Surely I did not know
That he, my sweet persuader—
My love who loved me so—
Would lead me to this anguish
And lock my heart away.
A prisoner, I languish;
My life has lost its day.

The ships at anchor riding
Await fair winds to start;
And all with him wait tiding
Who bears away my heart.
Oh Father who did make us,
Pray, guide them safe to shore;
They journey in your service
To free the cross you bore.

And you, my dear Dolcetto,
You know the pain I bear;
Write me a sweet sonetto
To send when you are there;
For I have nothing to withstand
This everlasting strife.
My love's gone to the Holy Land
And with him goes my life.

DANIEL J. DONNO

GUITTONE D'AREZZO

Have Mercy, Love! Give Ear

Amor, merze, intende s'eo ragione

Have mercy, Love! Give ear,
For I seek justice at your court:
You have taken away my liberty,
And delivered me into the power of my lady,

And always, in every way, you oppose me—
But why, since I am in your hands?
Why do you not strike her instead,
Who with her wit and her will makes war against you?

You show yourself an unjust lord
If you spare her and seek my death;
Unless it is that you lack the power.

Very easily, I believe, you could have her for your vassal,
But if you cannot subdue her,
At least have mercy on me, who am your servant.

MAURICE VALENCY

JACOPONE DA TODI

O Love, All Love Above

Amor de caritate, perche m'hai si ferito?

O Love, all love above,
Why hast thou struck me so?
All my heart, broke atwo,
Consumed in flames of love,
Burning and flaming cannot find solace;
It cannot fly from torment, being bound;
Like wax among live coal it melts apace;
It languishes alive, no help being found;
Seeking a grace to fly a little space,
A glowing furnace is its narrow pound.
In such a deadly swound,
Alas, where am I brought?
Living with death so fraught!
O leaping flames of love!

Before I ventured forth I dared demand
The love of Christ, expecting only sweet;
Thinking in peace of sweetness I could stand

Without a pain; but, being come to it,
I suffer torments of a molten brand;
And all my heart is melted by its heat.
    I find no figure meet
    To tell this curious smart,
    To live without a heart,
    Daily to die of love.

Ah! I have lost my heart and all my sense,
Desire and all delight and all sensation;
All beauty seemeth filth to me; and hence
Pleasaunce and power of riches are damnation.
A laden tree of love for recompense,
Set in my heart, doth yield me consolation;
    Maketh great alteration;
    Doth brook no least delay;
    Thrusts out and drives away
    Sense, strength and my self-love.

To purchase this one thing I ventured all
The world; in this exchange gave all I had.
If I had all things ever made, to call
My own, I give them freely and were glad.
But love deceived me somewhat; I gave all,
And now I know not whither I am led.
    And people think me mad.
    Now that I have been bought;
    They set my worth at naught;
    I am undone by love.

My friends imagined they could call me back;
My friends who travel by another road;
The slave is helpless to forsake his track,
Nor can the bondman lay aside his load.
Sooner the stone might soften and be slack
Than love, who holds me in his straït abode.
    Oh, to my soul a goad!
    Love burns it through and through.

Transformed, united, who
Can sunder it from love?

Not iron nor the fire can separate
Or sunder those whom love doth so unite.
Not suffering nor death can reach the state
To which my soul is ravished. From its height,
Beneath it, lo! it sees all things create;
It dominates the range of dimmest sight.
My soul, by what a flight
Hast thou this high reward?
It is of Christ the Lord;
Embrace the Lord of love.

I have no longer eyes for forms of creatures.
I cry to him who doth alone endure.
Though earth and heaven exhaust their varied natures,
Through love their forms are thin and no wise sure.
When I had looked upon his splendid features,
Light of the sun itself was grown obscure.
Cherubim, rare and pure
By knowledge and high thought,
The Seraphim, are naught
To him who looks on love.

If such a love confoundeth all my wit,
Against me let no blame henceforth be held.
No heart could fly if love should beckon it.
No heart could brave the anguish I have felt.
How is it able to endure such heat?
How is it that the poor heart doth not melt?
Ah! if I but beheld
A soul to take a part
Of pity for my heart,
To know the pains thereof!

I would love more and better if I could.
My heart hath uttered all it ever knew.
I am not able, freely as I would.

To give the already given gift anew.
I gave myself, to hold, for all my good,
This Lover who reneweth bone and thew.
Beauty antique and new,
Since that my heart hath found
Light without pause or bound;
Oh, splendor of thy love!

Seeing such wealth of beauty, I am drawn
Without myself; am borne I know not where.
My heart doth yield, and, being held in pawn,
Like wax receives the seal love setteth there.
So rash a bargain never yet was drawn.
To put on Christ I strip me stark and bare.
My heart, transformed and fair,
For very love doth weep;
Waves of its sweetness steep
My heart in boundless love.

My soul transformed, almost the very Christ;
One with her God, she is almost divine;
Riches above all riches to be priced,
All that is Christ's is hers, and she is queen.
How can I still be sad, despair-enticed,
Or ask for medicines to cure my spleen?
The fetid sweet from sin,
With sweetness overspread;
The old forgot and dead,
In the new reign of love.

In Christ a goodly creature am I born.
The old stripped off, I am a new made man.
But with a knife my heart is gashed and torn,
Where flaming love, a molten metal, ran.
Wisdom and sense burnt off and wholly shorn
Christ is my own, and beauty beyond ken.
Flung in his arms' great span,
The cry of love rings higher:

Love, whom I so desire,
Make me to die of love.

For thee, for love, I languish and I burn.
I sigh for thy embraces soon and late.
When thou art hence, I live and die; I yearn
And groan and whine in very piteous state
To find thee; and my heart, at thy return,
Fainteth with fear lest aught should separate.
Therefore no longer wait.
Come, love, to succor me.
Compel me; bound to thee,
Consume my heart with love.

I am grown dumb, discreet discourse who held.
Once I could see the light who now am blind.
Such an abyss has never been beheld.
But mute, I speak; I fly, in chains confined;
Falling I mount; I hold and am compelled;
I follow, my pursuer pants behind.
O passion unconfined!
My folly is complete,
By reason of the heat,
The fury of the stove.

CHRIST:
Virtue availeth not without control.
Control the love wherewith thou lovest me.
Do thou with virtue renovate thy soul;
Since thou desirest so to come at me.
Controlled and duly ordered, sane and whole,
I will the love which thou shalt offer me.
How doth one prove a tree,
If not by what it yield?
Worth in this wise is sealed
To all things, by a proof.

Everything which I have formed and made
Is made with number, measure and array.

Unto their end all things in rank are laid;
By order 'tis all things pass not away.
Love, more than all the rest, is held and staid
In order by its nature, in a way.
        But if the fervent ray
        Of love hath made thee mad
        And shapeless, be not glad;
        Fervor hath ruined love.

FRANCIS:
O Christ, now thou hast stolen my heart, thou say'st:
"Set thy soul's love in order," to thy worm.
But how, transformed in thee, so deeply graced,
Can I be lord of me, or rule the storm?
As iron in the fire grows plastic paste,
As air transfixed by sun grows light and warm,
        And lose their ancient form,
        And take a new allure,
        So be my soul, grown pure,
        Clad on with thee in love.

Why hast thou brought me to a fiery place,
If thou wilt have me to be temperate?
When without measure thou didst give thy grace,
Thou didst confound all sense of size and weight.
Small thou didst fill my small heart's utmost space:
I have no scope to hold thee being great.
        If I be desperate,
        The fault is thine, not mine,
        O thou who didst define
        Conditions of our love.

Thou canst not shield thyself from love. Love brought
Thee captive by the road from heaven to earth.
Thou didst descend to lowness to be naught,
To roam a man rejected from thy birth;
No house nor field enhanced thy lowly lot;
Poor thou hast given riches and great worth.
        In life, in death, no dearth

Of love hast thou declared.
Thy heart hath flamed and flared
With nothing else but love.

Wisdom remembered not to stint or rein
Thy love, when passion bade the whole be poured.
Thou wert not flesh, but love, in frame and brain;
Love made thee man to bear our sin's reward.
Thy love required the cross, the world's disdain.
Thou didst not profit thee to speak a word
To Pilate, or the horde
Of those who wrought thy woe;
Yearning to take the blow
Upon the cross of love.

Love, love, how thou hast dealt a bitter wound!
I cry for nothing now but love alone.
Love, love, to thee I am securely bound;
I can embrace none other than my own.
Love, love, so strongly hast thou wrapt me round,
My heart by love for ever overthrown,
For love I am full prone.
Love, but to be with thee!
O love, in mercy be
My death, my death of love.

Love, love, O Jesus, I have reached the port,
Love, love, O Jesus, whither thou hast led.
Love, love, 'tis thou hast given me support.
Love, love, for ever am I comforted.
Love, love, thou hast inflamed me in such sort,
The goal of love is reached, and I am dead.
To love for ever wed,
Love hath cemented both
Our hearts in perfect troth
Of everlasting love.

JOHN GRAY

FOLGORE DA SAN GIMIGNANO

Come, January, I Give You These Treats

I' doto voi, nel mese di gennaio

Come January, I give you these treats,
a courtyard warmed by a straw-burning fire,
and rooms and beds with elegant attire,
with coverlets of fur and silken sheets,
sugared nuts, sparkling wine and sweets,
imported clothes such as you may desire:
in this way, protection you would acquire,
if either the north or the south wind beats.
To go outdoors often each day in sport,
to throw the beautiful and clean white snow
at girls who stand about just to consort;
and, when their fatigue began to show,
the group would return to this court:
where rest would be found by the fire's glow.

JOY GOULD

In March, for You a Gift of Fish I Boast

Di marzo si vi do una peschiera

In March, for you a gift of fish I boast,
with sturgeon and salmon, I will embark,
and eels and dolphins and trout and blue shark,
and all kinds of fish found near every coast;
with boats in a fleet manned by a great host,
a sloop, a schooner, a galleon, a bark,
to take you oversea in light or dark
to whatever port pleases you the most;
there will be manors with servants and beasts,
and other luxuries furnished for you,

with people to please you with fairs and feasts.
You'll have no church there nor altar nor pew,
abandon the preaching of madmen priests,
who have many lies and little that's true.

JOY GOULD

For April I Give You the Countryside
D'april vi dono la gentil campagna

For April I give you the countryside,
its new-born grass and flowering expanse;
with fountains of waters that stream and prance;
and women and girls in whom to confide;
from Spain lively horses on which to ride
and people dressed in the style of France,
who as if in Provence, will sing and dance
to German music which I will provide.
And there'll be gardens east and west,
in which everyone's cares will soon take wing,
and their adoration each will bequest
to the sweet one to whom I gave the ring
of rare jewels for her head, the very best
that have Prester John or Babylon's king.

JOY GOULD

In October, Figuring up Your Share
D'ottobre nel contado a buono stallo

In October, figuring up your share,
good dwellings, good prayers, and good sons are due;
have a good time—there's a bird to pursue,
go after it now, on foot or on mare.
An evening of dancing must be your fare,

and getting drunk on a vigorous brew,
perhaps some red wine and I know it is true
that this way of life is superbly rare.
The morning after, the day will begin
with washing your hands and face and the rest;
the roast and the wine are choice medicine.
But the cure that will make you healthiest
is from lake, stream, or sea—some claw and fin;
of all Christian lives, this one is the best!

JOY GOULD

CECCO ANGIOLIERI

If I Were Fire, I'd Burn the World Away

S'io fossi foco, arderei lo mondo

If I were fire, I'd burn the world away;
If I were wind, I'd knock it to the ground;
If I were water, then it would be drowned.
If I were God, I'd make it Satan's prey;
If I were pope—ah! then I would be gay
With addling every Christian that I found.
If I were emperor, this would resound:
"Off with the head of each who's in my sway!"
If I were Death, I'd call upon my Dad;
If I were Life, I'd flee from him apace,
And toward my mother I'd be just as bad.
If I were Cecco—just as is the case,
I'd snap up all the young and pretty girls
And leave the sick and faded to the churls.

DANIEL J. DONNO

Despair Herself Regards Me as Her Son

La stremità mi richer per figliuolo

Despair herself regards me as her son,
And I, indeed, must hold her as my dame.
Great Pain begot me—thus was I begun.
Black Melancholy was my nurse's name.
My swaddling bands, of thorny fibers spun,
From tattered sheets of coarsest sackcloth came.
From tip to toe there's much in me to shun,
For nothing good has place within this frame.
Now, in my youth, to better my poor plight,
I am bequeathed a wife who deems it fit
To prate and quarrel long into the night
In tones such as unstrung guitars emit.
The widowed man alone is freed of blight.
If he reweds, his wits have taken flight.

DANIEL J. DONNO

GUIDO CAVALCANTI

You Have in You the Flowers and the Green Grass

Avete in voi li fiori e la verdura

You have in you the flowers and the green grass:
And what is shining or is fair to see:
Light of the sun your own light doth surpass:
Who has not seen you, worthless wight must be!

And in this world of ours, no creature is
So full of pleasure and delightfulness:
If any man fear love, new courage his,
Seeing your face, so much himself to bless!

The ladies all, that bear you company,
For your dear sake, are pleasing to my sight,
And I would beg them of their courtesy,

To do you honor, each to strive her best,
And in your sovereignty to have delight
Since of them all you are the loveliest.

G. S. FRASER

Who's This That Comes, as Each Man Looks at Her

Chi è questa che vien, ch'ogni uom la mira

Who's this that comes, as each man looks at her,
Makes tremulous with clarity the air,
And leads Love with her, so that speak or stir
Can none among us: all have sighs to spare!

Alas! How seems she when her eyes she turns?
Let Love relate what I may not explain:
Yet such esteem her modest bearing earns
Another in her place shall earn disdain.

Uncounted are the gifts that make her rich:
To her the Gentle Virtues are obeisant:
Beauty, as Beauty's Goddess, doth approve her.

Nor was our mind turned to so high a pitch,
Nor of its health so properly complaisant,
That we could have a proper knowledge of her.

G. S. FRASER

Beauty of Woman of Noble Heart

Beltà di donna di piacente core

Beauty of woman of noble heart,
And armed knights of gentle breeding,
Birds singing, and talk of love,
Brave ships running swiftly on the sea,

Soft breezes at the break of day,
And white snow falling in the still air,
Green river banks, and fields of flowers,
Jewels of gold and silver, and azure ornaments—

These, the beauty and the nobility of my lady
And her gentle heart so far surpass
That they seem base to the beholder.

So far she exceeds all other beauty
As the heavens exceed the earth:
Happiness comes soon with one of such nature.

MAURICE VALENCY

If Mercy Were a Friend to My Desires

Se Mercè fosse amica a' miei desiri

If Mercy were a friend to my desires
And took her motion from the very heart
Of my most fair, if Mercy could impart
That balm which my harsh suffering requires,
Then would the thrilling agony of sighs—sired
By a mind that dwells on Cupid's art
And never in discoursing will depart
From that great theme, though none be thus inspired
To pity me—then would those sighs ascend
With so much might and force that fiery tears
Would be transmuted into burning joys.
Instead they wreak the havoc that destroys
The heart, darkens the soul, rousing such fears
That men disdain me, for my looks offend.

DANIEL J. DONNO

You've Filled My Mind So Full of Grief

Tu m'hai si piena di dolor la mente

You've filled my mind so full of grief,
My soul now shudders to depart.
The sighs sent out by my unhappy heart
Testify my suffering will be brief.

Love, sensing your high nobility,
Says: "It hurts me much that you should die
For this cruel girl, who won't try
To hear you with a touch of sympathy."

I move like one who walks outside life's line,
Who seems, at glance, as if he might be pressed
From copper, or from wood, or stone,

Moving by outside governance alone,
Bearing a wound deep within his breast,
That is, of his sure death, an open sign.

JAMES J. WILHELM

O Lady Mine, Caught You No Glimpse of Him

O donna mia, non vedestu colui

O lady mine, caught you no glimpse of him
Who held his hand pressed down upon my heart
when I made answer to you, choked and hoarse,
shrinking before the fierce thrust of his dart?
That hand was Love's, who, having found us out,
followed me close even when I came away—
a Syrian archer, swift of pace and keen,
intent alone on killing his poor prey.

Out of your eyes thereafter he drew sighs
and plunged them with such force into my heart

that I fled off from him aghast with fear,
only to come straightway upon Lord Death
flanked by those savage bearers of his arms
who take men's lives and do not heed their tears.

IRMA BRANDEIS

We're the Pens, Saddened and Dismayed

Noi siam le triste penne isbigotite

We're the pens, saddened and dismayed,
The scissors and the sorrowing knife
Who cut these words of strife
That you've just now surveyed.

We'll tell you why we've moved apart
And come to you, reader, now and here.
The hand that formed us felt great fear:
O, fearsome forms beset his heart,

Forms that had him so unmanned
They almost forced him to his end,
For he had nothing left but sighs.

Now we beg you, strongly as we can:
Please consider us your friends.
Let us see *one* pair of gentle eyes!

JAMES J. WILHELM

A Lady Begs Me

Donna mi prega

A lady begs me, so I must now speak
of that accident, fierce so many a time,
and so sublime, which we on earth call love,
and I shall prove the truth to those who seek

it not. But one who understands I must now find,
since one whose heart is evil—there's no doubt—
to such a subject cannot raise his mind;
for, unless I can prove what I'm about
to sing, I do not wish at all to tell
where it does dwell, and who can make it be,
and what its virtue is, its power as well,
its essence and its motions, and why we
call love the thing we like, and whether men
can show it so that soon it may be seen.

Right in that part where our memory dwells
it takes life, just as the diaphanous
takes form from light. By some strange darkness' spell,
which from Mars, its abode, comes down to us,
it is created: though its name is sense,
it's the soul's habit and the heart's desire.
It starts out of a form, perceived by chance
yet understood, which soon comes to acquire
both place and home in the Possible Intellect,
as in a subject. There it feels no ache
since from plain quality you don't expect
it to be: in itself it shines, for its own sake,
a perpetual effect; it gives no pleasure,
but thought, unable to grant a face's features.

It is no virtue, but it learns its way
from what is called perfection—but not that
of reason, that of sentiment, I say.
In its own health its judgment's habitat
is not, for reason and intention, oh,
are worth one thing; its discernment is false
in vicious people. Often death can flow
from its great might, if the virtue that succors
its opposite path is strongly hampered: this
is not because it is opposed to nature,
but because, as we know, men's fate it is
to be so snatched away from perfect pleasure
as to be, so astray, no more alive:
when they forget, to this same death they arrive.

Its being is when such is the desire
as to go far beyond all nature's measures:
and it adorns itself with leisure never.
Onward it moves, changing hues, laughter, tears,
and disfigures its face with fear's displeasure;
little it stays; and you will find that ever
it lives with those whose worth is the most high.
The new quality causes many a sigh,
and makes man stare into the empty space,
while ire, ablaze, soon rises and (you must
experience it, to understand its rage)
makes him not shun the blows that are being thrust
at him, nor move at all to find some lull,
for his mind cannot offer help at all.

From likeness does the glance draw life and marrow,
which makes the bliss look like reality:
when it is struck, it cannot be concealed.
Oh, not in timid beauty hides the arrow,
for such a wish is chased away by fright:
a wounded spirit does achieve its boon.
And nothing will you learn just from the face
you look at: such a whiteness falls on it,
that (if you listen well) no form is seen,
unless a quick result proceeds from it.
Faint is the sheen of what in darkness lies,
far from the brightness of its life divided.
One whom I trust and is with truth adorned
affirms: from this alone can bliss be born.

Fearing no harm, my song, you can now go
wherever you wish: with such glow have I
adorned you, you'll be praised by those who know
when all your reasoning shall be revealed:
from others you can well remain concealed.

JOSEPH TUSIANI

Fresh Newborn Rose
Fresca rosa novella

Fresh newborn rose,[1]
My beauteous Spring,
Through field, by river,
Gaily singing
Your noble worth I bring
To nature.

Your truly noble worth
Renews itself with joy
In aged man or boy
With every setting forth.
Birds chant to it their vows,
Each in his Latin,
From evening to matin,
On greenish boughs.
The whole world's now with song
Since it's your season
And, with good reason,
Hymns your majesty:
For you're the most heavenly
Of creatures.

Heavenly features
In you, my lady, rest;
O God, how wondrous blessed
Seems my desire.
Lady, your glad expression,
As it comes and passes,
Nature and custom surpasses
In wonderful digression.
Together women admire
Your truly godlike form,
For you are so adorned
Your beauty's not transcribed:

---

1 *Secret name for the poet's lady.*

O, can't it be described—
Beyond nature?

Beyond our human nature
God formed your excellence
To show by its very essence
That you were born to rule.
Now, that your noble face
May rest forever near,
To me keep ever dear
Your most abundant grace.
And, if I seem a silly fool
To set you as my queen:
Know that I don't blaspheme,
For Love makes me courageous
Which still no force assuages—
Nor measure.

JAMES J. WILHELM

There in a Woodland, to My Thought More Bright

In un boschetto trova' pasturella

There in a woodland, to my thought more bright
Than a star's light, I found a shepherdess.

Her hair she had golden and ringleted,
And her eyes full of love, rosy her hue:
With a small switch her lambs she pasturèd,
And being barefoot, she was bathed with dew.
Singing she was, as though with love she burned,
And was adorned with all delightfulness.

With love I did salute her thereupon
And asked if she had any company
Whereto she answered in a gentle tone
Alone, alone she walked the woodland way,

And said: "Know thou, that when the birds complain
Then I am fain, a lover to possess."

No sooner had she told me her condition
And through the wood I heard the birds to sing
Than in myself I said: "Now is the season
Out of this shepherdess my joy to wring."
Mercy I asked her that to kiss with lips
And love with clips, she should have willingness.

And then my hand she took most amorously
And said her heart a gift to me she made
And led me underneath a shadowy tree
Where many a flower I saw of every shade
And such a joy and sweetness to me brought,
I saw, methought, the god of tenderness.

G. S. FRASER

Since I No Longer Hope, O My Sweet Song

Perch'i' non spero di tornar giammai

Since I no longer hope, O sweet song,
To see my Tuscan land,
Go, calm and quiet, and
Seek the fair lady to whom you belong
And who, when you reach her gentle face,
Will greet you with her grace.

You will bring news of sighs
Replete with anguish and bewilderment;
But try not to be caught by impure eyes
Of people who of love are diffident,
For so would they impede
Your loving speed
That I would suffer for it, and this ache
Would render my death painful and would make

Even my after-death
A thought of sorrow and immense distress.

You know well, little song, how death's strong grip
Now holds me and how life is failing me,
And you feel how my heart is beating fast
Now that each spirit says it cannot last.
My body's so worn out
That my own suffering I cannot feel
Any more: if you will
Help me, oh, carry my spirit along—
This is my last request—
That it may leave my heart's unrest.

Oh, little song, I do
Recommend to your friendship
This soul of mine that trembles in dismay:
Take it with you in all its pain
To that fair lady who lives far away.
When you are before her, tell her, pray,
With a sweet sigh: "This humble servant comes
To be with you forever,
And he has sent her here who never
Ceased to be servant of love."

You, my bewildered voice—oh no, a moan
Leaving my doleful heart as a last tear—,
Go with my soul and with this song of mine,
And say that my mind has been destroyed by fear.
You will soon find a lady sweet and fair,
And so considerate,
That it will be your joy and happiness
Ever to be before her.
Oh, quick, my soul, adore her
For all her worthiness.

JOSEPH TUSIANI

DANTE ALIGHIERI

To Guido Cavalcanti
A Guido Cavalcanti

Guido, I should wish that you, Lapo and I,
Caught in the net of the enchanter's spell,
Were set into a bark whose sails should swell
With every vagrant wind that happened by,

So that no turn of chance or change of sky
Should mar our ease or hinder our delight.
No, rather as we shared one hope we might
Share the desire to sail on endlessly.

And Monna Vanna and Monna Lagia too,
And she who's named among the thirty fair
Should join our crew through Merlin's sorceries

And join our talk of Love as Love might please;
And there with us, removed from every care,
Rejoice with us as we would wish them to.

DANIEL J. DONNO

Beyond the Sphere Which Turns Most Distant
Oltre la spera, che più larga gira

Beyond the sphere which turns most distant
Passes the sigh which issues from my heart:
A strange intelligence which Love,
Weeping, gives it, draws it ever upward.

When it has come where it desires to be,
It sees there a lady who receives such honor

And such light that by her own splendor
This pilgrim spirit sees her.

It sees her such that when it returns to tell me of her
I do not comprehend, so subtly does it speak
To the sorrowing heart that questions it.

All I know is that it speaks of that gentle one,
Because I hear it say Beatrice often,
And that I understand quite well, dear ladies.

MAURICE VALENCY

Nothing Will Ever Seem to Me More Cruel

Nulla mi parve mai più crudel cosa

Nothing will ever seem to me more cruel
Than she I serve, and serving waste my life,
For my desire is caught in flames of love
And hers is bound within a frozen lake.

So pitiless and cold is she, whose beauty
I gaze upon and thereby cheat myself,
So deeply do I yearn for my own torment
No other pleasure dares to tempt my eyes.

She who turns her face upon the sun,
And keeps her love unchanged through her own changing,
Had not so bitter a lot as I have drawn.

Then, Giannin, since that proud one binds
My heart to love until I breathe my last,
Out of compassion sigh a little with me.

JUDITH GOODE

To a Short Day and a Great Ring of Shadow

Al poco giorno, ed al gran cerchio d' ombra

To a short day and a great ring of shadow
have I come alas! and a whitening of hills,
as they lose color with the clouded grass.
And still my passion does not change its green,
so fast it is in the hard soul of stone
that looks and speaks and heeds me like a woman.

And in the same way this springtime woman
stands frozen like the snow in shadow;
because she is not moved, no more than stone
is, when the sweet weather warms the hills
and turns them back again from white to green
to cover them with little flowers and grass.

When she wears her hair in a garland of grass,
our minds are charmed away from every woman
save her who mingles curled yellow and green
so neat that Love comes there to stand in shadow,
Love who fixes me between small hills
more firmly than mortar fixing stone.

Her beauty dearer than a precious stone
works a wound not cured by healing grass,
and I have fled through plains and past the hills
with hope to save myself from such a woman;
yet her dazzle gives no rest in shadow
cast by wall or knoll or leafy green.

I have sometimes seen her dressed in green
so made she might have then provoked in stone
the love I suffer even for her shadow:
therefore in the fairest meadow grass
I craved to see her lovesick as ever woman
was—and bounded by the highest hills.

But rivers will return to run uphill
sooner than, for me, this damp green
wood take fire, as should a pretty woman;
so could I bring myself to sleep on stone
a lifetime and roam and feed on grass
only to watch her garments set a shadow.

And when the hills throw their darkest shadow,
under such green beauty this young woman
melts it, vanished like a stone in grass.

SONIA RAIZISS and ALFREDO DE PALCHI

I Seek to Make My Speech a Yawp as Bitter

Così nel mio parlar

I seek to make my speech a yawp as bitter
As is her every act, the stone I prize,
Who now and always petrifies
Anew her nature, her obduracy;
And clothes her in an adamantine glitter
That turns the arrow aside (or else she shies),
No matter from what bow it flies
Or quiver comes to pierce her nudity.
The other dies, although he tries to flee
Or shuts him in against the deathly blow
That goes as sure as wings can go
To where he is and shatters his defense.
Lost to myself, I make of her no sense.

There is no shield I find she does not shatter,
Nor place which grants asylum from her frown;
For, as the leaf can grow no other crown
But flowers, she blossoms from my topmost soul.
My anguish seems to her as small a matter
As mild waves' lapping to the galleon;
And yet the weight that weighs me down
Is one that no rime's counter-weight can equal.

Ah, agonizing lure, as deaf as cruel,
Who deafly wear my life away—say how
Can you not learn to disavow
This gnawing, rind by rind, toward my heart's core,
As I the baring of your source of power!

Thinking of her my heart begins to shudder,
Especially beneath the stranger's gaze,
For fear my shining thought betrays
Itself to others, shining out of me;
Nor death at my nerves' ends compels more utter
Terror, though with teeth of Love it graze;
Because that thought puts out of phase
The force that makes act out of energy.
Struck to the earth, I see still straddling me,
The sword in hand whose thrust made Dido die,
Love, for whose grace I cry,
Cry, "Mercy! Mercy!" pray him, bowing low,
Though merciless, he knows no word but no.

He lifts his hand from time to time and taunts
My ebbing life; for he is most perverse,
Who holds me racked upon the earth,
Back pinned, too tired even to buck or flail.
Cries rise within my mind, and blood that shunts
From vein to further vein and is dispersed,
Now fugitive, its course reversed,
Must hunt the heart that calls it, leave me pale.
Under the left arm, he aims a thrust so fell
It raises anguish in my heart again.
"Let him lift," I cry out then,
"That hand once more, and I within death's dark
Shall dwell before the blow complete its arc."
Would I could see Love split that bitch's heart
In half, who hacked my own till scarce a fourth
Survives. Death would not find me loathe,
Toward which for her fair sake I urge myself.
In sunlight as in shade she can impart
One solace only, thief and killer both.
Oh Christ, if she in hell's hot broth

For me, as I for her, would dog-like yelp,
How soon I'd cry to her, "I'll help! I'll help!"
And gladly help, like those who in the yellow hair
Of girls, entwine (so I with her)
Their hands. Ah, when I hold what love embossed
For my defeat in gold, perhaps she'll love me at last.

Once grasped, I would not loose those lovely tresses,
That serve me only as a scourge, a flail;
But seizing them at Matins bell
Hang on till Vespers and till Midnight ring.
Without courtesy or pity, my caresses
Would take the playful bear as their ideal;
And just as Love now makes me reel
Beneath their stripes, a thousand times I'd wring
From her exaction. In those eyes which fling
Live fire toward my heart that she's left dead,
I'd stare—head fixed to neighboring head,
Till vengeance cancel out rejection's pain;
And only then in love permit her peace again.

Go song, go straight, seek out my lady,
Who wounds my heart and steals from me
The sole hope of satiety.
Go, thrust an arrow through her heart,
For vengeance is a seemly art.

LESLIE A. FIEDLER

DANTE AND FORESE DONATI

Tenzone Sequence

BY DANTE ALIGHIERI
Chi udisse tossir la malfatata

Whoever's heard the run-down wife
Of Bicci—called Forese—cough

Might think she spends her winter-life
Up north, where the icicles drop.

Even in the middle of August, she sneezes.
(Think how she suffers the rest of the year!)
She wears her shoes to bed—but freezes.
Covers that cover cost too dear.

The cough, the cold and such distress
Don't come because the poor dear's overripe.
She's cold because Bicci's fled her nest.

Her mother's weeping for griefs that mount:
"To think! For just a dowry of tripe
I could've married her to a Guido count!"

BY FORESE DONATI
L'altra notte mi venne una gran tosse

The other night I had a coughing fit
Because there wasn't a cover for my back.
Soon as day dawned, out I tracked
For any gold I could walk off with.

Listen how fortune gave me riches:
Here I was looking for a pearl-filled box
Or pretty florins with gold-minted gloss—
But found Alighieri by the graveyard ditches,

Tied in a knot whose name I didn't know
(Maybe it's Solomon or some other prophet.)
I crossed myself, facing the eastern glow,

As he said: "For the love of Dante, undo
These knots." I tried—but to no profit.
Then I turned back and saw my journey through.

BY DANTE ALIGHIERI
Ben ti faranno il nodo Salamone

Solomon's knot will soon be wrapping you in,
Bicci junior, with those necks of quail.
Those expensive cuts of mutton will make you wail
Your sins recorded on the dead sheep-skin.

Your house'll be even closer to Saint Simon Jail
Unless, of course, you make a getaway.
But now, I'm afraid, it's too late to repay
Those debts—unless your appetite should fail.

They tell me, though, you've got a clever hand,
And if it's true, you'll be just like new,
Because you can pick up several thousand grand.

Maybe this art will ease gluttony's grief.
You'll pay your debts and stay in Florence too.
But is it better than being a glutton—to be a thief?

BY DANTE ALIGHIERI
Bicci novel, figliuol di non so cui

Bicci junior, son of I-know-not-who
(Unless I asked your mother, Lady Tess),
So much stuff goes in and out of you
That, naturally, you must turn to thievishness.

Already everybody's on his guard
Who has a wallet, when you're nearby,
Saying: "Look at that man, how scarred!
A common crook! He acts so sly!"

In bed your daddy keeps an all-night tryst
With his conscience, praying you're not caught.
Your dad? Yes. Like Joseph was to Christ.

Of Bicci and Brothers, I'd write many pieces:
How with tainted gold they pursue their lot,
But treat their wives politely—like nieces.

JAMES J. WILHELM

CINO DA PISTOIA

Ah Me, Alas! Am I So Very Base

Oimè lasso! or sonvi tanto a noia

Ah me, alas! Am I so very base
That you disdain me as your wretched foe
Because I love and strive against my woe,
Unable to unlove so fair a face?
I'll kill myself if you'll but think it grace;
For that faint hope that keeps my life aglow
Darkens to such despair words cannot say:
When pity stirs unpity that's the case.
All that from which before I nourished peace—
Sweet love by which I found me comforted—
Now turns to strife from which there's no surcease.
Thus it is fit that, since you wish me dead,
I kill myself and thus obtain release;
Thus wrong prevails where right should win instead.

DANIEL J. DONNO

Love Is a Subtle Spirit That Can Slay

Amore è uno spirito ch'ancide

Love is a subtle spirit that can slay:
Begotten by delight, born at a glance,
It pierces with the fury of a lance;
And those poor faculties that bar its way
Stand unavailing to prevent such prey,
While Mercy's mute to halt its dire advance.
Such were the words my mind in its mischance

And my bewildered soul had cause to say
When my unweary eyes, too bold for fears,
Chanced on the fairest wight I ever met,
By whom my heart, as now too well appears,
Was shattered quite. Better that Death had set
On me instead, for unremitting tears
Were all my love begot or will beget.

DANIEL J. DONNO

Ah, Woe to Me Alas, for Love Has Bound

Omè! ch'io sono all'amoroso nodo

Ah, woe to me, alas, for Love has bound
Me straight with two bright tresses, silken blond,
And, like the poor belimèd bird, I've found
That every struggle but secures the bond,
Whereat I'm lost, unless I hear the sound
Of her sweet voice whence Pity may respond;
For still I strive and thus I still confound
Desired escape, and thus I more despond.
And, more bewildering still, I see increase
Of radiance in those precious knots of gold,
Those glowing tresses that will not release
The fearful fluttering heart that they enfold.
Ah, Pity, help me; you alone may ease
Where Love with but one charm has taken hold.

DANIEL J. DONNO

ONESTO DA BOLOGNA

To Cino da Pistoia

A Cino da Pistoia

Mind and *humble* and more than a thousand
Basketfuls of spirits and your air of walking
in your sleep

Make me think there is no way
To make sense of you in your rhyming mood.

I know not what makes you do it,
Whether it is love or death, but with your
philosophic airs
You have wearied even the strongest
Of those who hear your beautiful, conceited song.

Moreover we all find quite burdensome
Your colloquies of three with another person,
And your four-voiced discussions with yourself:

Truly, all human burdens seem sweet
In comparison with what you cause
A man to endure who reads you.

MAURICE VALENCY

FRANCESCO PETRARCH

If Life Survives These Years of Bitter Woe

Se la mia vita da l'aspro tormento

If life survives these years of bitter woe
Which I have suffered through your loveliness,
One day, toward the end of my distress,
I shall perceive your eyes have lost their glow,
Your golden hair is gray upon your brow,
Your garlands faded, and your verdant dress,
And all these beauties vanished which oppress
My fainting spirit, hesitant and slow.

Perhaps then I will find at last the strength
To tell you of the torments I endure,
And how it was with me this day and year.
And if, by chance, desire has fled at length,

At least my agony will then secure
The comfort of a sympathetic tear.

MAURICE VALENCY

It Is the Evening Hour; the Rapid Sky
Ne la stagion che 'l ciel rapido inchina

It is the evening hour; the rapid sky
Bends westward; and the hasty daylight flees
To some new land, some strange expectant race.
An old and weary pilgrim-woman sees
The lonely foreign desert-dark drawn nigh.
Fearful, she urges on her stumbling pace.
And to her resting-place
At length she comes, and knows
The sweetness of repose;
The pains of pilgrimage, the road's duress
Fade in enveloping forgetfulness.
But oh, alas, my hurts that ache by day
Are but more pitiless
When the light sinks into the west away.

When the sun's burning wheels have sped along,
And night pursues, rolling its deepest black
From highest peaks into the sheltered plain,
The sober woodsman slings upon his back
His tools, and sings his artless mountain-song,
Discharging on the air his load of pain.
And yet his only gain
Is, on his humble board,
The food the woods afford,
Acorns, which poets honor, yet abjure.
Let him be happy, let him sleep secure,
Though I no happiness have ever won,
No rest, no ease, no cure,
For all the turning of the stars and sun.

And when the shepherd sees the evening shade
Rising and graying o'er the eastward land,
And the sun dropping to its nightly nest,
He rises; takes his well-worn crook in hand;
And leaves the grass, the spring, the beechen glade,
And quietly leads the tired flock to its rest.
He finds a cave, recessed
In crags, wherein to spread
Green branches for his bed,
And there he sleeps, untroubled, solitary.
But then, O cruel Love, the more you harry
My breaking strength to that most hopeless chase
Of her who flees apace,
And Love will never aid to noose the quarry.

In the sea's vales the sailors on their bark
Throw down their limbs on the hard boards to sleep
When the sun dips beneath the western main.
Oh, though he hide within the farthest deep,
And leave Morocco's mountains to the dark,
Granada and the Pillars and all Spain,
And though the worldwide pain
Of suffering man and beast
In the first night have ceased,
There comes no night with mercy to conclude
My ardor, ever in suffering renewed.
My love grows old; soon shall my captor see me
Ten years in servitude.
And still no savior comes with strength to free me!

And as I seek with words my wounds to numb,
I watch at eve the unyoked oxen turning
In from the fields, down from the furrowed hill.
My yoke, alas, is never lifted from
My shoulders, and my hurts are ever burning,
And in my eyes the tears are springing still.
Alas, it was my will
To carve the unearthly grace
Of her most lovely face

In the immutable matter of my heart.
Now it is carved so deep that strength nor art
May rub it thence until that final day
When soul and the body part.
Even then, perhaps, it will not pass away.

O my unhappy song,
My grief has made you grieve,
You will not dare to leave
My heart, to show your sorrows anywhere;
And yet, for others' praise you shall not care,
For all your burden is the weight of pain
Left by the flames that flare
From the cold rock to which I cling, in vain.

MORRIS BISHOP

Father in Heaven, after Each Lost Day

Padre del ciel, dopo i perduti giorni

Father in heaven, after each lost day,
Each night spent raving with that fierce desire
Which in my heart has kindled into fire
Seeing your acts adorned for my dismay;

Grant henceforth that I turn, within your light
To another life and deeds more truly fair,
So having spread to no avail the snare
My bitter foe might hold it in despite.

The eleventh year, my Lord, has now come round
Since I was yoked beneath the heavy trace
That on the meekest weighs most cruelly.

Pity the abject plight where I am found;
Return my straying thoughts to a nobler place;
Show them this day you were on Calvary.

BERNARD BERGONZI

She Used to Let Her Golden Hair Fly Free

Erano i capei d'oro a l'aura sparsi

She used to let her golden hair fly free
For the wind to toy and tangle and molest;
Her eyes were brighter than the radiant west.
(Seldom they shine so now.) I used to see

Pity look out of those deep eyes on me.
("It was false pity," you would now protest.)
I had love's tinder heaped within my breast;
What wonder that the flame burned furiously?

She did not walk in any mortal way,
But with angelic progress; when she spoke,
Unearthly voices sang in unison.

She seemed divine among the dreary folk
Of earth. You say she is not so today?
Well, though the bow's unbent, the wound bleeds on.

MORRIS BISHOP

Pale Beauty! and a Smile the Pallor There

Quel vago impallidir che 'l dolce riso

Pale beauty! and a smile the pallor there
Hung over tenderly, a veil of love
Which sent such awe into my heart that above
In my face it moved and shone out everywhere.

I knew then how the saints in heaven's air
Gaze on each other; what she was thinking of,
In pity, to my eyes held shape enough,
To others unseen; I cannot look elsewhere.

The most angelic glimpse, the humblest deed
Of any woman deep in love, to this
Would be a theme of scorn, it's praise unjust.

She bent her kind sweet glance, but I could read
What fell, these silent words I could not miss:
Who is it steals from me the friend I trust?

EDWIN MORGAN

From Thought to Thought, from Mountain Peak to Mountain

Di pensier in pensier, di monte in monte

From thought to thought, from mountain peak to mountain,
Love leads me on; for I can never still
My trouble on the world's well-beaten ways.
If on a barren heath there springs a fountain,
Or a dark valley huddles under a hill,
There may the grieving soul find quiet days;
There freely she obeys
Love's orders, laughing, weeping, hoping, fearing,
And the face writes a gloss upon the soul,
Now glad, now charged with dole,
Not long in any manner persevering.
At sight of me a man of subtle wit
Would say, "He burns, and sees no end of it."

In the high mountains, in the woods I find
A little solace; every haunt of man
Is to my mood a mortal enemy.
At every step a new thought comes to mind
Of my dear lady, whose remembrance can
Turn all the hurt of love to gayety.
I would no sooner be
Quit of this bittersweet existence here,
Than I reflect, "Yet even now Love may

Destine the better day;
I, loathing self, may be to others dear!"
So I go thinking, hoping, sighing, now;
May it be true indeed? And when? And how?

And in the shade of a pine tree or a hill
I halt, and all the tumbled rocks near by
Are pictured with the beauty of her face;
And tears of tender melancholy fill
My bosom; and "Alas! alas!" I cry,
"What have I come to! From how far a place!"
But, for the little space
That the uneasy mind thus looks on her,
Rapt out of self into another sphere,
Then I feel Love so near
That the tricked soul rejoices it should err.
So clear I see her, and so fair and pure
That I pray only that the fraud endure.

Often I've seen her—who'll believe me now?—
Treading the grass, cleaving the lucid water,
Alive, alive, in a forest beech-trunk caught,
White mid the clouds; so fair, Leda would vow
The famous beauty of her lovely daughter
Is dimmed as a star when the broad sun beams hot.
And, in what savage spot
I chance to be, in what most barren shore,
Ever more beautiful she walks with me.
Then, when Truth makes to flee
My darling cheat, I find myself once more
A dead stone statue, set on living stone,
Of one who thinks and grieves and writes alone.

Now it's my whole desire and all my pleasure
Up to the highest mountain-pass to climb
To dizzy and unshadowed solitude.
And thence I send my flying gaze to measure
My length of woe; I weep a little time;
The mist of grief blows from my dismal mood.
I stare afar and brood

On the leagues that lie between me and that face,
Ever so near and yet so far away.
Soft to myself I say,
"My soul, be brave; perhaps, in that far place,
She thinks of you in absence, and she sighs!"
And my soul suddenly wakes and gladly cries.

My song, beyond these alps,
In the land where skies are gladder and more clear,
You'll see me soon, where a quick streamlet flows,
And where the fragrance blows
Of the fresh Laurel that I love so dear.
There is my heart, and she who reft it me;
Here you may see only my effigy.

MORRIS BISHOP

I Find No Peace, yet Am Not Armed for War

Pace non trovo, e non o da far guerra

I find no peace, yet am not armed for war,
In hope I fear, in ice I burn and gasp;
I lie on earth, and in the sky I soar,
Embrace the universe, and nothing clasp.

She holds me trapped with neither lock nor noose,
Nor keeps me for her own, nor breaks the chain;
And Love itself will neither slay nor loose,
Nor let me live, nor free me from my pain.

I have no eyes, yet see; no tongue, yet cry,
I long to perish, yet I voice my fears;
Myself I hate, and for another sigh,
I joy in sorrow, and I smile in tears:
For death and life alike I am unfit,
And you, my lady, are the cause of it.

MAURICE VALENCY

Now Skies and Earth Are Stilled and Winds Are Dead

Or che 'l ciel e la terra e 'l vento tace

Now skies and earth are stilled and winds are dead,
The beasts and restless birds are tethered in sleep,
Night's starry car moves on in darkness deep,
Unstirring seas lie quiet in their bed;
I wake, brood, kindle, weep. She whose caprice
Commands me gives this sweet pain no relief;
My state is open war, dire anger, grief,
Yet thoughts of her are all I know of peace.

Constant from one pure, living source outpour
The sweet, the bitter, to fulfill my need;
One hand still heals my wound and makes it bleed;
I die, am born, a thousand times each day
Lest ceaseless struggle cast me safe ashore,
Being ever from salvation far away.

DWIGHT DURLING

Absorbed in One Fond Thought That Makes Me Run

Pien d'un vago penser che me desvia

Absorbed in one fond thought that makes me run
A solitary course, companionless,
Sometimes, rapt deep in reveries, I confess,
I seek out her whose pathways I should shun:
I see her pass, so sweet, so cruelly
Lovely my soul trembles and turns in flight,
Such troops of sworded sighs throng there, unite
Behind my own and Love's dear enemy.

Yet surely, unless I err, a pitying gleam
Illumines now that clouded, lofty brow;

This partly summons hope, gives me new heart;
I call my soul to stand its ground; I seem
About to stammer some audacious vow—
But have so much to tell I dare not start.

DWIGHT DURLING

The Woods Are Wild and Were Not Made for Man

Per mezz' i boschi inospiti e selvaggi

The woods are wild and were not made for man.
Now men and weapons fill them with their fear.
I walk there free, the only terror near
Being my Sun and the bright rays I scan—

Her piercing Love! And I walk singing (but can
Such thoughts be wise?) of her who in absence is here,
Here in my eyes and heart to make me swear
I saw girls, ladies, where beech and fir trees ran!

I seem to hear her, when I hear the air,
The leaves, the branches, and the plaint of birds,
Or waters murmuring on through the green grass.

Never so happy, never in silence so rare,
Alone in a grim forest, without light, without words—
But still too far out from my Sun I pass!

EDWIN MORGAN

Love, We Attend the Vision of the Rose

Stiamo, Amor, a veder la gloria nostra

Love, we attend the Vision of the Rose,
Things above Nature unsurpassed and new;

See how in her the sweetness falls like dew!
See how on earth that radiance Heaven shows!

See now how Art, pearls, purple and gold bestows
On that rich-favored person no man knew
But here; who sweetly feet and eyebeams through
Shade cloistered by the hills, moves as she goes.

The emerald grass and thousand-colored flowers
Sparse in the shade of that dark ancient tree
Pray her white feet may touch their leaves of green;

Blue sky all around the leafy sunlit bowers
Bursts into flame and visibly makes glee
That such bright eyes should make it all serene.

PETER RUSSELL

Nowhere So Clearly Have My Inward Eyes

Mai non fui in parte ove si chiar vedessi

Nowhere so clearly have my inward eyes
Beheld her whom my longing sight must lose,
Nowhere am I so free as in Vaucluse,
Nowhere so fill the air with amorous cries.
No valley ever offered sorrowing guest
Such deep seclusion, leafy, overgrown;
I cannot think that Love has ever known
On Cyprus or other shore so sweet a nest.

These waters speak of love, the air, each tree.
Bird, fish, and flower, the vines and grasses say
Together, live and love while life is yours!
But you, O noble lady summoning me,
By memories of your bitter death, Oh pray
That I despise the world its hooks and lures.

DWIGHT DURLING

The Eyes That Drew from Me Such Fervent Praise

Gli occhi di ch'io parlai si caldamente

The eyes that drew from me such fervent praise,
The arms and hands and feet and countenance
Which made me a stranger in my own romance
And set me apart from the well-trodden ways;

The gleaming golden curly hair, the rays
Flashing from a smiling angel's glance
Which moved the world in paradisal dance,
Are grains of dust, insensibilities.

And I live on, but in grief and self-contempt,
Left here without the light I loved so much,
In a great tempest and with shrouds unkempt.

No more love songs, then, I have done with such;
My old skill now runs thin at each attempt,
And ears are heard within the harp I touch.

EDWIN MORGAN

Great Is My Envy of You, Earth, in Your Greed

Quanta invidia io ti porto, avara terra

Great is my envy of you, earth, in your greed
Folding her in invisible embrace,
Denying me the look of the sweet face
Where I found peace from all my strife at need!

Great is my envy of heaven which can lead
And lock within itself in avarice
That spirit from its lovely biding-place
And leave so many others here to bleed!

Great is my envy of those souls whose reward
Is the gentle heaven of her company,
Which I so fiercely sought beneath these skies!

Great is my envy of death whose curt hard sword
Carried her whom I called my life away;
Me he disdains, and mocks me from her eyes!

EDWIN MORGAN

The Nightingale Whose Ardent, Soft Despair

Quel rosignuol che si soave piagne

The nightingale whose ardent, soft despair
For mate or offspring lost, unceasingly
Sweetens the fields and skies with melody,
With plaintive, brilliant notes suffusing the air,
Accentuates my solitary pain
And night-long, as it seems, accompanies me
Who mourn my former self too blind to see
That Death in goddesses could fix his reign.

The easiest to deceive feels more secure!
That two such lovely lights, outvieing the sun,
Could ever darken to dust—who could believe?
Now my unpitying fate I know; undone,
Weeping, to learn that ecstasy must grieve.
No joys that here below delight endure.

DWIGHT DURLING

Go, Grieving Rimes of Mine, to That Hard Stone

Ite, rime dolenti, al duro sasso

Go, grieving rimes of mine, to that hard stone
Whereunder lies my darling, lies my dear,

And cry to her to speak from heaven's sphere.
Her mortal part with grass is overgrown.

Tell her, I'm sick of living; that I'm blown
By winds of grief from the course I ought to steer,
That praise of her is all my purpose here
And all my business; that of her alone

Do I go telling, that how she lived and died
And lives again in immortality,
All men may know, and love my Laura's grace.

Oh, may she deign to stand at my bedside
When I come to die; and may she call to me
And draw me to her in the blessèd place!

MORRIS BISHOP

Small Wandering Bird Who Singing Go Your Way

Vago augelletto che cantando vai

Small wandering bird who singing go your way
Or rather weeping, it may be, your past,
Seeing your night and winter approaching fast
Bright day behind you and the month of May—
As you know well your own long-borne dismay
So should you know I likewise am downcast:
You'd come into this yearning heart at last
To share its grievous pains if not to allay.

I know not if your fortunes be the same
For She for whom you weep perhaps still lives
For whom, to rob me, greedy Death soon came;
This season, this unwelcome hour revives
Alike of bitter years and sweet the name,
Courage with you to speak of pity gives.

PETER RUSSELL

Death Cannot Sour the Sweetness of Her Face

Non po far Morte il dolce viso amaro

Death cannot sour the sweetness of her face,
Her sweet face can the sour of death dispel;
She taught me the good life, and now she shall
Teach me to die the good death, in its place.

And He who shed His blood to give us grace,
Who with His foot broke ope the gates of hell,
Comforts me by His blessèd death, as well.
So come, dear Death; come, with thy kind embrace.

And it is time, O Death, do not delay;
It was high time after thy cruel power
Had made Madonna from the world ascend.

We'd walked together all along the way;
Together did we come to the utmost hour;
And where she halted is my journey's end.

MORRIS BISHOP

FAZIO DEGLI UBERTI

I Gaze upon Her Light Crisp-Curling Hair

Io guardo i crespi e li biondi capelli

I gaze upon her light crisp-curling hair
Whereof Love weaves a net entangling me
And sometimes to ensnare more cunningly
Baits it with strings of pearls or a vivid flower.
I gaze into her eyes, at once aware
How they through mine make entrance piercingly
And strike my heart with such sharp energy
That it might seem a sun's immediate power.
Their influence, more ascendant hour by hour,
Enthralls me; and my soul, subjected, sighs

Within itself, and speaks in an undertone,
"Oh, would I were alone
With her, alone, that I might make her eyes
Two mirrors to my own—usurping too
Her lovely hair, undo
Its beauty wave by wave, and so hold fast
In love's employment radiance unsurpassed."

And then I gaze upon her ardent mouth,
Her broad forehead, her deep expressive eyes,
White teeth, straight nose, brown eyebrows' traceries
Outvieing strokes of art. Soliloquy
Resumes, and thus again my amorous drouth
Finds words, "Consider her lips and realize
The joy of besieging and taking that scarlet prize
Wherein all nectar and spices seem to be.
And hear her speak, how well, how charmingly,
Soft-toned, with gentle courtesy. Confess
How well divided, well ordered, her words unfold.
Now see her laugh—behold
How she receives and gives delightfulness!"
Thus dwelling upon her mouth, my revery
Says irresistibly
That all I could possess would be well spent
If those lips might say yes with full assent.

And then I gaze upon her slender throat
That sweetly rises from her shoulders and breast,
Her chin, small, round, and dimpled; east or west
None yields to favored eyes such sheer delight.
My thought, allured by all these may denote,
Continues, saying, "Consider the perfect zest
Of holding that neck and shoulders tightly pressed,
Of making a tiny mark on a throat so white."
Thus thought, emboldened further, says, "Invite
Your fancy. If what you see can so excel
In beauty, how rich must be what hidden lies,
For men put Paradise
Beyond the visible sun and stars and tell

How it eclipses splendors seen in the skies.
Look long, and let your eyes
Imagine beauty exceeding all they know,
That lies beyond where their keen glances go."

And then I gaze at shapely arms, a pair
Of soft hands intertwining, comely, neat,
Their slender tapering fingers made complete
By one bright ring that borrows beauty of them.
My thought now urges me, "What if you were
Even now in those arms where all delights would meet
In concentration, confluence so sweet
That I could find no words for such a theme!
See how all members of her body seem
Rounded and full, as is most fitting for her,
And touched with delicate tints of pearl-like hue.
Her captives, gladly we view
Her bearing, though she can frown if boldness err;
But she is mild and modestly discreet,
In virtuousness replete,
In all her ways so high in excellence
And grace that she commands all reverence."

She walks with soft step as the peacock treads,
Her figure erect and straight as the elegant crane;
All that to womanly charm may appertain
Is hers by incontestable birthright.
"If you would see," thought counsels, "how she sheds
Lustre about her, go survey the train
Of ladies lovely and gay; the loveliest wane
When she approaches, as the stars less bright
Pale at the first effulgence of sunlight.
Thus does she vanquish all among the throngs
Of rival ladies who each other excel.
Judge then, acknowledge well
Her rarity when even to love belongs
No more than the beauty and goodness found in her.
Whatever to her is dear

Is seemly, decorous, always worthy one
Who puts her hope in fair deeds meetly done."

Declare it all with confidence, my song,—
That since the dawn of womankind's first days
Not one has known such praise—
Or favor comparable; she draws
The world's stintless applause
For inward and outward beauty. Such her estate,
She may, I fear, be somewhat uncompassionate.

DWIGHT DURLING

FRANCO SACCHETTI

An Amorous Thorn
Inamorato Pruno

Never in all my days
Did I behold, as yesterday to my amaze,
An amorous thorn. Upon an emerald green
Beneath a prickly press
Of boughs reclined a gleaming girl;
And when a spiny branch with threatening mien
Snatched at a golden tress,
She would reclaim the curl
With flashing hand of pearl,
Emboldening the bough upon its thievish ways.
Never have I beheld such amorous strife
As then when all set free
Her tresses shone, and wild
Her eyes blazed fire. Never, upon my life,
Did my heart strive with glee
As outwardly I smiled
And whispered, self-beguiled,
Who would have thought a thorn could merit praise?

DANIEL J. DONNO

O Lovely Mountain Shepherd Lasses
O vaghe montanine pasturelle

O lovely mountain shepherd lasses,
Whence do you come, whose beauty all surpasses?
What country bears such fruit beyond all others,
What far-off joyful lands, what happy races?
Children of Love you seem, nor men your brothers,
So well your gracious presence daylight graces.
Nor gold nor silver gleams against your faces,
And yet you walk as if an angel passes.

High up upon the mountain is our place,
A little cabin on the mountainside,
And thither to our parents we retrace
Over the slopes our steps at eventide,
Over the flowered meadows which provide
Our nourishment, and for the flocks the grasses.

Then doubtless must your beauty suffer greatly
If only fields and mountains look upon her,
For there exists no steepled town nor stately
City which your presence would not honor—
Oh, tell me, are you happy in this manner,
Ragged, roaming in the mountain passes?

Far happier are we living as we do,
Following our flocks upon the open downs,
Than you and yours can ever be when you
Sit at your banquets in the well-walled towns.
We want no riches, gems, nor costly gowns—
Content to live and sing where green the grass is.

Ballad, if I could live my life once more,
A mountain shepherd I should choose to be—
No spoken word would pass my lips before
I too was of their joyous company,
Calling now Martin, now Blondel to me,
Following ever the lovely shepherd lasses.

MAURICE VALENCY

NOTES AND BIOGRAPHICAL SKETCHES

The dominant influence which may be traced in the lyric of medieval Italy is that of the wandering Provençal troubadours who first appeared in Italy toward the end of the twelfth century. Their influence was so great that initially imitation of their poetry went beyond matters of form and technique; even their language was borrowed, and native poets like Rambertino Buvalelli, Lanfranco Cigala, Sordello, and Brunetto Latini actually wrote in the idiom of Provence. Among the first to adapt the Provençal lyric to the *volgare locale* were the poets of the Sicilian (or Frederician) school—Pier delle Vigne, Giacomo da Lentino, Cielo D'Alcamo, Enzo Re, and others—who, coming from many parts of Italy, found a congenial home at the learned, cosmopolitan court of the Emperor Frederick II (d. 1250). The work of this group furnished the model for the poets of the various Tuscan schools—Guittone d'Arezzo, Bonagiunta Orbicciani and a host of others—who, like their predecessors, remained essentially "provençalizers," faithful to the amatory aspirations, the motifs, and the rigorous technique of the troubadours.

Despite its popularity and technical excellence, the work of the Provençal poets and their imitators were not entirely suited to the modified feudal conditions of Italian society. Inevitably there was a reaction in taste, ushered in by the poets of the so-called *dolce stil novo,* who, without abandoning the themes and forms of their predecessors (chiefly the sonnet, *canzone,* and *ballata*), sought for greater delicacy of expression, greater transparency, and fresher diction. The father of this group of poets, so Dante tells us, was Guido Guinizelli, whose canzone *Al cor gentil* introduces the idea of the lady-angel, the lady whose presence bestows beatitude, dispels ill thoughts, and inspires her lover to desire spiritual perfection. In her fullest manifestation (i.e., Dante's Beatrice) the lady becomes, so to speak, the vehicle of divine illumination and grace. The poets who adopted and developed Guinizelli's innovations were not numerous. Guido Cavalcanti, Cino da Pistoia, and, of course, Dante were the only ones to leave a substantial body of poetry. But their influence was far-reaching. It is prominent in the sonnets of Petrarch, who perhaps more than any other single poet helped to determine the shape the Renaissance lyric was to take in nearly every country of Europe.

Standing largely apart from the tradition of the "provençalizers" and the stilnovists were the so-called bourgeois poets—Cecco Angiolieri, Fazio degli Uberti, Folgore da San Gimignano—comparatively unpolished and unlearned, whose chief merit lies in their vigorous, earthy realism.—DANIEL J. DONNO

BONAGIUNTA ORBICCIANI (c. 1220-1300), also known as Bonagiunta da Lucca, a Tuscan poet, followed in the tracks of Guittone d'Arezzo (q.v.) and the Provençal poets, opposing the upsurge of the *dolce stil novo* poets, especially Guinizelli (q.v.), for their obscurity. In *Purgatorio,* Dante depicted him as the best representative of the pre-*dolce stil novo* period.

CECCO ANGIOLIERI (c. 1250-1319) was born in Siena to wealthy parents who later tried to curb his bohemian tendencies, but failed. He fell in love with his shoemaker's daughter and dedicated to her many sonnets (he wrote only sonnets), fought her and other wenches so ferociously that his anger verges on the farcical. He wrote disrespectful sonnets to Dante, whom he probably met at the battle of Campaldino (1289). In the *Decameron* (IX, 4) Boccaccio reveals how once a merrymaker stole Cecco's clothes. Cecco's hectic life, with all his quarrels and roguery, with his biting satires and witty perversity (cf. the sonnet included here against his parents, "If I were fire"), reminds one of his French superiors: Rutebeuf (q.v.) and Villon (q.v.).

CIELO D'ALCAMO (fl. 1231), probably wrote in the court (1220-1250) of Frederick II, Emperor of Sicily, and therefore is grouped with the Sicilian School, writers concerned primarily with love poetry. He adapted the Provençal debates (*tenzone*) into the memorable *contrasto,* or dialogue, included here.

CINO DA PISTOIA (c. 1270-1336), born in Pistoia, studied law in Bologna and other universities, and after the Guelph victory lived in exile, teaching in various law schools. With his *canzoni* and sonnets to a lady (probably Selvaggia Vergiolesi) he won honors from Henry VII of Luxemburg and praises from Dante, who calls him the Poet of Love and assigns him a lofty place in *Paradiso* (XXX, 136-138). Indeed, Cino rejected most of the artificial elements in the Provençal poets and put greater warmth and psychological depth into his lyrics, clearing the way for Petrarch.

DANTE ALIGHIERI (1265-1321), the Florentine author of the *Divine Comedy* is Italy's greatest literary genius, whose *canzoni* and sonnets are perhaps not as well known among readers of English as they deserve to be. The *Sestinas* here included, also called "stony poems," were written to a lady named Pietra (stone) and rank with his sonnets and *canzoni* among the most magnificent lyrical utterances in the Italian language.

ENZO RE (c. 1220-1272), the illegitimate child of Frederick II, rivaled his father in courage and leadership. In 1239 he conquered the island of Sardinia, of which he was made king. After years of warfare, he was captured near Modena, at the battle of Fossalta (1249) and brought to Bologna. During his long years of inprisonment he came to know the literary figures of his day, who stimulated him to write.

FAZIO [BONIFAZIO] DEGLI UBERTI (c. 1310-1370), born probably in Pisa of an illustrious Florentine family, lived in many Italian courts while an exile. A militant Ghibelline, he wrote political verse, the allegorical treatise *Dittamondo* (in *terza rima*)—whose only saving grace is its historical and biographical wealth—and sundry love lyrics, remarkably graceful.

FOLGORE DA SAN GIMIGNANO (c. 1250-1317), whose real name was Giacomo di Michele, was born in Siena. After 1305, drawing a pension for military services rendered, he lived in San Gemignano a splendid (hence, *folgore*) life of leisure. In a sonnet sequence reminiscent of the Provençal *plazers,* he presents the pleasures of the months of the year—thus mirroring the daily life and occupations of the Sienese nobility. Cenne dalla Chitarra parodied this sequence with an *enueg,* listing all the unpleasant aspects of each month and the gross manners of the peasantry.

FRANCIS OF ASSISI, ST. (c. 1180-1226), was born at Assisi, where his wealthy father wanted him to follow a commercial career, but he was more fond of amusements. However, after his miraculous recovery from a dangerous illness, he devoted himself to the care of the poor and the sick, repented his sins, became a soldier of Christ and founded the Franciscan Order. Two years after his death he was made a saint. His *Canticle* expresses his extraordinarily deep, all-embracing charity toward all created things.

GIACOMO DA LENTINO (c. 1189-1240), born in Tuscany, studied at the University of Bologna with Pier della Vigna and Mostacci, and in 1233 became one of the chief notaries of Frederick II (that is why Dante called him the Notary in *Purgatorio,* XXIV, 56). One of the most gifted poets of the Sicilian School, he has left us poems in the sonnet form, which it is claimed he invented, and canzoni—in all some forty poems.

GUIDO CAVALCANTI (c. 1255-1300), born in Florence of noble parents, participated with his friend Dante in the political strife of the day, and suffered exile, dying of malaria in Sarzana. He is mentioned by his father, Cavalcante de' Cavalcanti, in a moving scene in the *Inferno.* With his famous song "*Donna mi prega*" the *dolce stil novo* reached its apogee, this canzone being one of the purer and most genuine expressions of these poets' philosophy of love. Dante dedicated his *Vita Nuova* to Cavalcanti.

GUIDO GUINIZELLI (c. 1225-1276), born in Bologna of a distinguished Ghibelline family, became a judge (like his father) in 1268. On the victory of the Guelphs he was exiled, and died two years later. He is considered the first practitioner of the *dolce stil novo,* and Dante and Cavalcanti referred to him as their master. His poem "The Gentle Heart," included here, holds an importance far beyond its modest poetic merits. It is commonly cited as the source for the concept of the angelic lady (*donna angelicata*), which attained its highest expression in Dante's Beatrice as presented in the *Vita Nuova* and the *Divine Comedy.* Modified and attenuated, it also reappeared in Petrarch's sonnets and, largely through their influence, became a commonplace in Renaissance love poetry.

GUITTONE D'AREZZO (c. 1230-1294), born in Santa Formena, near Arezzo, joined the Guelphs, and was exiled about 1260, entering soon thereafter the Order of Knights of Saint Mary, composing from then on only religious poems and *laudes* in ballad form. In addition to these, there are also extant many lyrics, epistles in verse and in prose on moral, political, and religious subjects. The year after his return to his native city he died. He has been held to be one of the most distinguished among the Tuscan poets.

JACOPONE DA TODI (1236-1306), born in Todi, in Umbria, of a noble family, studied law and became rich and famous. He married a beautiful lady and upon discovering at her premature, tragic death that she wore sackcloth under her elaborate gowns, he renounced his life of pleasure and became a Franciscan monk To him is ascribed the *Stabat Mater* and deeply religious poetry, such as the *laudes,* included here.

ONESTO DA BOLOGNA (fl. 1301), was a lawyer—a deed drawn by him in 1301 is preserved in the archives of Bologna.

PETRARCH, FRANCESCO (1304-1374), one of the world's greatest lyric poets, was born at Arezzo, where his Florentine father lived in exile. For years he lived in Avignon and Vaucluse, studied law at Montpellier and Bologna (1323), beginning there his writing. He met Laura de Sade, a married woman, in a church in Avignon, and she may have been the Laura he continued to love even after her death (1348). Most the poems included here show his love for Laura while she was alive, except for the last eleven, written after her untimely death. "Gluttony, Torpor, Pillowed Slothfulness" was addressed to a friend who devoted himself to the study of literature and philosophy; "Weep, Ladies All! Let Love Too Weep with You!" was written at the death of Cino da Pistoia (q.v.).

RINALDO D'AQUINO (?-1279), probably of the same family as St. Thomas Aquinas, held office as falconer (1240) of Frederick II and later joined Charles d'Anjou. Of the twelve songs ascribed to him, the most beautiful is the one here included, the lament of a girl whose lover has left for a crusade. Since the Emperor mentioned is Frederick II, the crusade in question is either that of 1228 or 1240.

SACCHETTI, FRANCO (1335-1400), derived from a noble Guelph family. A man of sterling character, he filled many public offices in Florence and was named ambassador to Bologna in 1376. Highly cultured, he wrote verse and some of the finest stories of early Italian fiction, the *Trecentonovelle,* which, despite his claim that he imitated Boccaccio, show his originality and satiric qualities.

THE IBERIAN PENINSULA: SPAIN AND PORTUGAL

Arabic Poets From Andalusia

Anonymous Mozarabic Jarchas (c. 1040)

William M. Davis

Hebrew Poets

William M. Davis

Arabic Poets From Andalusia

BEN SUHAYD

The Storm

The flowers lift their open mouths in the dark,
seeking the bountiful udders of the rain,

and the black clouds parade in grand battalions,
armed with golden sabers of the lightning.

LYSANDER KEMP

BEN HAZM

The Visit of the Beloved

When you came to me, it was a little before
    the Christians rang their bells,
when the half moon was climbing up the sky.

It was like the raised eyebrow of an old man,
    each hair of it white,
or like the delicate arch of your white foot.

The dawn had still not risen, yet the great
    bow of the Lord
shone against the horizon at your coming,
    radiant with every color
    like the peacock's tail.

LYSANDER KEMP

ABU-L-HASAN AL-HUSRI

In Mourning

White is the color worn for mourning
in Andalusia, and that is just.

Why do I wear the grief-stricken
white of these white hairs?
Because I am in mourning for my youth.

LYSANDER KEMP

IBN AL-TALLA

The Artichoke

Daughter of earth and water, her bounty
Is offered to him who awaits her
Locked in a castle of greed.

By her whiteness, and the fastness of her refuge,
She seems like a Greek virgin
Concealed in a veil of spears.

WILLIAM M. DAVIS

ABU-L-HASAN BEN AL-QABTURNUH

In Battle

I remembered Sulayma when the passion
of battle was as fierce
as the passion of my body when we parted.

I thought I saw, among the lances, the tall
perfection of her body,
and when they bent toward me I embraced them.

LYSANDER KEMP

ABU SALT UMAYYA

The White Horse

It was as white as the morning star at dawn,
and it marched proudly, bearing its golden saddle.

A man who envied me asked, when he saw it
prancing behind me to the combat:

"Who has bridled the daybreak with the Pleiades,
and saddled the lightning with the half moon?"

LYSANDER KEMP

ALI BEN HARIQ

The Oars of the Galley

It seems there are only reptiles in the hold,
which entered in Noah's day to escape the Flood.

They think the waters are rising again, and each
serpent, alarmed, flickers its tongue at an opening.

LYSANDER KEMP

SAHL BEN MALIK

The Dawn

When the first light came and I saw her brush
the dew from her smooth brow, I said to my love,

"I fear the sun has discovered our secret."
She answered, "Please God that my brother has not!"

LYSANDER KEMP

ABU ZAKARIYYA

The Spear

It was dark till the dust of battle covered
its head with white hair:
old age has always followed after youth.

When I thrust it toward the enemy, it seemed
the rope with which I drew
blood from the deep well of a hero's heart.

LYSANDER KEMP

BEN SAID AL-MAGRIBI

The Battle

Dear God, the standards of the knights
hovered like birds round your enemies!

The spears punctuated what the swords wrote;
the dust of battle was the sand that dried
the writing; and the blood perfumed it.

LYSANDER KEMP

QADI BEN LUBBAL

Night Fiesta on the River

By day the river's throat was bare of adornments,
but later, in the night, it gleamed with jewels.

The lantern-lights outshone the stars; their bright
reflections were like spears lost in the water.

When the ships loomed on the spread wings of their sails,
the rowboats fled on the long legs of their oars,

escaping as the hare escapes the falcon.

LYSANDER KEMP

Anonymous Mozarabic Jarchas

So Much Loving, So Much Loving
Tant' amare, tant' amare

So much loving, so much loving
Darling, so much loving
Made gay eyes grow dim
With so much longing!

WILLIAM M. DAVIS

✖

What Shall I Do or What Become of Me?
Qué faré yo o qué seråd de mibi?

What shall I do or what become of me?
Lover,
Don't abandon me!

WILLIAM M. DAVIS

✖

My Lord Ibrahim

Mio sidi Ibrahim

My lord Ibrahim,
Oh dulcet name,
Come to me
By night.
If not, if you will not,
Then I shall come to you.
Tell me where
To find you.

WILLIAM M. DAVIS

❖

Come, Bewitcher!

Ven, ya sahhara!

Come, bewitcher!
Morning, fair with vigor
Rising, seeks your love.

WILLIAM M. DAVIS

❖

If You Truly Want Me

Si queres como bono mub

If you truly want me,
Kiss this string of pearls:
This little mouth of cherries.

WILLIAM M. DAVIS

❖

Comes Easter, Ah, without Him

Venio la Pasca, ay aun

Comes Easter, ah, without him,
My heart is wounded for him.

WILLIAM M. DAVIS

⁂

No, Little Sweetheart, No

Non, quero, non jillello

No, little sweetheart, no,
I only want the dark one.

WILLIAM M. DAVIS

⁂

Mother, See My Love!

Mamma, ayy habibi

Mother, see my love!
Under his golden ringlets
His neck so white,
His little mouth of crimson.

WILLIAM M. DAVIS

⁂

Mother, I Shall Not Sleep

Non dormireyo, mamma

Mother, I shall not sleep
When morning rises

But dream of Abū-l-Qāsim,
His features dawning.

WILLIAM M. DAVIS

⁂

Now Like Another's Child

Como si filiolo alieno

Now like another's child,
My breast is not your pillow.

WILLIAM M. DAVIS

⁂

Mercy, Lover Mine!

Amau, ya habibi

Mercy, lover mine!
Leave me not alone.
Beauty, kiss my lips:
I know you will not go.

WILLIAM M. DAVIS

Hebrew Poets

SOLOMON IBN GABIROL

She Looked at Me and Her Eyelids Burned

She looked at me and her eyelids burned,
While her goblet brimmed with tears;

The words overflowed her mouth, like strings of pearls,
And the smile on her lips defied compare with gold.
But the rebuke she sent my soul
Wounded me like the words of the creditor
to the poor debtor.
Meanwhile, the cup passed from hand to hand
like the sun amid the heavens,
And day receded, fleeting, like waves along the shore,
But my blood, receding at unison of day,
Tinged my cheeks bright red: she will not return.

WILLIAM M. DAVIS

Behold the Lovely Maid!

THE LOVERS:

Behold the lovely maid! The bracelets
On her arms gleam like the tiles of Ahasuerus
Her walk is comely, with sprightly step
And the sound of them
Is as the tinkling of her jewels.
The moon would be her diadem
And the Pleiades her bangles.
While the sun, at its height, turns pale,
And, shamefaced, hides behind her veils.
Her lover beholds her with loving looks
For until the dawn, he has kept his vigil.
But she counts your hopes; be aware
That in her eyes your vigils are as gifts.
Surely her curving breasts are ripe for love,
For the folds of her tunic cannot conceal them.

THE POET:

Seek not to incite your lover's heart
For now in him the fires of love are quenched;
The burning embers quickly turned to ashes
And the sun of his love grew dark.

They told me, "Go and serve the world!"
But one who is its master cannot become its servant.

WILLIAM M. DAVIS

JUDAH HALEVI

Afráh

Afráh laves her garments in the waters
Of my tears, and spreads them
In the sunshine of her glow.
She begs no water of the fountains,
Having my two eyes;
Nor any sunshine but her beauty.

WILLIAM M. DAVIS

✖

Cups without Wine Are Lowly

Cups without wine are lowly
As a pot thrown on the ground
But, full of juice, they shine
Like the body with a soul.

WILLIAM M. DAVIS

✖

The Earth, like a Girl, Sipped the Rains

The earth, like a girl, sipped the rains
Of winter past, and those the ministering cloud
distilled
Or perhaps, like a secluded bride in winter,
Whose soul longs for the coming of love's time
She waited, and sought the season ripe for love
Till summer came, and calmed her anxious heart

Wearing golden tunics and white embroidered flax.
Like a girl who delights in her finery and raiment,
Every day she renews the grace of her embroiderers
And provides all her neighbors with new garments.
Every day she changes the colors of her fields
Now with strings of pearls, now with emeralds or rubies,
Offering her meadows now white or green or gold
Or blushing like the sweetheart kissing her beloved.
Her trellises display such gorgeous flowers
It seems as if she stole the stars from heaven.
Here is paradise, whose sheltered buds are clustered
Among the vines, kindled with blushes that incite to love.
The grapes are cold as snow in the hand of him
who plucks them.
But in his entrails, they burn as hot as fire.
From the whirling cask, the wine, like sun, is rising.
And we shall bring our onyx cups to pour it.
In the love of wine we shall stroll beneath the bowers
Around the garden, and smile with tears of rain,
Bright with shining drops spilled by the clouds
That scatter round like strings of pearls.
She finds joy in the song of the swallow,
and in the song of the vintagers,
And in cooing pigeons tamed by love.
She twitters in the branches, as the maiden sings
Behind her zither, swaying as she dances.
My soul is attentive to the breeze of dawn,
For it fondles the breath of my beloved.
A wanton breeze it is, that steals the scent of myrtles
To waft it off to lovers apart.
The heads of the myrtle rise and nod in turn
While the tremulous fronds of the palm tree
Seem to applaud the singing of the birds.

WILLIAM M. DAVIS

⌘

One Day I Fondled Her on My Knees

THE LOVER SPEAKS OF HIS BELOVED:
One day I fondled her on my knees,
And she saw her image reflected in my pupils;
And then, sporting, she kissed my eyes,
Yet kissed not them, but her image.

WILLIAM M. DAVIS

Galician-Portuguese Poets

AIRAS NUNES

The Summertime Delights Me

Que muyto m'eu pago deste verão

The summertime delights me
With branches, buds, and flowers,
With birds that twitter lovesongs
And carefree, happy hours.
Then, like every lover
I'm joyful and content
I stroll along the river
By trees, and through the glen.
When lovebirds sing their lovesongs
I sing of love a while
And follow them, inventing
A thousand tunes a mile.
I'm full of joy and happiness
To hear their summer smile.

WILLIAM M. DAVIS

✲

Let the Three of Us Now Dance, Oh Friends

Baylemos nós ia todas tres, ay amigas

Let the three of us now dance, oh friends,
beneath these flowering hazel trees,
and whoever is beautiful, as we are beautiful,
if she loves a lover,
under these flowering hazel trees
she will come to dance.

Let all three of us, oh sisters,
under this branch of these hazels,
and whoever is pretty, as we are pretty,
if she love a lover,
under this branch of these hazels
she will come to dance.

For God's sake, oh friends, while we are idle,
under this flowering branch let us dance,
and whoever is comely, as we are comely,
if she love a lover,
under this lonely branch where we dance
she will come to dance.

LAWRENCE A. SHARPE

✠

When Truth Disappeared from the World

Porque no mundo menguou a verdade

When truth disappeared from the world
I ventured to inquire
Where she might have gone.
All said, "Seek her elsewhere,
For she has strayed so far
No news of her can come,
Nor is she at the friars'."

At the cloister of the friars,
This is what I heard:
"Don't seek truth among us,
She doesn't live here now:
We don't know where she's moved to,
For much concerns us more."

In Cistel, where truth once dwelt,
They said she dwelt no more,
Nor had she now, for years.
No friar or abbot knew her,
And one quite simply said:
"I hope she doesn't come here;
She lives uncloistered now."

At Saint James of Compostela
The pilgrims at my inn
Said, "By God, you've strayed afar
But truth is not this way.
Go try another road
She's left no message here."

WILLIAM M. DAVIS

NUNO FERNANDEZ DE TURNEOL

Arise, Fond Lover, Who Sleeps on Chilly Mornings

Levad amigo que durmides as mañanas frias

Arise, fond lover, who sleeps on chilly mornings,
All the birds are chirping lovesongs,
Merrily I go!

Arise, fond lover, who sleeps on mornings chill,
All the birds are singing lovesongs,
Merrily I go!

All the birds are chirping lovesongs
To lie about your love and mine.
Merrily I go!

All the birds are singing lovesongs
To lie about your love and mine.
Merrily I go!

To lie about your love and mine
And so you cut their branches fine,
Merrily I go!

To lie about your love and mine
And so you cut their perches fine,
Merrily I go!

And so you cut their branches fine
And dried the springs they drank in.
Merrily I go!

And so you cut their perches fine
And dried the springs they bathed in,
Merrily I go!

WILLIAM M. DAVIS

ALFONSO X [King Alfonso the Wise]

Song VII

Cantiga VII

This is how Saint Mary saved the pregnant abbess, who weeping had fallen asleep before her altar.

We should love Saint Mary
much, and we should beseech
her to cast her grace o'er us,
so that the shameless
fiend will not make us sin.

Therefore I shall tell you
a miracle which I found
that she, Mother of the Great King,
performed for an abbess,
for, according as I have learned,
she was her devotee.
But the devil beguiled her
so that she became pregnant
by a man from Bologna,
a man who took great care
to conceal his deed and her need.
We should love Saint Mary . . .

The nuns, when they found out
and had sure knowledge of it,
were highly delighted;
For because she had never
wished to let them sin,
they held her in malice.
And they went to accuse her
to the bishop of the place,
and the good man arrived there
from Cologne, and when he had
called, she came without delay,
happy and smiling.
We should love Saint Mary . . .

The bishop addressed her so:
"Madam, according as I hear
Wickedly indeed have you acted;
and therefore I have come here,
so that now before me, you
may make amends for it."
But the lady without delay
began to call the Mother of God;
and, as from one who was dreaming,
Saint Mary had the child taken
and sent for rearing to Saxony.
We should love Saint Mary . . .

When the lady awakened
and found herself delivered,
quickly she came to the bishop;
and carefully he examined her
and ordered her disrobed;
and as soon as he saw her body,
he began to praise God
and to curse the nuns, who were
of the Order of Onna, saying:
"As God helps me, I can declare
This one saved from all accusation."
We should love Saint Mary . . .

JOHN E. KELLER

⁂

Song XVIII
Cantiga XVIII

This is how Saint Mary caused the silkworms to make the silk for two head veils, because the woman who kept them had promised one and had not given it to her.

In order to remove us
from doubt it pleases
Saint Mary to show us
her beautiful miracles daily.

And so that we might see
her loveliness
she performed a great miracle
in Extremadura,
in Segovia, where dwelt
a lady of hers,
who in her house
produced much silk.
In order to remove us . . .

Because she was losing her silkworms
and had little silk,

she therefore promised
          to give a veil,
so as to honor the image
that stood above the altar
of the Virgin without par,
in whom she greatly trusted.
In order to remove us . . .

Because she had made the vow,
          the silkworms always
increased from that time
          and did not perish;
but the lady in the great leisure
that she enjoyed there
ever forgot to give
the silken veil
In order to remove us . . .

Hence it befell her
          that in a great festival
in August that she came there,
          during the height of siesta,
to pray before the image;
and as she lay there
at prayer she remembered
the veil which she had vowed.
In order to remove us . . .

With heartfelt weeping
          she went running home
and beheld then
          that the silkworms were
weaving and working
earnestly at the veil,
and she began to weep
with the greatest of joy
In order to remove us . . .

And as she wept thus,
          She pondered about

the veil and therefore called
　　a great many people in
so that they might see
how the Mother of God
knew how to labor
with holy skill.
In order to remove us . . .

The people, with great joy,
　　when they beheld this,
giving praise to the Mother
　　of God, went forth
to proclaim it in the streets,
saying: "Come, come
to behold the great miracle
that she who guides us wrought!"
In order to remove us . . .

One by one, and two by two
　　Swiftly they came there;
meanwhile the silkworms
　　fashioned another
veil to make it just that
if anyone should desire
to carry one away,
he should leave the other
In order to remove us . . .

Therefore Don Alfonso, the King
　　in his own chapel
keeps, according as I hear,
　　the most beautiful veil,
and that he has it brought out
in festivals to uproot heresy
from those who doubting the Virgin
go in their great folly.
In order to remove us . . .

JOHN E. KELLER

PERO MEOGO [Peter the Monk]

Tell Me, Daughter, Pretty Daughter

Digades, filla miña, filla belida

Tell me, daughter, pretty daughter,
Why did you tarry by the spring?
"Mother, I'm in love!"

Tell me, daughter, lovely daughter,
Why did you tarry by the stream?
"Mother, I'm in love!"

Mother, I tarried by the spring
To see the stags at dawn;
"Mother, I'm in love!"

Mother, I tarried by the stream,
To see them drink at dawn;
"Mother, I'm in love!"

You're lying, daughter, you lie for a friend,
I never saw stags at the spring;
"Mother, I'm in love!"

You're lying, daughter, you lie for some boy
I never saw stags at the stream;
"Mother, I'm in love!"

WILLIAM M. DAVIS

In the Green Grass

En as verdes ervas

In the green grass
I saw the prancing does
My lover.

In the green lea
I saw the angry stags
My lover.

And with the scent of does
I sat and washed my braids
My lover.

And with the scent of stags
I sat and washed my hair
My lover.

As soon as it was washed
I bound it up in gold
My lover.

I bound it up in gold
And waited for you there,
My lover.

In gold I bound it up
And waited for you there
My lover.

WILLIAM M. DAVIS

❖

My Friend Is Going, Mother

Tal vai o meu amigo

My friend is going, mother,
With love I gave, and he
Goes wounded like a hart
From huntsmen of the king.

My lover's going, mother,
My love he takes, and he
Goes wounded like the stag
The huntsman shot for me.

And if my love goes wounded
He'll go to die at sea;
My friend will board a ship
And drown himself at sea.

Watch yourself, my daughter,
For such I'll never see;
He makes himself look woeful
To win his cause with me.

And watch yourself, my daughter,
For such I'll never see;
He makes himself look woeful
To win his way with me.

WILLIAM M. DAVIS

JOAN ZORRO

Hair, My Pretty Hair

Cabelos, los meus cabelos

Hair, my pretty hair,
The king sent for it to me:

Mother, what shall I do?
Daughter, give it to the king!

Tresses, my pretty tresses,
The king sent for them to me:
Mother, what shall I do?
Daughter, give them to the king!

WILLIAM M. DAVIS

¤

In Lisbon by the Sea
En Lixboa, sobre lo mar

In Lisbon by the sea
New ships I ordered built
Alas, my pretty lady!

In Lisbon by the shore
New ships I ordered made
Alas, my pretty lady!

New ships I ordered built
And ordered them to sea
Alas, my pretty lady!

New ships I ordered made
And ordered them away
Alas, my pretty lady!

WILLIAM M. DAVIS

¤

Along the River Shore
Per ribeira do rio

Along the river shore
I saw them tip the oar
And loved the river more!

Upstream along the shore
I saw them speed the oar
And loved the river more!

I saw them tip the oar
To reach my friend afar
And loved the river more!

I saw them speed the oar
To reach my love afar
And loved the river more!

To reach my friend afar:
I longed for him, ashore,
And loved the river more!

To reach my love afar:
I yearned for him, ashore,
And loved the river more!

WILLIAM M. DAVIS

Let's Dance, Let's Dance, Us Pretties

Bailemos nós xa todas, ay amigas

Let's dance, let's dance, us pretties,
Under the blossoming trees
And the prettiest pretty her love will prance
Under the nut trees, and see him dance.

Let's dance, let's dance, us lovelies,
Under the crimsoning trees,
And the loveliest lovely her friend will prance
Under the nut trees, and see him dance.

WILLIAM M. DAVIS

MARTIN CODAX

O Waves of the Sea of Vigo
Ondas do mar de Vigo

O waves of the sea of Vigo,
Have you seen my friend?
Ah Lord, let him come soon!

O waves of the rolling sea,
Have you seen my love?
Ah Lord, let him come soon!

If you've seen my friend,
The one I sigh for,
Ah Lord, let him come soon!

If you've seen my love,
The one I burn for,
Ah Lord, let him come soon!

WILLIAM M. DAVIS

Ah, Waves, I Come to See
Ai ondas que en vin veer

Ah, waves, I come to see
If you could only say
Why my love delays
without me!

Ah, waves, I come to say
If you could only see

Why my love delays
without me!

WILLIAM M. DAVIS

AFONSO LOPES DE BAIAN

They Have Told Me Some News
Diseron mi hunhas novas

They have told me some news that I am glad to hear:
my lover has arrived, and if he comes there,
to the shrine of Santa Maria das Leiras
I shall go, in my beauty, if my lover comes there.

They have told me some news which gives me great joy,
my lover has arrived, and if he goes there,
to the shrine of Santa Maria das Leiras
I shall go, in my beauty, if my lover comes there.

They have told me some news which greatly pleases me,
my lover has arrived, but I, in order to see him,
to the shrine of Santa Maria das Leiras
shall go, in my beauty, if my lover comes there.

Never was a woman so happy with such news,
as I alone am with this, and if he comes there,
to the shrine of Santa Maria das Leiras
I shall go, in my beauty, if my lover comes there.

LAWRENCE A. SHARPE

ROI FERNANDEZ

When I See the Waves
Cand'eu vexo las ondas

When I see the waves
And rocky shores

My heart sends waves
To her ashore:
    Curst be the sea
    So cruel to me!

When I see the waves
And hills depart
The waves rise up
And drown my heart:
    Curst be the sea
    So cruel to me!

WILLIAM M. DAVIS

JOAN DE GUILHADE

For Mr. X I've Only Mischief

A don Foam quer'eu grã mal

For Mr. X I've only mischief;
For his wife, I've only love.
We three have lasted through
The years, as such things do.
For, ever since I saw her
His wife I've always served
And sought what he deserved.

Here's what I'd like to show:
(It will hurt someone, I know,
Who'll die, in any case)
So I'll talk about Mr. Bad
And the goodness his Mrs. had
Which has no peer, I know:
Here's what I'd like to show.

In wisdom and good looks
And courteous remarks
No woman (this I'll swear)

Could match her or compare.
She'd charm Our Lord Himself
(He'd charm the Devil more)
With charming, dev'lish talk.

And since they both are such,
I've taken them to heart:
Let Him Who Watches, judge!

WILLIAM M. DAVIS

✠

Alas, Ugly Lady, You Complained

Ai, dona fea, foste-vos queixar

Alas, ugly lady, you complained
My verses never sang your praise
But now I will compose a song
And laud you all the same.
You'll see it's meant for you:
Ugly lady, nasty old shrew!

Alas, ugly lady, I'll not say
You've taken fame to heart:
And so these lines proclaim
And laud you all the same.
You'll see they're meant for you:
Ugly lady, nasty old shrew!

Ugly lady, I never praised
Your vice in verse, though much I've made
But now I'll make a song of praise
And laud you all the same:
Ugly lady, nasty old shrew!

WILLIAM M. DAVIS

✠

Friend, I Can't Deny

Amigo, non poss'eu negar

Friend, I can't deny
I'm all aflame with love,
For I'm at my wits' end,
And witlessly I'll say:
    Those green eyes I see
    Are tantalizing me.

But, whoever understands
Whose pretty eyes I mean,
That someone will lament
About my life, and grieve:
    Those green eyes I see
    Are tantalizing me.

But men should not be swayed
Because their wits are weak
And witless in their sorrow
Let their sorrow speak:
    Those green eyes I see
    Are tantalizing me.

WILLIAM M. DAVIS

JOÃO ROIZ DE CASTELO-BRANCO

Song of Parting

Cantiga, partindo-se

Milady, by departure
My eyes you so bedim
That ne'er you've seen such sorrow
For man or maid or whim.

So sorrowful, so mournful,
So dolorous my eyes

So weary, and so tearful,
I long for death and prize
This life as but a whim.
My sorrows part so sorrowed
So scarce my hope and slim,
That ne'er you've seen such sorrow
For man or maid or whim.

WILLIAM M. DAVIS

KING DINIS OF PORTUGAL [Dom Dinis]

O Flowers, O Flowering Green Pine

Ai flores, ai flores do verde pĩo

O flowers, o flowering green pine,
What news of my sweet friend?
O Lord, and where?

O flowers, o flowering green boughs,
What news of my sweet love?
O Lord, and where?

What news of my sweet friend,
Who lied to make me bend?
O Lord, and where?

What news of my sweet love,
Who lied of what he swore?
O Lord, and where?

"You ask for your sweet friend;
I say he's live and sound."
O Lord, and where?

"You ask for your sweet love;
I say he's live and sound."
O Lord, and where?

"I say he's sound and live
And yours before his time."
O Lord, and where?

"I say he's live and sound
And yours before he grounds."
O Lord, and where?

WILLIAM M. DAVIS

⌘

A Shepherdess Well Made

Ua pastor ben talhada

A shepherdess well made
Was longing for her friend
And was, I will relate,
From what I saw, irate,
And said, "There's nothing more
To trust a lover for;
A girl in love should scoff
For mine, oh mine, ran off."

On her hand there perched
A parrot, with a glimmer
Of mischief in his song,
For it was nearly summer.
And said, "Sweet friend, explain
What shall I do for love
Now that you've strayed in vain
And fallen in the flowers?"

A great part of the day
She sported there, relying
At times on old regrets
And sometimes merely sighing
And said, "Ah Good Saint Mary,
How shall I manage now?"

And then the parrot cackled,
"Well enough, I vow!"

"If you would grant a boon,
Oh lover, please be true,
Be charitable, too,
For life is death enough."
And the bird said, "Dearest lady
Don't weep, but lend an ear
For him who served you once,
Look up, you'll see him here!"

WILLIAM M. DAVIS

⌘

Provençals Right Well May Versify

Proençaes soen mui ben trobar

Provençals right well may versify
And say they do with love
But those with verse in flowertime
And never else, I'd vow,
Their heart is not in torment
As mine is for my lady.

Although they're bound to versify
And praise as best they can,
Nonetheless, I'd vow
That those with verse in spring
And never else, will bring
No grief as deep as mine.

For those who versify with joy
About the verdant time,
The flowers do their bidding,
In spring, but soon decline,

Nor is their life perdition
Nor death in life, like mine.

WILLIAM M. DAVIS

⌘

John Bolo's Acting Grim
Joam Bol'and mal desbaratado

John Bolo's acting grim
And sad and very cross
For though he's gained, he's lost
All his mother left him:
His servant, who's no fool,
Stole his nag and left his mule.

If the knave who stole his mule
Had left John Bol' his nag,
John wouldn't wring his hands
Or think it was so cruel:
But his servant, who's no fool,
Stole his nag and left his mule.

If the knave who stole his nag
Had carried off his mule,
John, though I'm sure he'd bleat,
Wouldn't whimper in the street.
But the knave, when treated cruel,
Stole his nag and left his mule.

WILLIAM M. DAVIS

MACIAS O NAMORADO

I Went in Quest of Measure
Provei de buscar mesura

I went in quest of measure
Where measure could but fail,

And lacking in good fortune
Was judged by folly's rule;
And so I tell you frankly,
Beset by growing pain,
A verse, with this refrain:
The heart I had
Has reason to be sad.

Mine eyes have seen such beauty
I'll perish, and for sure
My heart will burst with sorrow
So great that love's no cure;
Thus I would advise you,
Don't speak to me of joy,
But hear my verses through:
Well may God maintain
Great pleasure after pain.

Woefully these verses
I've sung e'er since the day
I went in quest of measure
And found there was no way.
Measure I die calling,
Sighing to maintain
A verse, with this refrain:
My dazzled eyes depart
Struck dead by you, my heart.

For I did not find measure
Where measure seldom failed
But willingly took pleasure
And all that it entailed;
And so, still sad and grieving,
I'll sing, and e'er maintain,
A verse, with this refrain:
Good Lord, please bring
Great pleasure after pain.

WILLIAM M. DAVIS

Castilian Poets

GONZALO DE BERCEO

Lament of the Virgin
Duelo de la Virgen

To the tomb they did return in coats of mail all dressed,
Saying dirty, foul insults till all were sore distressed,
Inventing at that moment songs in cheap and vulgar style,
Playing their accompaniments on zither, harp, and viol.

Rhyming songs the rascals sang as they continued thither,
Harsh and bitter were their words to the Virgin Mother:
"Oh Jews, let us keep watch, let us with care proceed,
Lest they make cruel mock of us both in word and deed."

SONG OF THE GRAVE-WATCHERS:

Keep watch, keep watch, keep watch!

Keep watch, O Jews, with care and zeal
Keep watch!
Lest they the Son of God do steal.
Keep watch!

Peter, John, and Andrew too,
Keep watch!
Will try to steal Him, woe to you.
Keep watch!

Nor rest nor peace will e'er be known,
Keep watch!

To come out from beneath the stone,
Keep watch!

They are all as little thieves,
Keep watch!
Who like to peep through holes of keys.
Keep watch!

Your tongue that wags so loose and free,
Keep watch!
Has made you suffer painfully.
Keep watch!

They are all vile and lowly creatures,
Keep watch!
Mixed and base, with mongrel features.
Keep watch!

Your loose tongue, careless and unwise,
Keep watch!
Has put you in this troubled guise.
Keep watch!

Nor guile nor tricks can you envision,
Keep watch!
To put you forth from out the prision.
Keep watch!

You have not reason nor have you sense,
Keep watch!
By year's end to get you hence
Keep watch!

Thomas and then Matthew too,
Keep watch!
Will want to steal Him, to your rue.
Keep watch!

He was betrayed by His disciple,
Keep watch!

But understood not, not one trifle.
Keep watch!

Philip, Judas, and Simon Peter,
Keep watch!
Look for help to steal their leader,
Keep watch!

If they wish to do this deed,
Keep watch!
Today's the day they surely need!
Keep watch!

Keep watch!
Keep watch, keep watch, keep watch!

As they joked and boasted, saying foul and shameful things,
Full villainous and unseemly, their insult wounds and stings,
Their folly grieved the King of Heaven
and made his heart all sore,
At the malice they toward Jesus Christ
and His companions bore.

BEATRICE P. PATT

JUAN LORENZO

From *The Book of Alexander*
Libro de Alexandre

Alexander, that good magistrate without frontiers
Had a thought while strolling down the road:
How he could make a ladder or a hill
To climb, and see the world spread out below.

He caught a pair of griffons, valiant birds,
And had them fed on meats, both salt and fresh,
Until they were accustomed to the taste
And eating, grew quite fat and very strong.

He planned to make a supple leather cape
About the length a man would go, stretched out,
And tied it to the griffons with a chain
Like one a heavy man could never break.

He took the meat, well skewered on a spit,
Stretched it far before his griffons twain,
Who lunged at it and strained and flapped their wings;
They thought to wolf it down, but they could not.

As they rose, Alexander stood erect
And kept on rising up into the sky
Sometimes higher, sometimes dipping low,
And made them take him where he wished to go.

He raised the meat, whene'er he wished to rise
Or lowered it whenever he did not,
And where the griffons saw it, they were sure to go,
Nor did he scold them, for hunger's hard to bear.

So far did Alexander push upward toward the clouds
That hills and valleys spread out for him below;
The rivers plunged down deep into the sea,
But just how deep, he never could conceive.

He saw the harbors where oceans narrow down;
He saw great perils in many wondrous spots;
He saw great galleys crashing on the rocks,
And others enter port, and take their meals.

Thus he learned of Africa's great form
And where effecting entry might be best;
Then suddenly he found the best way out,
For vast the journey was, and hard and slow.

It takes too long to tell you all he saw;
Half a day would hardly be enough;
But at a certain time he came to know
What no scholar ever thought to show.

WILLIAM M. DAVIS

ANONYMOUS

Dispute of Elena and Maria
Disputa de Elena y María

(Elena extols the way of life of her lover, the Knight, and makes fun of that of Maria's lover, the Clergyman.)

To the palace goes my lover,
But he's not starved or cold;
He goes along on horseback
Nobly shod and clothed.
Knights seek out his company,
Squires serve his wants,
They give him princely wages
And render him accounts.
When visiting the palace,
Spruced up, and very well,
Along with arms and horses,
His squires and his men,
He always brings his goshawks,
And falcons, purest bred.
When hunting by the river,
He makes the biggest kill:
Bitterns and bustards,
And other birds as well.
When he nears the palace,
God! how good he looks!
Goshawks shriek,
Horses neigh,
And merrily he sings.
He honors me and buys me
The finest shoes and clothes,
Pretty silks and satins,
And things I won't disclose.
Believe me, his one kiss

Outdoes an abbot's five,
Like yours, with his scrapy beard,
Always bundled in his cloak,
His head and chin and neck
First cousin to a toad.
But what your lover cares for,
Your priestie's great concern,
Is counting up his rosaries,
And getting brats to learn:
Battling with his hands,
To baptize godsons live;
Eating food and spending,
Sleeping and cavorting,
Seducing good man's daughters,
Both married and engaged.
If he can't tell right from wrong,
A man's not worth a drat:
Mine knows which is which;
He's a better man for that!

WILLIAM M. DAVIS

JUAN RUIZ, ARCHPRIEST OF HITA

From *The Book of True Love*
[*Libro de Buen Amor*]

Encounter of the Archpriest with Ferrand García
De lo que acontesció al Arcipreste con Ferrand García

I swear my eyes won't see the light
Now their Cross is lost for life.
This Lady Cross, the baker's wife,
I came across, all set to browse on,
Like any other Andalusian.
I thought she'd be my private lane—
She was Public Highway One.
And the pains I took to get her!

I told that poacher, "Now, García,
Be my go-between and clear
A path for me—be nice and tender."
Yes, he said, he'd gladly do it,
But got *himself* set up and rooted
In her private crossroad bed.
I got the crusts that he spat out.
He got all the softest bread.
Through him I told her she would get
Every bit of my best wheat.
But he charged her with his rabbit—
That dirty, double crossing cheat!
God cripple all these go betweens,
These lowdown leaping rabbiteers!

EDWIN HONIG

Don Pitas Payas
Don Pitas Payas

A man once left his wife—I'll tell you all about it—
And if the tale's no good, then tell me one to match it.
His name was Pitas Payas, a lusty Breton painter
Who married a young wife, who liked her man to romp her.

Before one month was up, he told her, "Wife,
I'm off to Flanders, I'll bring you lots of presents."
"My lord," she cried, "Godspeed,
But don't forget my person."

"Mistress of beauty," Sir Payas said,
"On your body I long to paint
A figure to curb more folly:"
She answered, "My lord, then paint it on my belly."

Under her navel he made a lamb
And then flew off, as cocky as a merchant

To spend two years—and not by chance—
Each month she thought a year had passed.

She'd only just been married
And not dwelt long with him:
A willing friend took over
And wore away her lamb.

When she heard her spouse was coming
She ran to tell her friend
And said, "Please paint, as best you can,
Another lamb right here."

But in his rush, he made a ram
With horns and whatsis sprouting
For just that day, a herald told
Of Pitas Payas' coming.

When he finally came from Flanders
His wife gave scornful welcome
And when the two were snug in bed
He asked to see his token.

"Forgive me, wife," Pitas Payas said,
"Let's strip and see our token."
"Husband," she said, "go look for yourself,
Now do your will; be bold!"

He looked at the accustomed place
And saw the ram with horns.
"Wife," he said, "can you tell me this,
How I made a lamb and find this dish?"

As women in all such arguments
Are always smooth and clever, she said:
"What, husband, two years, and can't a lamb grow?
If you hadn't delayed, the horns wouldn't show!"

So watch your step, don't leave the goods,
Don't be Pitas Payas, and force your wife to look:

With pretty speeches, praise her all the way,
And when she's yours, be sure you never stray.

WILLIAM M. DAVIS

Hill Song [Near Tablada]
Cantica de serrana [*Cerca la Tablada*]

Near Tablada
Past the crest
I met Aldara
Close to dawn.

Atop the pass
I thought I'd die
Of snow and cold
And frosty dew.

Down the slope
I made a turn
And met a hill girl
Buxom red.

"I bow, my pretty,"
"Just don't," she said,
"Keep on running
And go your way."

I said, "My beauty,
I'm cold as sin.
Please, for measure,
Take me in."

She thought it over:
"Friend," she said,
"It's either marriage,
Or pay the bride."

I told her, "Gladly,
But I've been wed
Here in Herreros:
I'll pay, beloved."

She said, "Gee haw,"
So off we sped
And lit the candle
As hill folk do.

She gave me rye bread
Black with soot
Stale, thin wine
And salted meat.

She gave me goat cheese
"Hidalgo," she said,
"Open the satchel,
There's more inside."

She said, "Drink up
And warm your gizzard,
We won't be home
Till round the bend.

"Who gives good gifts
Gets what he likes:
Free bed and supper
And more, besides."

"Now tell me," said I,
"Just what's the price?"
Said she, "I'm thinking—
Will you be nice?

"Well, give me a ribbon
Dyed bright red—
A fancy tunic
With high frilled edge.

"Give me a string
Of bright tin beads,
A sparkling jewel
And furs I need.

"Give me a kerchief
With skirtsy stripes,
A pair of heels
And all one piece.

"With jewels like that
I'll serve you well:
You'll be my husband,
And I, your girl."

"Milady hill girl,
I left 'em home,
But here's a pledge
For round the turn."

Miss Ugly told me:
"No cash, no trade.
I give no credit
Till I've been paid.

"No cash, no credit,
No fun for free:
Who gives no treasure
Gets none from me.

"Honor never foots the bill,
Cash takes care of
What men will:
Proof's not wanting,
That's for sure."

WILLIAM M. DAVIS

✖

Easter Day

De cómo clérigos e legos e flayres e monjas e dueñas e joglares salieron a recebir a don Amor

This is a holy, festive Easter day,
The happy sun has leaped with brightest ray,
And all created things join bird and flower
To welcome Love in His triumphant hour.

The swelling choirs against the darkness fling
Their sweetest song and merry choraling;
Parrot and jay and lark and nightingale—
Both great and small, their risen Love they hail.

The branches of the woods with buds are bent,
Bursting with living hues, with odors blent,
And all men lift their hearts in harmony
To greet their Love, praising orchestrally.

JAMES EDWARD TOBIN

Of the Characteristics of Small Women

De las propiedades que las dueñas chicas han

I'd like to cut the preaching short,
For sermons brief are best, I've thought,
And so for ladies as for speech
What's short and pithy moves us each.

A babbler is a laughing stock; a laugher often cracks his crock
Love in short women is great, not small:
Some tall women few short can top,
But tall for short's a lucky swap.

Cupid told me: Praise 'em short,
Sing their glories, and report,

And so with tongue in cheek I'll show
They're hot as fire, cold as snow.

They're cold outside but hot in love
In bed a comfort, light as fluff,
Around the house, wise, good, and gay,
You'll find out more, so pay good heed.

The zircon's small, but what a gem!
A little sugar's succulent:
In little women, there lies great love:
Few words suffice for clever men.

Good peppercorn's exceeding small
But more than nutmeg spiced and warm:
A little woman, when she's in love,
Every pleasure's hers to give.

As roses small are color bright
In little gold, great treasure;
In little balsam, great perfume,
Small women's love's not measured.

As little rubies sparkle best
With goodness, pride and virtue,
So women small are prettiest
Most loving, loyal, and graceful.

Small's the lark and nightingale:
No larger bird sings sweeter:
A little woman's tenderness
Outsweets all flowers and sugar.

The oriole and popinjay
Are tiny, but sweet shouters:
A little woman who's in love
'S a prized and gifted singer.

With little women naught compares,
She's paradise and comfort,

Joy and solace, pleasure blessed,
And more in proof than greeting.

I'll always take small for big or great:
To flee great evil I deem discreet;
"Choose the lesser," says the sage,[1]
And so, in women, least is best.

WILLIAM M. DAVIS

SEM TOB

From *Moral Proverbs*

Some I've Seen So Crudely

Unos vi con locura

Some I've seen so crudely
Building up large sums,
While others go so shrewdly
Losing all they won.

NORMAN T. DI GIOVANNI

⁂

There's No Day without Night

Non ay syn noche día

There's no day without night,
Nor without heat, cold's bite;
Sowing first, reaping after,
Without weeping there's no laughter.

NORMAN T. DI GIOVANNI

⁂

---

[1] *Aristotle*

There's No Finer Treasure
Non ay buen thesoro

There's no finer treasure
Than doing right,
Or sweeter pleasure,
Or coin so bright.

NORMAN T. DI GIOVANNI

✖

Whether Long or Sparing
Quier larga, quier escasa

Whether long or sparing,
Speech is like
A passing shadow
That leaves no trail.
There is no lance
That pierces every armor,
Nor aught that transfixes
Like what is written.
The flying arrow
Hits the mark,
And letters hark
From Burgos unto Egypt.

WILLIAM M. DAVIS

DIEGO HURTADO DE MENDOZA

That Tree with Its Leaves Atremble
A aquel árbol que mueve la foxa

That tree with its leaves atremble:
It is possessed of something.

That tree so lovely to look at
Seems as though it would bud now:
It is possessed of something.

That tree so lovely to behold
Seems as though it were a flower:
It is possessed of something.

Seems as though it would bloom now:
They can be seen already; come out and watch them:
It is possessed of something.

Seems as though it would flower:
They can be seen already; come out and look:
It is possessed of something.

They can be seen already: come out and behold them.
Let the ladies come cut down the fruit:
It is possessed of something.

KATE FLORES

FERRÁN SÁNCHEZ CALAVERA

By God, My Lords, Let us Lift the Veil

Por Dios, señores, quitemos el velo

By God, my lords, let us lift the veil
That clouds and blinds our view:
Let us gaze on death, which rules the world
Dashing high and low aground:
Our moans transpierce the skies
To God, as we seek pardon
For sins of every age:
Childhood, youth, decay.

For life is not what we have lived
For, living, we grow closer

To cruel, elusive death; and when
We live our life the most, we waken, finding death.
Most certain is the time of birth
Less certain, when we die;
Life's certainty lasts not an hour;
With grief we come, with grief we go.

What became of emperors
Great prelates, popes, and kings?
Dukes and counts and gentle knights,
Rich men, strong, and wise?
How many righteous lovers served
Everywhere bearing arms
And how many skilled in learnèd arts:
Doctors, troubadors, and bards?

Sons and fathers, cherished kin,
Friends we dearly loved:
We ate and drank and romped with them,
Fair and gracious, all!
Duennas, girls, and valiant youth,
Who brawl about below,
And some, who just the other day
Were present here above.

The Duke of Cabra and the Admiral
And great men of Castile:
Now Ruy Diaz, whose standing
Was so high, his praises ran
From Spain unto the Orient
Ringing out in feats of excellence
So great, he dazed the court
With his kind and noble mien?

Of those that I have mentioned
Some are ash and dust
Others, bone and putrefaction
Left scattered to the dogs.
Others are broken skeletons

Heads without hands or feet;
Others make good meals for worms
Others are first interred.

Now where are the kings and emperors
The rulers, rents, and lords?
Where are the pride and arrogance,
The courage and reports?
Where are the ventures, where the deeds?
Where are the crafts, and learnèd skills?
Where are the masters of poetry,
Where, the rhymesters of mastery,
Where the songs, and tambourines?

Where are treasures, serfs, and vassals,
The brooches and precious stones?
Where are the pearls and costly trimmings,
The musk and fragrant oils?
Where are the golden fabrics, and lustrous chains,
The garters and the necklaces,
The black and silver furs,
The tinkling timbrelines?

Where are the banquets, feasts, and dinners,
The tournaments and jousts?
Where are the gaudy dresses, the swayed and mincing steps?
Where is the art of dancers,
Where the meals and the repasts;
Where is the frankness and the splurging,
Where the pleasures and laughs;
Where are the minstrels and buffoons?

I believe with all my being
That now the time is come
As told of by Isaiah:
When cities shall be desolate
With the stench of rotting corpses
When noble men of quality shall die

With mourners at their gates,
And every habitation lie in ruins.

Such death and great destruction
Jeremiah once foretold:
His wrathful eyes repenting
For errant ways of old.
And in that verse and chapter
The careful reader finds
That now, indeed, is time.

Thus it is wisest to provide
And clothe bare souls with virtues:
And castigate our bodies,
For we are sure of loss.
Who ventures to advise this
Need never fail for death,
But shall pass from death to triumph
In everlasting life.

WILLIAM M. DAVIS

IÑIGO LÓPEZ DE MENDOZA, MARQUÉS DE SANTILLANA

Far from You and Close to Care

Lejos de vos y cerca de cuidado

Far from you and close to care
Poor in pleasure and rich in sorrow,
Deprived of rest and well provided
With mortal pain, anguish and fury;

Stripped of hope and cloaked in
Immense affliction and vested with bitterness,
My life escapes me, against all efforts,
Death pursues me without ceasing.

Not enough to satisfy at present
The burning thirst of my great desire
Is Tagus; nor, to succor me, I think

The sickly Guadiana:
Only Guadalquivir has power
To cure me and that only I desire.

FRANCES FLETCHER

Mountain Song of Finojosa
Serranilla de la Finojosa

No lovelier lass have I seen
than one standing on the green
tending her cows
at Finojosa

Making my way from Calatraveño town
to Saint Mary's
by sleep led astray
and mistaking my course
through scrubby gorse
I saw the girl
tending her cows
at Finojosa.

Gay was the meadow
a-bloom with roses,
and there she stood
among all the others;
yet so lovely was she
that she simply could not be
just tending her cows
at Finojosa.

In truth I could not sing
in any way proper

of the roses of spring
had I not first
—to be quite frank—
laid eyes upon the girl
who tended her cows
at Finojosa.

Yet I did not dare
to rest my gaze
upon such beauty rare
and so lose my liberty.
But said I: "Fair lady,
(to find out who she was)
where is the girl
who tends her cows
at Finojosa?"

With lips in curl of smile
she said: "Welcome be.
But it takes such little guile
to find out what you're after.
She needs no love,
nor thinks thereof,
that girl who tends the cows
at Finojosa."

MARTIN NOZICK

JUAN DE MENA

Mourning of the Mother of Lorenzo Dávalos

Duelo de la madre de Lorenzo Dávalos

With jagged nails she tore her face
And rent her breasts with little measure.
She kissed her son's dead lips grown cold
And cursed the hands that wrought his murder.
She cursed the war and its beginning
And wrathfully spewed cruel complaints

Denied herself her due reprisal
And close to living death, she stopped.

Weeping, she cried with rabid tongue:
"Oh murderer who killed my son,
Why not me, instead of him?
I would be no stubborn victim
And death would be a worthy thing.
You would not bear so steep a burden
Or show yourself so cruel to him
As this has been to me."

"If his mother died the first,
These hands would close my eyes;
My son would tell his brothers
I died a single time.
Now I perish wretched,
And suffer for his wounds
With sad unanswered tears
Though wept in my despair."

Thus the pious matron
Lamented her dear son
And hovered by his body
Like a lioness with cubs.

WILLIAM M. DAVIS

JORGE MANRIQUE

Stanzas on the Death of His Father

Coplas por la muerte de su padre

Let the drowsy soul awake!
Let the mind rise quick from sleep
To think of this:
How the living meet their fate,
How we feel the silent feet

That death imprints;
How soon we see our pleasures go,
How easily they are recalled
But with what pain;
Now, as it seems, we've only known
A past far better when it's gone
Than present days.

Well: if we look about the world—
Time in a moment lost from sight
And smuggled away—
If we can look, and judge things well,
We'll count all past and future times
At the same rate.
Let no one fool himself, not here!
Let one think a wished-for thing
Is to endure
Longer than what his eyes have seen—
For all things, like all days, go in;
All doors shut to.

These lives of ours are living streams
But all the streams wind to the sea
And the sea is death.
There, the great estates retreat,
Moving headlong to be seized
And lost to earth;
There, the most imposing floods,
There, the undistinguished, there
The puny rills
Become obliviously one:
Hands that had to toil and scrape,
And hands with rings.

. . . .

Let the men of Troy lie by,
For what have our eyes seen of them,
Their glories or griefs?
Let the men of Rome sleep quiet,

For all the exploits that invest
        Our books and ears!
What have we to do with those
That lived in days long gone, their cares
        Are not our care!
But those of yesterday we know
And sing, though even yesterday
        Evades, and fades.

Where have they gone, the King Don Juan,
The princes and the sons of Aragon,
        Where are they now?
What has become of that brilliant band
Of knights, where are their stirring thoughts
        Like seed on the ground?
That jousting and those tournaments,
The array and the embroidery,
        The crests of arms—
Did we just dream them while we slept?
Are they more now than the green ear
        That's dust in the barn?

What has become of the ladies there,
The coiffures and the gowns they wore,
        The scents they breathed?
What has become of all those flames,
Those fires the lovers struck alone
        From hearts and tears?
Where has the poetry slipped away,
And sweetness of musicians
        Drawn from the strings?
Where is the dancing or the air?
Where are the silks and elegance
        The dancers bring?

And then the next in line to the throne,
Don Enrique, what powers grew
        Between his hands!
With what deceitful soft approach

The world and its delights seduced
        That happy man!
But who can hide how the world bent
Its enmities against him, cruel
        In their reversal—
How it had barely been his friend
When all it gave him was removed and
        Proved unperpetual!

The indiscriminate largesse,
The kingly edifices crammed
        With a king's gold,
The brightly shining banquet-sets,
The treasury with coins like sand
        On a golden shore,
The horses and caparisons
Of all his folk, and such a flash
        Of garb and arms:
Where shall we go to see these things?
What were they but the dews that star
        A field of grass?

. . . .

There is one man, and master of men,
Rodrigo Manrique, whom I'd extol
        If there was need;
But his great acts are known, he's blessed
By the good people he upholds,
        They love his deeds,
And men can see why he is loved,
His courage, his audacity
        Blaze out, so that
I have no wish to gild a sun
Appearing in such clarity
        Through crystal fact.

What a friend to friends, how intimate!
What a gentleman to kinsmen
        And servants alike!

What a foe he was to foemen,
What an example to his own men,
        Bold, brisk in fight!
What wisdom to delight the thinker!
What elegance to meet the witty!
        What reach of mind!
With what a mild hand he commanded,
Till rebel and vainglorious banners
        Unloosed a lion!

. . . .

It was no mountain of treasure he left,
It was no glitter of riches and plate
        That he amassed;
But the Moors knew the armies he led,
And lost the fortresses he gained
        And the towns he attacked;
And those were battles that he won
Where Moor on Moor and horse on horse
        Lay dead and still,
And only by exploits did he come
Into such lands and servitors
        As were given him.

And for those other times in the past,
How did he defend his name
        And his estate?
Finding himself left poor in arms,
He by his servants and brothers saved
        What he maintained.
After the famous deeds were done
In this war that engaged his sword
        As I have said,
His treaties were so honor-hung
That he was given even more
        Land than he held.

The legends that he painted once
By his main strength so long ago

When he was young
He now restored in age, his brush
Tracing new victories as of old,
In new wars won.
And so, for his abilities
And great renown, and good old age
Harvested home,
He was granted then the dignity
Of the crown of knighthood, the great
Order of the Sword.

And when he saw the tyrants come
To occupy his fields and homesteads
He rose up
And by his arm they were undone,
By sally and by siege he forced their
Armies to turn.
And whether all the deeds he did
Were deeds that dutifully served
Our lawful king,
Let him of Portugal admit,
Or him who followed at his death,
Of Castile's kin.

After he had so many times
Gambled his own life-blood to keep
Good rule in force,
After he had with single mind
Served the true crown he so revered,
And the true throne,
After all the adventurous acts
So crowded that no numbering them
Is possible,
There came to his town, to Ocaña,
Knocking at the door of his house, Death
To call on him,

Saying: "O admirable knight,
Leave the deceitful world to those

It flatters yet;
Let your heart of true steel shine
With all the fortitude you've known,
In this distress;
And since you cared so little once
For life and safety, when you aimed
At glory alone,
Now let your good name fear no hurt
And strongly meet the insolent pain
Which calls you to go.

"The battle you expect is terrible?
Reject a tempting bitterness;
You stand exposed:
But here, remember, you have left to us
Your second, larger life, which spreads
Its fame, and grows;
And though this life of honor is
No more eternal than the first,
Nor yet more real,
It is better and more glorious
Than life that runs through dying earth
On vanishing heels.

"The truly lasting life is won
Not by possessing great estates
Here in the world,
Nor by brimming a joyous cup
In which the sins of hell can dare
The unwary to err;
But rather is it won by tears,
By prayers that the good monks make
To bring it near,
By labors and by difficulties
Where knights attack the Moors to gain
The fame they seek.

"And since, O famous fighter, you
Have scattered so much pagan blood

Deep in the ground,
For your hope a reward is sure:
You with your own hands have built up
Life here and now;
Let this become your confidence,
And let the faith that clothes your stride
Complete and true
Console your hopeful parting steps
And take you where that far third life
At last is yours."

"Ah, let us waste then no more time
In speaking of this petty stir
Of soil and air!
For my will with the will divine
In every element concurs
That words can say,
And I consent to dying now
With a will that breathes in joy,
So pure, so clear
It sees the madness in the frown
Of dying men who clutch too long
What God has seized.

"You who took degraded form
And humble name to save the souls
Of sick mankind:
You whose divinity was drawn
To bitter unity below
The stars, with life:
You who were willing to endure
In life and flesh such tortures as
Bad men could mete:
Not for my merits, only yours,
Only through your grace, I ask:
Lord, pardon me."

So, in that state of understanding,
With every human feeling sharp

In consciousness,
Surrounded by his wife, his family
Of sons and brothers, in the heart
Of his serving-men,
He gave his soul back to its giver,
And may that giver set it in
A glory undimmed.
It is true that his life is finished.
We have good consolation still,
Remembering him.

EDWIN MORGAN

ANONYMOUS

The Barbs of Mingo Revulgo
Las coplas de Mingo Revulgo

I

GIL ARRIBATO:
Ah, Mingo Revulgo, Mingo!
Ah, Mingo Revulgo, hallo!
What's happened to your blue tunic?
Isn't that your Sunday best?
And what of your scarlet doublet?
Why do you look all but pleased?
After a sleepless night,
You scowl about, unkempt;
Why don't you speak out loud?

II

Your face is sad and grieved,
Your body's full of aches;
You cross from hill to valley
Like a beast that's gone astray.
You don't watch where you're going
Straight forward or straight back

And spreading out your legs,
You make great sideward strides
Not knowing where you are . . .

III

MINGO REVULGO:
By my faith, Gil Arribato,
We must have lost our minds
When we let old Candaule[1]
Be shepherd of our flock.
He struts about after shepherd boys[2]
In these secluded parts
All day in sheer delight
Playing the hare-brained idler
And shrugging at our ills.

IV

Look now, look at those flocks[3]
And the she-ass with the hounds[4]
How they wander in the hills
Lost, and gone astray.
By all the saints, I swear
That big pot-bellied oaf
(May his eyebrows never prosper!)
Has gone off without his sheep
To hide behind every hedge.

V

Yonder, in those ravines,
You'll find some bleating lambs
Here, a few dead sheep
That fell into the ditch.
The grass has all been grazed,
Forbidden fields are bare
And even the trees in town:

---

[1] *A vicious and extravagant King of Lydia, mentioned by Herodotus.*
[2] *Courtiers and favorites.* [3] *The people.*
[4] *The Church and the clergy.*

Such havoc in Esparilla[5]
Was never seen by living men.

VI

May a wicked poison take him
And shepherds of his ilk
Whose horn is full of turpentine
But neglects his mangy flock.
He sees the wolves a-prowl
He hears the livestock bleat
But only bursts out laughing when he does.
And so he never ceases
To pray his shepherds' pipes.

XIII

The hound Justine[6]
So dauntless, as you know,
Grew raw-boned on thin air
And died. I swear to God, you'd pity her
With her courage and her strength
She attacked the fiercest lions
And could kill a sly, old wolf.
Now a sorry rabbit
Has packed her in a corner.

XIX

GIL:
Of course, brother Revulgo,
You're grieved about your sins;
If you do no good works
Another ill will stare you in the face.
For if you had confidence
You'd have warm land for grazing
And green pastures all year long.
You'd not have any losses
Of harvests or of sheep.

---

[5] *Spain.* [6] *Justice.*

XX

But you're not well-advised
On how to act with profit.
You stretch flat on your belly
For seven hours,[7] like dead.
Courage, now, be confident again,
And purify your conscience
So you can rise again
For, if you don't, death just
May strike you down by chance.

XXII

I dreamt this very night
And tremble at the thought
That this time neither beards
Nor beardless would be spared.
So go to bed and sleep!
For, as far as I can see,
About the way things are,
I guess the three mad wolves[8]
Will hunt throughout the land.

XXIII

I'm sure that you've seen sallowness:[9]
Always out of breath,
Declining, lean, and sighing,
And pitiful to all;
Who, though she may devour, is never satisfied;
With her fangs she never ceases
To bite and dodge and nip;
The flock will not be long
In spreading far and wide.

XXIV

The other scurvy traitor[10]
Cruel and fierce to fight

---

[7] *Because of Seven Deadly Sins.* [8] *Hunger, War and Plague.* [9] *Hunger.* [10] *War.*

Handmaid of every evil
And born a thief
Knows farms very well
And leaves no mother or child
Alive in their smoky hovels
In the valleys or the pens:
She knows where people hide.

XXV

And even the three-pronged one[11]
Who eats up little lambs
And never spares the yearlings
When she's the least bit peeved,
I fear she won't forget
To come and divvy up
Her portion of the loot.
Tell me, with such a team
Who would not be scared?

XXXII

I think it less harmful
To thread the middle way
For high or low
No road is safe.
Remember now, you must
Be firm. Don't let your foot
Slip off its rightful place
For many woes beset
This vale of tears.

WILLIAM M. DAVIS

---

[11] *Plague.*

ANONYMOUS TRADITIONAL SONGS
[*El Cancionero*]

If You Go to Bathe, Juanica
Si te vas a bañar Juanica

If you go to bathe, Juanica,
tell me where you go.
For I, Juanica darling,
admire your figure so.

JAMES DUFFY

⁂

Those Mountains, Mother
Aquellas sierras, madre

Those mountains, mother
are steep to climb,
where streams rush down
to fields of thyme.

Those mountains, mother
have flowers above:
up where they are,
I have my love.

JAMES DUFFY

⁂

I Refuse to Be a Nun
No quiero ser monja, no

I refuse to be a nun,
for I'm a girl who's found a boy.

Leave me with my pleasure,
with my pleasure and my joy,
leave me with my stubborn ways,
for I'm a girl who's found a boy.

JAMES DUFFY

I Will Not Pick Verbena

Que no cogeré verbena

I will not pick verbena
on the morrow of St. John,
for my lover has gone.

I will not pick sunflowers,
honeysuckle or carnations.
Only sorrows will I pluck
and cruel frustrations,
for my lover has gone.

JAMES DUFFY

Do Not Speak to Me, Count

No me habléis, conde

Do not speak to me, count,
of love in the street,
for my mother will say
you are indiscreet.

Tomorrow I'll go, sir,
to wash at the stream.
Then I promise, sir count,
to fulfill your dream.

Do not speak to me, count,
of love in the street,

for my mother will say
you are indiscreet.

JAMES DUFFY

⁂

Hill Song of La Zarzuela

Serranilla de La Zarzuela

I was going, Mother, to Villa Real,
And lost my way where it was wild.
No bread had I for seven days,
My hawk no meat, my mule no grain.
Between La Zarzuela and Darazután,
I raised my eyes up toward the sun.
I saw a cabin, and there was smoke;
I spurred my mule, and then rode up.
The shepherd's dogs came out to bark
And then a pretty highland girl
Said, "Stranger, do not be afraid,
My parents now have gone to town,
My darling Mingo's gone for bread,
We'll have two days before they're back.
You'll drink this milk while I make cheese,
We'll make a bed beside the field,
And make a son, and call him Paul,
He'll be a bishop, priest, or pope,
Or else the swineherd of Villa Real;
Well, by my life, you must find this a joke!"

WILLIAM M. DAVIS

⁂

Gentle Knight/Now Give Me a Kiss

Gentil caballero/dédesme hora un beso

Gentle knight,
Now give me a kiss,

Perhaps for the harm
You've done me.

The knight rode on,
He rode from Seville:
And in a convent garden,
Picked lemons,
And the prioress
Asked for pretty favors:
Perhaps for the harm
You've done me.

WILLIAM M. DAVIS

⁂

To Whom Shall I Tell My Sorrows?

¿A quién contaré mis quejas?

To whom shall I tell my sorrows
My handsome love,
To whom shall I tell my sorrows
If not to you?

WILLIAM M. DAVIS

⁂

I Grew Up in a Village

Criéme en aldea

I grew up in a village
And then I turned nut-brown;
I would have been more beautiful
If I'd grown up in town.

WILLIAM M. DAVIS

⁂

Out of Love
Por amores lo maldijo

Out of love
The bad mother
Cursed the good son.
"I wish to God in heaven
and his mother, good Saint Mary,
that you were not my son,
so I could be your mistress!"
Thus the bad mother
Called, and cursed the good son.
Out of love, she cursed him.

WILLIAM M. DAVIS

ANONYMOUS

The Romancero or *Book of Ballads*
[*El Romancero*]

Ballad of Juliana
Julianesa

"Get on, you hounds, get on,
    And may the furies take you.
Thursday you kill the boar
    And eat the meat on Friday.

"Today makes seven years
    I've wandered in these hills.
Now both my feet are bare,
    Blood spurts from my toenails.

"Now I drink fresh gore,
    The meat I eat is raw,

And sadly seek Juliana,
Who was the emperor's daughter.

"Early St. John's morning,
While she gathered flowers,
The Moors took her away
From her father's bowers."

Juliana hears this said
Wrapt in the Moor's embrace;
Twin tears her two eyes shed
Fall on that Moor's face.

EDWIN HONIG

Count Arnaldos
El Conde Arnaldos

Who can tell of such adventure above the bounding main
As befell good Count Arnaldos, the morning of St. John?
He readied for the hunt, with a falcon in his hand
And saw a ship approach, veering toward the land
With sails of purest silk, and shrouds of finest crepe
And at the helm a sailor, who made the winds abate.
He sang the waves to sleep, and made the deep fish rise
And to the mast birds flocked, and perched there
in surprise.
Then spoke Count Arnaldos, then he spoke at last:
"By God, I beg you, sailor, now tell me of your song."
Then the sailor answered: his answer was not long,
"Only those who travel with me will ever know my song."

WILLIAM M. DAVIS

Ballad of the Fair Melisenda
La linda Melisenda

The people all were sleeping
All in God's protection,
But the emperor's daughter
Melisenda was awake.
Her love for Count Airuelo
Would not let her rest.
She leapt naked out of bed,
Putting on a smock
When she could not find a skirt,
And went across the halls
Where her ladies slept.
Slapping every one,
She began to shout:
"Arise, if you are sleeping,
Maidens mine, arise, arise.
And you know of love,
Give me some advice.
You who do not know of love,
Spare me by keeping quiet.
My love for Count Airuelo
Will not let me rest."
Up spoke an old woman,
A woman ancient of days:
"Now is the time, my lady,
To enjoy yourself,
For if you wait till you are old,
No young man will want you.
I learnt this as a girl,
And never did forget it,
From the days when I was raised
In your father's house."
No sooner did she hear this
Than Melisenda heard no more;
She went to find the Count

In the palace where he was.
She ran into young Hernando,
Her father's constable.
"What is all this, Melisenda?
What can all this mean?
You are either lovesick
Or else are going mad!"
"No, I am not lovesick,
For no one do I grieve,
But when I was a child
I was taken very ill,
And swore to say novenas
At St. John Lateran's.
There the ladies go by day,
And at night we maidens."
When Hernando heard this,
He spoke no further word.
The princess in her anger
Sought revenge on him.
"Lend me now, Hernando,
Please lend me your dagger,
For I am very frightened
Of the dogs that roam the street."
He held the dagger by the point,
She took it by the hilt
And gave him such a thrust with it
He fell dead upon the floor.
She went on to the palace
Where Count Airuelo was.
She found the doors shut down,
And not knowing how to enter,
By magic opened them up wide.
When he heard the din and clatter,
The Count began to shout:
"Come and help me, knights,
Help me without delay;
I fear my enemies are here
Who come to murder me."
Discreetly Melisenda

Began to speak to him:
"Do not be alarmed, sir;
Do not be surprised.
I am but a Moorish maiden
Come from overseas."
As soon as he had heard her,
The Count knew who she was.
The Count drew closer to her
And took her hands in his,
And in a laurel shade
They played the Venus game.

EDWIN HONIG

The Prisoner
El prisionero

Ah, for the month of May, of May,
When the days grow warm,
When the wheat-ear's sprouting
And the fields with flowers swarm,
When to the song of the skylark
The nightingale replies,
And when the lovers set about
To wait upon their brides;
And I, poor wretch, disconsolate
Behind these prison walls,
Know neither when 'tis daytime
Nor when nighttime falls,
Except that once a little bird
Would sing to me at dawn.
But oh, the archer shot him—
May God avenge the wrong!

KATE FLORES

Ballad of the Cool Fountain

Fonte Frida

Fountain, coolest fountain,
Cool fountain of love,
Where all the sweet birds come
For comforting—but one,
A widow turtledove,
Sadly sorrowing.
At once the nightingale,
That wicked bird, came by
And spoke these honied words:
"My lady, if you will,
I shall be your slave."
"You are my enemy:
Begone, you are not true!
Green boughs no longer rest me,
Nor any budding grove.
Clear springs, when there are such,
Turn muddy at my touch.
I want no spouse to love
Nor any children either.
I forego that pleasure
And their comfort too.
No, leave me: you are false
And wicked—vile, untrue!
I'll never be your mistress!
I'll never marry you!"

EDWIN HONIG

❖

Abenámar

Abenámar

Abenámar, Abenámar
Moor of Moor's delight
The hour of your birth

Comets filled the night.
The sea was calm as glass
The moon was waxing full
A Moor with stars like yours
Must never break the spell.
"I tell the truth, my lord,
Though it be death to tell."
"I thank you, Abenámar,
Your birth bespeaks you well.
What castles are those shining
High on yonder hill?"
"The Alhambra there, my lord,
The mosque tower further still,
And there, the Alixares,
Built so wondrous well.
A Moor was paid to build them
A hundred crowns a day
And lost, for each day idle,
As much as he was paid.
When all was built and ready
The architect was slain
So he could build no others
For Andalusia's reign.
There lies Crimson Towers
A castle of renown
And there, the Generalife,
Of matchless garden fame."
Then spoke King don Juan,
Mark what he will say:
"With your consent, Granada,
I'd marry you today;
With Córdoba for dowry,
Sevilla for display."
"I am a wife, King John,
No widow, but a wife,
The Moor who is my husband
Loves me more than life."

WILLIAM M. DAVIS

✖

Delgadina
Delgadina

The good king had three daughters,
All graceful and all fair,
The youngest was Delgadina.
"Now come, my Delgadina,
For you must lie with me."
"Neither the Lord of Heaven
Nor our most sovereign Lady
Wishes that I should lie
With the father who begot me."
Her father in his anger
Locked her into a room,
With nothing for her hunger
But a little salted meat,
With nothing for her thirst
But the drip of a green orange.
When it was morning she looked
Out of a high window,
Down in the garden her mother
Sat in a golden chair.
"My mother, because you are
My mother, bring me water,
I am dying of thirst, I want
To give up my soul to God."
"Be quiet, bitch of a daughter,
Be quiet, you are to blame
That for seven years I have known
The shame of a bad marriage."
On the next morning she looked
From another high window,
Down in the yard her sisters
Were spinning out the silk.
"My sisters, because you are
My sisters, bring me water,
I am dying of thirst, I want

To give up my soul to God."
"If only we had a knife
We would throw it in your face."
On the next morning she looked
From another high window,
Down in the court her brothers
Were practicing with their spears.
"My brothers, because you are
My brothers, bring me water,
I am dying of thirst, I want
To give up my soul to God."
"No, Delgadina, no,
We cannot bring you water,
For if your father knew,
Our punishment would be death.
On the next morning she looked
From another window,
Down in the hall her father
Was pacing to and fro.
"My father, because you are
My father, bring me water,
I am dying of thirst, I want
To give up my soul to God."
"Yes, I will bring you water
If you will do as I wish."
"Yes, I will do as you wish."
"Now run, my pageboys, run,
Bring water to Delgadina:
The first of you to arrive
Shall have her hand in marriage,
The last to arrive shall die."
Some ran with silver pitchers,
Some with pitchers of gold,
While the church bells were ringing
For Delgadina's soul.
When the first page arrived,
He found that she was dead,
Around her bed a ring
Of blessèd angels stood,

The bed of the king her father
Was crowned with a ring of fiends.

LYSANDER KEMP

⁂

Moriana's Poison
El veneno de Moriana

At daybreak Don Alonso rises with the sun
To call on friends and neighbors each and every one.
At Moriana's gate he hitches up his roan.
"Good tidings, Moriana." "Alonso, welcome home!"
"Moriana, drink a toast—my wedding's Sunday noon."
"By rights the bride, Alonso, is me, and me alone.
But I'm not one for grudges and so I'll surely come,
But first, to prove my friendship a glass of wine you'll down."
Moriana, sly and crafty, goes inside her room
To find her rod and pestle and grind the seeds of doom.
Three corrosive sublimates, blood from four black toads,
Viper eyes and scorpion stings, she mixes, stirs, and pours.
"Drink this down, Alonso. Drink the good, fresh wine."
"Drink first, Moriana, or else I must decline."
Moriana lifts the goblet and purses tight her lips:
Her teeth are close together so not a drop she sips.
Alonso, hale and hearty, downs a gulp of his.
"What is it, Moriana? What is it makes me swoon?
I know the sun is shining but I can't see my roan."
"Three corrosive sublimates, blood from four black toads,
Viper eyes and scorpion stings, to make you writhe and moan."
"Cure me, Moriana—I'll marry you today!"
"It cannot be, Alonso, your heart has died away."
"Pity my poor mother, weeping and bereft."
"I've pitied mine, Alonso, since the day we met."

WILLIAM M. DAVIS

⁂

The Mistress of Bernal Francés
La amiga de Bernal Francés

At night I hug my pillow
And lie in bed alone;
Who goes there proudly knocking,
Calling "open" at my door?
"Bernal Francés, my lady,
Your love who serves you true;
At night we share the covers,
By day, the garden view."
She rose from linen sheets,
A flowing robe she wore,
With golden candelabra
Downed the stairway to the door.
When the door was but half open
He blew the candle out.
"Protect me, Holy Virgin,
Protect me, good Saint Gil;
Whoe'er put out my candle
May put out my life."
"Fear not, Catalina,
Make no hue or cry,
I killed a fellow fighting
And justice seeks my hide."
To her chamber in the tower
She led him by the hand;
In a silver chair she sat him,
Backed in ivory, and then
Bathed him all in sweet balm gentle
His skin in rare perfume,
Prepared a bed of roses,
With gillyflowers festooned.
"What ails you, Bernal Francés,
Why sorrow at my side?
Do you fear for justice?
No sheriff enters here.

Do you fear my servants?
All are fast asleep."
"I do not fear for justice,
I seek it for myself
Nor less do I fear servants
Who sleep their honest sleep."
"What is it, Bernal Francés?
You never acted thus—
In France you have a sweetheart
Or heard bad news of me."
"I have no loves in France,
Another ne'er I served."
"If you're thinking of my husband,
He's far away from here."
"Distance oft grows narrow
For him who wants to come:
Your wedded husband greets you,
For I in truth am he.
In token of my coming,
A gown and gift I bear:
A dress of finest scarlet,
All crimson-lined to wear;
A necklace stained incarnadine,
That ladies never see,
The necklace of my sword,
Your pretty throat will sheathe.
News will reach the Frenchman—
He'll mourn you in despair."

WILLIAM M. DAVIS

Catalan Poets

RAMON LLULL

To You, Lady Virgin Santa Maria
A vós, Dona Verge Santa Maria

To you, Lady Virgin Santa Maria,
I give my will that wills your love
So much that were it not for you
I would not want desire or love
For every will has betterment
Above all others that are not
Enwilled to you, love's fountainhead:
Who wills you not, has naught of love.

As my will enwills your mastery,
I give to you my memory and mind:
Else, Lady, what then should I do?
And you, Milady, I pray you, keep in mind
The clergy, love and understand
They journey off to Syria
To preach, converting infidels
And Christian men to peace.

Many a man is proud to die
For your Son, as people say,
But few will go to preach His Word
To infidels, and brave the sword.

WILLIAM M. DAVIS

✖

When the Star Appears at Daybreak

Quan par l'estela en l'albor

When the star appears at daybreak
And flowers all adorn
The fields with many colors
    And hope begins to dawn,
I am garbed with happiness,
With tenderness and confidence
    That dwells in lady Love;
And then I ask to be confessed
By her, and have my sins redressed
    And make amends
To those who are the serving men
    Of Valor's Queen,
And so I don't expect such help
    That to no sin
    I'll be impelled
Since there be true confession.

WILLIAM M. DAVIS

ANONYMOUS

Alas! If I Had Married

Lassa! Mais m'agra valgut/que fos maridada

Alas! If I had married
Or had a courtly lover—
But I became a nun.

A nun to my lasting sorrow
And great the sin
Of those who put me here.
And those who put me in
Great sorrow,
May God's wrath do them in!

For if I had ever known
—But then I was a fool—
Though they gave me all Montagut,
I'd never have gone in.

WILLIAM M. DAVIS

PERE MARCH

The Widow Wearing White or Saffron

Viuda que port color blanch ne saffra

The widow wearing white or saffron,
Powder or perfumes, will give and take
And joke a lot, and have a mind to sell.
And if she can, she'll get her price;
If not, she'll go for nil:
But since she plays the bargainer,
She'll show her talents well;
And so I really doubt she lacks
In virtues straight from hell!

WILLIAM M. DAVIS

Ladies I Like Well Dressed

Dompna'm platz ben arreada

Ladies I like well dressed,
And gentlemen well armed,
And pretty hair well curled,
And working sleeves well rolled,
And horses stoutly breasted,
And bridles rash and bold
To hold old ladies well.

And I like to ride
Across the busy plain

And look at smoke and fires
And enemies besieged
Forced to keep watch
And feel unsafe
Outside the walls.

And I like the sweetheart
Built delicate and slim
Providing that she's glad
That I'm her sweetheart, too,
And flirts and rolls her eyes
To pay me for returning
And when I ask her to.

Here's what I like even better,
A wise and prudent lord,
One not served in vain,
Frank and brave, but honest,
Whose retinue is large
For the opposite's too dull.

And I like the wintertime
Before the sun is up,
When mass is said
By a priest who's on his toes,
A low mass, and not sung,
Except on holy days
To celebrate the feast.

WILLIAM M. DAVIS

AUSIÀS MARCH

The Time Is Such That Each Brute Beast

Lo temps es tal que tot animal brut

The time is such that each brute beast
Needs love, and finds a mate.

The fearless stag howls through the wood,
His bellow judged a tender song;
The magpie chats so loud and long
That every creature's bound to join.
The nightingale in doleful croon
Sings: Where has my sweetheart gone?
And if I grieve, then grief is right
When I see lovers poor at love
Or clumsy lovers pass for skilled
Or see not what is wrong.
And so I make a just complaint
How Desamor beguiles my lady:
For, unaware, she wounds her slave
Not knowing how his love is steady.
Unlike the man who lost his wealth
And risked his all in hope of gain,
I love you, and would fain be loved
Deliberately, but I am not.
Stark naked in my heavy cloak,
I find that Love has pawned my Will:
And that for which my Heart is ill
Is as my Need, which is so much.
Lady mid thistles, the stork hunts with the kite,
The lapdog with the bounding rabbit;
The world's a much too lively place
While my frail breast sings Passion of the Palms!

WILLIAM M. DAVIS

Where Is the Place My Thought May Find Repose?

On és lo lloc on ma pensa repose?

Where is the place my thought may find repose?
Where, I ask, may longing be content?
I plumb the depths, and there I find
No anchorage, no port where I would dare.
What once from every tempest kept me safe

Has turned on me, a cruel deserted shore:
Abandoned lies the house where I was sure;
Where I am now, the toil is great, and more.

Where is that joy I bring to mind
Of being loved by one who understood?
All my will and hers could put no end
To love, because its power was enough.
All the signs that love makes understood
I saw in her, nor will their work relent.
Who can say his love reveals so much
That he would feel no anguish at our plight?

Now naught on earth is my defense:
For me, all life has lost its joy:
To friends, perhaps I write of grief
Though time cannot repair
The grief that wears my mind:
For all I hear or see is grief,
So much, that now I fear to think
That grief itself may be defense.

As love sets free the firmest heart
To grant us hope of joy,
I feel the world is in despair
For, stripped of love, all joy's offense,
God's weapon, which he made to thrust
The body from its wicked star
And longings, from the bitter trace
Of pain, still indiscreetly veiled.

Like that sage, who living out his life
Right pleasantly, in art's pursuit,
Was made to see his art's scant good,
I know not where my mind should stray
And see the gates of love are shut
Nor can I say what course is best
Or change my ways instead.

O Foolish Love, how wrong it is
To risk one's love for virtue in a lady!
Her quality and station make her good:
But, truly, who can live that way forever?

WILLIAM M. DAVIS

JORDI DE SANT JORDI

Below the Brow I Bear Your Lovely Countenance
Sus lo front port vostra bella semblança

Below the brow I bear your lovely countenance
That night and day my body celebrates
For gazing on that very lovely shape
The imprint of your features shall remain
Unchanged in me as death's unyielding form.
And when I part entirely from this world
Those who bear my body to the grave
Upon my face shall contemplate your sign.

As the child who sees the altarpiece
And dwells upon the images of saints
Cannot be swerved for purity of heart
But revels in surrounding gold,
So I, before the loving circle
Of your body, by delights embowered,
Do dwell upon it more than God,
So great's the joy that pierces me!

Thus prisoner of ardent love I'm bound
Within my jail, as if within a coffer
With lock secured, and all of me inside
The place where all escape is but encounter.
For so great and firm's the love I have for you
That my heart, for fear, will never aught desist
From loveliness, but firmly as a tower
Love you alone, white dove!

Peerless beauty, nobly you prevail!
God made your lovely body loveliest of all,
Gay and graceful, bright as precious stone,
Amorous and lovely, more piercing than a spear
For, grouped with others, I see you humble all
In virtues, as the carbuncle that glows
Surpassing every stone
As the hawk outshines the lanner!

My love for you thus spears me from all sides
For no man's love was ever so sincere:
So strong a love as that which rends my soul
Was never found in human mind or breast.
I am more vexed than Aristotle
By love that burns, unleashing every sense:
And like the good monk, who never left his cell,
I stray from you no more than the finger from the nail.

Oh graceful body, pure of fraud and crime,
Have pity on me, fair and regal lady,
And do not let me perish of your love
For I love you more than anyone affirms
And beg you, tree of all good fruits
Wherein great valor's overcast,
Retain me in your queenly room
For I am yours until I die.

Rich ruby, now your crest adorns
The highest worldly register
For kindliness and good reborn
In you, more than Penthesilea.

WILLIAM M. DAVIS

✖

Vexation, Enemy of Youth
Enuig, enemich de jovent

Vexation, enemy of youth
And foe of thought
You vex me so
That nothing makes me glad
You often bring such grief
I feel my heart will burst
        Out of its lodgings.
In the first place, I am vexed
With the world, because it sits
And lets men get away with
        Frightful acts.
        So I am vexed
        With the world
        Whichever way
        I turn.
        Finally, I see
        That absolutely nothing
        Is loyal or true
But only wrong or wretched.

And so I'm vexed with love
For the way that it's abused
And with all the foolish boasters
        Who never did a thing.
Others squawk of love
Whose hearts ne'er felt its pangs
        Or even understood it.
And I deem it a great vexation
When I'm with her I love
To keep my languor silent
        Because someone is there.
        Another far worse
        (And well I know)
        Is waiting long,

And I'm vexed by the clumsy dolt
Who tries too hard
To please, and never does.

Another thing that irks me:
When I am speaking somewhere
And someone interrupts me
Just as I make my point.
Another, when I make a witty crack
And no one can see why
Which makes me mad
Because I try
To tell it to a numbskull
Who to everything says no.
Stubborn enemies
Bring great vexation
And irk me, too.
But it vexes me more
When someone I dislike
In spite of me
Tags onto me
Which really eats my heart.

Then, too, it vexes me
To snooze at night between
Two in a crowded bed
And more so
When I'm dressed
And shod and squeezed;
But I'm more vexed and irked by sleepy loafers
And the cold.
For I'm vexed by the churlish fool
Who, without my asking,
Butts in when I want to write
A secret letter, dealing with my affairs;
By children crying
By sleeping on a board
By being indisposed
At sundown, alone with a woman;

When I'm locked in;
Or when my charger
Loses his hobnails in a lonely gulch.

I wish to complain of other vexations
That have made my heart grow old:
Of piggish men
Who have everything to say
And don't believe a thing;
Of sermons preached by fools;
Of sleeping with a filthy woman
When I have to;
Of riding a palfrey
That shuffles, bumps, and lurches;
Of barking dogs at night;
Of dealing with a miser
[Line missing in manuscript]
Of the sun in June
Of my helmet when I'm fighting
And then again
Of the lady who spreads
Her favors wide, casting off all shame.

I am also vexed as death
When I'm stranded out at sea
Or else hemmed in and comfortless
When I feel sick;
When I hear songs out of tune
Or in winter, when I go down
The gully in a storm;
When there's a howling wind;
When I travel on sandy ground;
When there's smoke without a fire at an inn;
And by one who ambles down
The open road
And then is lost;
By anyone who wakes me up
Too suddenly from sleep;

By a man who somehow
Is of my class
And in an instant
Takes a shine to me, and never lets me go.

Also, I'm vexed when I shoot dice
And, just my luck, some blockhead
Sits near me and tells me
Something vexing;
When I travel long in summer;
Or carry an angry goshawk on my wrist
And I am clawed;
When I sleep with a man who coughs;
Or a quarrelsome old man;
And by mosquitoes
When at night
I'm sound asleep;
By a sick man
Who complains too much;
By a hard lance;
By hard bread
Grown hard too long;
Or by living inside bad walls.

Oh, what vexations I've put up with
So many, that now I have lost count!
But I'm very vexed by a shiftless,
Stupid, foolish man;
With cloth that is threadbare;
With mud, at night, when it drizzles
And I slip;
With someone who says No when I ask him;
When I often meet a creditor;
With dried up, squalid women;
With long advice
I never asked for;
With sleeping alone;
With hearing only

[Line missing in manuscript]

With a woman who shows
Lack of judgment
And a weak man who shakes his fists.

Of all the vexations I've mentioned
I know of none so stark
As poverty, which strikes fear
Into young and old alike
And when Fortune has wounded with its sword
Capriciously
And raises some not worth a fig,
And strikes down and makes a shambles
Of pure gold and sterling men,
It keeps no law
Or right or service
Which is why we must
Praise God
Who owes us nothing,
And thus I end
My ballad is complete
Let each man turn his will to where it leads him.

WILLIAM M. DAVIS

I Have No Liking for One Who in All Things Is Not

No m'asalt d'om qu'en tots afars no sia

I have no liking for one who in all things is not
Loyal and pure, like a finely-balanced scale.
I have no liking for one who five days out of seven
Lies in his words, and wants company of lovers.
I have no liking for one who picks a feather or a straw
From my garments, or brags of battle;
I have no liking for a man without shame,
For he gluts his craw with every food, like a stork.

WILLIAM M. DAVIS

NOTES AND BIOGRAPHICAL SKETCHES

The Arabic Poets

The Arabs developed a highly artistic poetry in quantitative meters as early as the end of the fifth century A.D. Descriptions of nature, camels, desert wanderings, praise of self and tribe abound. After Mohammed's death, poetry suffered a setback; it revived again under the Ommayads (661-750 A.D.) in Syria and especially in Mesopotamia. Under the Abbasids (750-1258 A.D.) a new poetry of drinking- and hunting-songs arose in the urban centers of Iraq, and after the fall of the Caliphate, the poetry flourished in the courts of the minor princes, especially at Aleppo. From the tenth century on, short forms gained increasing favor, side by side with poems in praise of princes, Anacreontic love and wine songs, and poetic descriptions of objects, landscapes, and situations. Spanish Arabic poetry derives from the Oriental, and in it the foregoing changes are reflected. The development in Spain of an Arabic poetry worthy of the name roughly coincides with the last two hundred years of the golden age of Arabic culture (eighth to eleventh centuries) which saw the assimilation of Hellenistic and Persian culture, and especially of Persian literary influence.

In Arabic poetry, lines are usually end-stopped and detachable from their context. Thus it is no surprise that Ibn Sa'id's anthology (compiled in 1243) consists mainly of metaphorical or descriptive fragments. The best-known form that flowered in Arabic Spain during the eleventh century, called *jarchas* and composed by Arabs and Jews, were short bi-lingual songs. Longer poems, called *muwassahas,* contained a *finida* or refrain in Spanish. In the *jarchas* are to be found the earliest lyrical blossoms of the Iberian peninsula. Because of the scarcity of biographical material, the Arabic poets are not listed here individually.

The Hebrew Poets

Another interesting contribution to the poetry of the Iberian peninsula came from Jewish writers who composed their lyrics in Hebrew, Arabic, and Spanish. The two outstanding figures of the eleventh and twelfth centuries were Gabirol and Halevi.

SOLOMON IBN GABIROL, also known as Avicebron, (1021-1058), the "Jewish Plato" and "most original philosophical writer among Jews and Arabs," derived from a family from Cordova which was forced to move to Malaga during a period of wars. While still very young, Gabirol became the protégé of Yequéliel Ibn Hazan, then an extremely influential personage in the service of the Tuyibi rulers of Saragossa. In that city Gabirol continued his philosophical studies and wrote poems in Hebrew based, to a large extent, on the Hispano-Arabic themes then in vogue: friendship, spring, rural life. When dealing with the ever recurrent motif of wine and women, he expressed himself with restraint. Gabirol also initiated metrical and linguistic innovations that revitalized Hebrew verse. His hymns are still sung in the synagogues of the world.

JUDAH HALEVI (c. 1078-1140), born in Tudela, traveled at an early age to the centers of intense literary activity: Granada, Cordova, Seville, attaining fame for his power of improvisation and for his originality in metrical experimentation. He composed secular and liturgical poems, which judiciously combined Biblical and Arabic influences. Deeply religious, he succumbed late in life to an irresistible urge to see the Holy Land. According to tradition, he was ridden down and slain by an Arab horseman outside the gates of Jerusalem. He is best known among Jews for his poignant *Ode to Zion*, a model for such utterances down through the ages.

The Galician-Portuguese Poets

Between the twelfth and fourteenth centuries, there flourished in the western part of the Iberian Peninsula an extremely rich lyrical poetry in the language spoken in Galicia and Portugal. The 2,000 poems extant fall predominantly into four categories: some seven hundred love songs (*cantigas d'amor*)—a substantial number have been attributed to King Dinis of Portugal—which are, ostensibly, imitations of Provençal *cansos;* folk poems, vaguely linked with the Arabo-Andalusian tradition, wherein a young woman tells her mother about the "amigo," with whom she has fallen in love—hence, they are called *cantigas d'amigo;* religious songs, in praise of the Virgin Mary; coarse, abusive songs, corresponding to the Provençal *sirventes: cantigas d'escarnh,* or veiled attacks—often so veiled that they are difficult to decipher—against individuals or institutions; and *cantigas de maldezir,* or vitriolic attacks against specific persons, mentioned by name—and, it must be added, in this group are to be found some of the most obscene poems ever written.

The finest work of the Galician-Portuguese was done either in the court of Alfonso X (Alfonso the Wise of Castile) or in that of King Dinis of Portugal, but biographical material about the poets is extremely scarce.

ALFONSO X *el Sabio* [Alfonso the Wise] (1221-1284), Castilian king, scholar, and promoter of science and literature, also wrote in Galician *Cantigas de Santa María* and about thirty *cantigas d'amor* and *maldezir.*

CODAX, MARTIN (fl. 1250), *a jogral* (i.e., jongleur), whose seven *cantigas d'amigo* refer to Vigo and the sea and are of unusual interest, since their musical notation has been found.

DINIS [King Dinis, also known as Dom Dinis] (1261-1325) King of Portugal, founder of first Portuguese university and Portugal's greatest medieval poet, noted for his lovely *cantigas d'amigo.* Though a cultivator of the Provençal type of lyric, his taste for the indigenous parallelistic songs indicates that he enjoyed most of the popular songs sung by the *jograis* at his court.

FERNANDEZ, ROI (XIIIth century), priest and contemporary of Alfonso the Wise (q.v.); wrote *cantigas d'amor* and *d'amigo,* and is noted for his passionate sea melody, which, even as it upbraids the sea, is filled with the sea's music and rhythm.

FERNANDEZ DE TURNEOL, NUNO (fl. 1225), who was perhaps a knight and cultivated all the various types of lyrics, is remembered especially for his *alba* or dawn-song, a rarity in the Portuguese poetry of his day.

GUILHADE, JOAN DE (XIIIth century) was a back-country esquire who led a soldier's life, and is best known for the technical virtuosity and lively wit of his *cantigas d'amigo* and satiric poems.

LOPES DE BAIAN, AFONSO (fl. 1253-1278), a *trovador* of the highest nobility, he held the position of governor and wrote numerous *cantigas.*

MACIAS (fl. 1360-1390), a Galician *trovador,* whose name recurs in romantic legends because he was slain by the jealous husband of his mistress.

MEOGO or MOOGO, PERO [Peter the Monk] (fl. 1250), probably a converted Jew, left us nine lovely *cantigas d'amigo.*

NUNES, AIRAS (c. 1175-1250), probably a priest at the court of Alfonso the Wise (q.v.), also a brilliant and original *jogral.* His beautiful sonnet-like "The Summertime Delights Me," included here, is one of the few *cantigas* in which nature is described; he wrote songs in Provençal, and his rich lyrical vein seems to foreshadow the *dolce stil novo,* two centuries before its arrival in Portugal.

ROIZ DE CASTELO-BRANCO, JOÃO (late XIIIth century), best known for his *Song of Parting,* wrote a letter in verse to a friend in Lisbon, in which he said that after living at court he had retired to his estate at Beira, where he felt happy and did not miss palace life.

ZORRO, JOAN (fl. 1250), a humble court *jogral,* known as "Foxy John," during the reign of Afonso III, was one of the earliest singers of Lisbon. His version of the dance-song (*bailada*), clearly of popular origin, received more literary, but less successful, treatment from Airas Nunes (q.v.).

The Castilian Poets

ANONYMOUS:

The Barbs of Mingo Revulgo (*Las coplas de Mingo Revulgo,* 1464), an allegorical dialogue between two shepherds satirizing the political and social scene during the reign of Enrique IV. Mingo Revulgo represents the people; Gil Arribato, the prophet; Enrique's kingdom, a herd abandoned by its shepherds to the ravenously powerful.

Dispute of Elena and María (*Disputa de Elena y María,* XIIIth century) consists of 402 lines in Leonese dialect, in predominantly octosyllabic, irregular versification, treating a subiect much in vogue in Latin and French—who is to be preferred as a lover: an abbot (or lettered man) or a knight (or man of arms).

The Cancionero is the body of anonymous medieval songs; the earliest compilation, by King Dinis of Portugal (q.v.), dates back to the thirteenth century; in Castilian there were several compilations: among the earliest, the *Cancionero de Baena,* containing courtly lyrics, and the *Cancionero de Stúñiga,* containing popular ones.

The Romancero is the body of *romances* or ballads which became popular throughout Spain after the twelfth century. Some claim that they derived from the epics, that they were brief elaborations of crucial moments. However this may be, the form took root in Spain and is still alive. The typical *romance* verse has eight syllables and penultimate stress; the form of the stanzas varies, and in a later phase of development the quatrain became the norm. The *romances* have been classified according to theme: the Breton cycle (dealing with King Arthur and the Round Table and the fabulous world of Lancelot, Tristan and the Holy Grail); the Carolingian cycle (highlighting Charlemagne and his twelve Peers and other Peers invented by the jongleurs); historical ballads about the Spanish heroes and their deeds of arms; frontier or border ballads, concerned with the conflicts between Moors and Christians; and fictional or lyrical ballads, borrowed from sundry myths or newly invented by the anonymous poets.

BERCEO, GONZALO DE (1195-1246), born in the town of Berceo, diocese of Calahorra, studied in the Benedictine monastery of San Millán de la Cogolla in Rioja. A "monastery-bred priest but not a monk," Berceo is the first Spanish poet known by name, an erudite writer affecting simplicity, concealing a sense of humor beneath a grave manner. He chose the vernacular for his biographies of local saints; his poems reveal a feeling for nature, and pathos and the comic spirit seem to fuse with his deep religious spirit.

HURTADO DE MENDOZA, DIEGO (c. 1364-1404), Admiral of Castile, was one of the first noblemen to write lyrics in the Provençal tradition. Seven of his poems have been preserved, he is remembered chiefly for the *cosante* included here, technically of Galician-Portuguese origin, comprising two-lined stanzas, each with an invariable single-line refrain, the whole of it in charmingly interlacing phraseology. Don Diego was the father of the exquisite Marqués de Santillana (q.v.).

IÑIGO LÓPEZ DE MENDOZA, see SANTILLANA, MARQUÉS DE.

LORENZO, JUAN (fl. 1250), a native of Astorga, wrote a 10,000-line erudite epic recounting the legendary enterprises of Alexander the Great. Although the poet unquestionably possessed encyclopedic knowledge, he also had a rich and colorful imagination. In his *Libro de Alexandre* he mingles allegorical inventiveness with a truculent, anachronistic history: Mérimée did not exaggerate when he considered it a blend of Dante, Sinbad the Sailor, and Jules Verne.

MANRIQUE, JORGE (c. 1440-1478), born at Paredes de las Navas and related to the Marqués de Santillana (q.v.), his great-uncle, and other lofty personages, immortalized his name through his elegy on the death of his father, don Rodrigo Manrique, Grand Master of the Military Order of Santiago. Both father and son were killed in action fighting for their king. Although the elegy is not original—death and life's vanities being an ever recurring theme in medieval Europe (cf. the *danse macabre,* and the poems of Sánchez Calavera [q.v.], and Villon [q.v.], included in this anthology)—Manrique succeeded in endowing it with unforgettable pathos and musicality.

MENA, JUAN DE (1411-1456), the son of a Cordovan official, was educated at Salamanca and Rome. During his Italian sojourn he saturated himself in the Renaissance spirit. In his long allegorical poem *Laberinto de Fortuna* (1444), the influence not only of Ovid and Lucan but also of Dante is readily discernible. His *Mourning of the Mother of Lorenzo Dávalos* displays lyrical intensity and suggests new poetical horizons, departing as it does from the narrow confines of the jongleurs as well as the repetitious imitations of the Provençal poets.

RUIZ, JUAN (c. 1283-1350), the greatest poet of medieval Spain, was Archpriest of Hita, a town near Guadalajara. Sent to prison by order of the Archbishop of Toledo, probably for his unsaintly conduct and licentious writings, he wrote c. 1330 the Spanish masterpiece *Libro de Buen Amor,* which, though supposedly religious in intention, glorifies the life of the senses and satirizes human frailty. The *Libro de Buen Amor* is a colorful panorama of Spanish medieval life.

SÁNCHEZ CALAVERA, FERRÁN (d. 1450), also known, wrongly, as Sánchez Talavera, was a Master of the Order of Calatrava who left us an elegy (*decir*) on the death of Admiral Ruy Díaz de Mendoza, the King's chief majordomo. The deep note, so eloquent and moving, has been considered precursory and comparable to Jorge Manrique's *Coplas* (q.v.). Sánchez Calavera's poem is written in *octavas* of anapaestic type (*arte mayor*), previously used by Juan de Mena (q.v.).

SANTILLANA, MARQUÉS DE (1398-1458), the courtier and warrior Iñigo López de Mendoza, was born in Carrión de los Condes, near Burgos, into a noble family of poets and statesmen: his father, the Admiral of Castile, Hurtado de Mendoza (q.v.), penned the lovely *cosante* included here. Conscious of Dante and Petrarch, Santillana's poetry seems to combine traditional forms with the new Italian currents. However, rather than his didactic and allegorical poetry, which bulks so imposingly in the totality of his work, it is the delicate *canciones, villancicos* and hill songs that have made him famous.

SEM TOB or SANTOB (c. 1290-1369), Rabbi of Carrión de los Condes, who wrote both in Spanish and Hebrew, made his name famous with his *Proverbios Morales* (c. 1350), some 400 quatrains of gnomic verses, Biblical in phrasing and didactic in style, dedicated to Peter the Cruel of Castile and Chancellor Pero López de Ayala (1322-1407), also a poet and a leading political figure. Each of the quatrains contains a moral, expressed often in intense lyrical phrasing, delicate and subtly ironical.

The Catalans

LLULL, RAMON, more universally known as *Raimundo Lulio* or *Lully* (c. 1233-1315), was born in Palma de Mallorca, served in his youth as page of Jaime I the Conqueror, and then wrote love songs. At the age of thirty, after the birth of his two children, he changed the course of his dissolute life, became converted and devoted his life to penitence and meditation. He broke his family ties and set out on long pilgrimages as a beggar, visiting Santiago de Compostela, Rome, and the Holy Land, and then studied in the outstanding universities of Europe. In his eighties he was stoned to death by an angry mob in Tunis. He was a prolific writer—more than 200 works survive—and excelled for his allegorical novels and mystical works. His mysticism also pervades his lyrics. His *Cant de Ramón* as well as his *Desconhort,* depicting his spiritual crisis and conversion, are essentially personal utterances. The dramatic and majestic *Plant de nostra dona Santa Maria* is comparable in style to the *laudes* of Jacopone da Todi (q.v.)

MARCH, AUSIÀS (1397-1459), the greatest poet in Catalan, Valencian nobleman and soldier, held a prominent position in the court of Alfonso the Magnanimous and owned considerable lands. He fought in Italy and retired at the age of thirty to Valencia, serving then as Chief Falconer to the King. His poetry excels in psychological depth and metaphysical anguish; he uses Provençal metres, and was especially influenced by Arnaut Daniel and to some extent by Dante and Petrarch.

MARCH, PERE (c. 1338-1413), Valencian narrative and lyric poet possessed of strong ethical concern. Of his poems included here, one deals with a flirtatious widow and the other imitates the Provençal school, especially the Monk of Montaudun (q.v.), for it is a *plazer,* enumerating all the things and actions which he found pleasant. His *esparças,* couched in free verse, are characterized by their simplicity, humor, and sensuous qualities.

SANT JORDI, JORDI DE (c. 1399-1430),Valencian aristocrat in the service of Alfonso the Magnanimous, took part in numerous military engagements in Italy and the Mediterranean. In 1423 he was captured and held prisoner by the condottiere Francesco Sforza. A delicate poet, who put his verse to music himself, he underwent both Provençal and Petrarchan influences. In his charming *Enuigs,* such as "I Have No Liking for One Who in All Things Is Not," he imitates the Monk of Montaudun (q.v.). His unrhymed *Stramps,* "Below the Brow I Bear Your Lovely Countenance," is perhaps his finest single work, a veritable milestone in the development of Catalan poetry.

GERMANY

ANONYMOUS

The Lay of Hildebrand

Hildebrandslied

I heard it told
that challengers singly met:
Hildebrand and Hadubrand between two hosts.
Son and father they; saw to their armor;
made fast their mail-shirts; girded their swords on,
over the rings, to ride to such striving.
Hildebrand first spoke; higher in years he,
master of men, measured his words,
first asked wisely, who his father was,
prince of the people. . . . .
. . . . "or of what clan thou art.
If thou but tellst me this, well I shall wot the rest.
Lad, in the lands of kings, few are unknown to me."
Hadubrand, he spoke—Hildebrand's son:
"This our folk told me,
old folk that were there before,
that Hildebrand was my father, my name is Hadubrand.
Eastwards he fared once, fleeing from Odoacer
thence with Theodoric and all his thanes.
He left in his lands: his lady, his lad,
home in his house, a beardless boy.
Left son and heir, riding to eastward,
for that Theodoric longed so to have him
stand at his side, that was a friendless man.
He was to Odoacer boundless in ill-will,
and was of his thanes all Theodoric's dearest.
He rode at the horde's head; loved all too well fighting.
Dear he was to daring men.
Nor do I hope have he is alive now. . . .
Witness is God on High up in the Heavens
Thou never yet hast stood up to one like him,
of such a lineage . . ."

He wound from his arm the winding bands:
gold worked for kaisers e'en as the king gave him.
The lord of the Huns spake: "This gift I give you."
Hadubrand answered, Hildebrand's son:
"With spear and gear such gifts should be greeted
point against point.
Thou art, old Hun, monstrous sly,
wooest with words me, wouldst spend thy spear on me.
Art such an ancient man, yet so full of guile thou.
They told me who plow the sea
west o'er the world's waves: war took him away.
Dead is Hildebrand, Herbrand's son.
Well do I see by thy fine trappings
that thou at home hast a good lord and master,
no outcast thou that ridest and fleest."
Hildebrand answered, Herbrand's son:
"Verily, wills it God, woeful our fate's way.
Abroad I've dwelt summers and winters full sixty,
since I was chosen one of the fighters:
Whom no man's weapon ever laid low,
Now shall my own son's brand best me,
blade bore through me or I bring his blood-death.
Yet if thy zeal be strong, canst thou today gain
armor and arms of this ancient and agèd man,
booty for boldness, if right thou hast any.
He would be the most craven of cowards from eastward
who turned away one like thee thirsting for fight.
The two-man fight, try it who must,
See which today must leave empty his armor
or both our byrnies be his alone."
They let first of all ash-spears whirr
in sharp showers—stood in the shields fast.
Then closed in together, splitting the shield's edge,
hewing harm into the heavy circles,
till shields were but shards, worn with their weapons.

HERMAN SALINGER

✠

Magic Spells

Go out, Worm, with Nine Little Worms

Geh aus, Wurm, mit neuen Würmlein

Go out, worm, with nine little worms,
Out of the marrow into the bone,
Out of the bone into the flesh,
Out of the flesh into the skin,
Out of the skin into the arrow,
So be it.

✠

Phol and Wotan Were Riding in the Forest

Phol ende Uuodan vuorun zi holza

Phol and Wotan were riding in the forest.
There the horse of Baldur twisted his foot.
Sinthgunt cast a spell,
The sister of Sunna,
Then Freya cast a spell,
The sister of Uclla,
Then Wotan cast a spell,
As only he could cast a spell:
Be it twisted bone
Be it twisted blood
Be it twisted joint
Bone to bone,
Blood to blood,
Joint to limb—
Let them be glued together.

RUTH YORCK and KENWARD ELMSLIE

✠

Thou Art Mine, I Am Thine

Dû bist mîn, ich bin dîn

Thou art mine, I am thine;
Certain be, in this heart of mine
Locked thou art,
Here within;
Lost for ever is the little key:
Herein must thou always be.

ELIZABETH CLOSS

✠

Stetit Puella

Stetit puella

Stetit puella
rufa tunica:
si quis eam tetigit,
tunica crepuit eia.

Stetit puella,
tanquam rosula
facie splenduit,
et os ejus floruit eia.

Stetit puella
by a tree,
scripsit amorem
on the leaves

There came Venus at once,
caritatem magnam,
great was the love
she offered her leman.

ELIZABETH CLOSS

✠

Never the Summer Seemed to Me

Ich gesach den sumer nie

Never the summer seemed to me
more gloriously fair than now.
With many blossoms beautiful
The meadow richly decks itself.
Field and wood is full of song,
The birds are singing the season long.

ELIZABETH CLOSS

✠

Floret Silva Undique

Floret silva undique

Floret silva undique,
For my lover I pine away.
The forest burgeons everywhere,
Where bides my lover so long?
Alas, he has ridden o'er the lea
Who will love me? Woe is me.

ELIZABETH CLOSS

✠

If the World Were Mine

Waer diu werlt alliu min

If the world were mine
From the ocean to the Rhine,
I'd renounce it without qualms
If the Queen of England[1]
Were lying in my arms.

RUTH YORCK and KENWARD ELMSLIE

---

[1] *The Queen of England referred to is probably Mathilda de Poitou, who married Henry the Lion in 1168.*

Song for the Virgin Mary [1]
Marienlied

O, into the earth
Aaron set a rod,
Which then bore almonds,
A most noble seed,
You brought forth their sweet taste,
Mother, without a man's embrace.
Sancta Maria.

In the dense undergrowth
Moses saw a fire.
The branches were not burning,
Above he saw the flame,
Blazing brilliantly,
Proof of your purity.
Sancta Maria.

Gideon, leader of Israel,
Spread out a lambskin
So the dew of heaven
Would rain upon the wool.
Thus you remained chaste
While becoming fruitful.
Sancta Maria.

Sea-star, red dawn,
Soil never ploughed,
There a flower grows,
Bright and beautiful,
She stands among the others,
A lily among thorns.
Sancta Maria.

---

[1] *From a song sequence written at the monastery at Melk, Donau.*

A fishing line was braided
At the time you were born.
Involving all your folk.
The hook was God's own will,
And strangled Death to death
Which was concealed from you.
Sancta Maria.

Isaiah the wise seer,
He has predicted you.
He said from Jesse's root
A slender branch would sprout,
Blooming to a flower.
He meant you and your child.
Sancta Maria.

They belong to each other,
Heaven and earth together,
Like the ox and the ass
Who at once praised the Child.
And so your womb became
A cradle for the lamb.
Sancta Maria.

You gave birth to the Child of God
Who henceforth released us all
With his holy blood
From eternal suffering.
He shall be forever praised.
You have brought us countless joys.
Sancta Maria.

Locked portal,
Open to God's word,
Overflowing honeycomb
Laden with sweetness,
You are without gall,

Like the turtledove.
Sancta Maria.

Sealed well,
Walled garden,
Where balsam grows,
Spiced with cinnamon,
You are the cedar tree
Avoided by the snake.
Sancta Maria.

Cedar in Lebanon,
Rose in Jericho,
Choicest myrrh,
Subtly scented,
You are above all angels.
You atone for Eve.
Sancta Maria.

Eve brought us double death,
One still condemns us.
You are the opposite,
You have brought us life.
The Devil counsels death for us,
Gabriel sings the word of God.
Sancta Maria.

You, a virgin, bore a child,
The noblest in the world.
You resemble the sun,
Risen in Nazareth,
Jerusalem Gloria,
Israel Laetitia.
Sancta Maria.

Queen of heaven,
Portal of paradise,
You were chosen House of God.

Sacrarium Sancti Spiritus.
You guide us on our way,
To our Judgment Day.
Sancta Maria.

RUTH YORCK and KENWARD ELMSLIE

✠

Mary Magdalene's Song[1]
Lied der Maria Magdalena

Peddler, sell me a shade of red
To make my cheeks glow brightly,
So I can teach the fine young men
Not to treat love lightly.

Young man,
Look at me,
I'll please you if you please me

Go and find some lovely maid
Shower love upon her.
Love's sweet harvest, fine young men,
Will bring you joy and honor.

Young man,
Look at me,
I'll please you if you please me

Bless you, world! For you are thus
Rich in earthly pleasure.
I'll serve you in my own sweet way
By giving love full measure.

Young man,
Look at me,
I'll please you if you please me

RUTH YORCK and KENWARD ELMSLIE

---

[1] *From the Easter play at Benedikt Beuren.*

DER VON KÜRENBERG

The Falcon
Falkenlied

I raised a falcon for more than a year.
When he was tamed to my heart's content,
I wound in his wings a golden band
Then he swooped up high and flew to other lands.

I watched the falcon in perfect flight,
From his talons trailed thongs made of silk.
In his wings there gleamed red and golden feathers.
May God help all lovers who long to be together.

I take it to heart and I must cry
I and my love are forced apart
Because of liars, may God give them pain.
Whoever reunites us will make me glad again.

The dark star goes into hiding
Like you, my beauty each time you see me.
Let your eyes glance at another knight
Then no one will know our bitter plight.

Both woman and bird are easy to tame.
They search for the man who can tempt them best.
Thus a fair maid is wooed by a knight,
When I think about this, I am filled with delight.

RUTH YORCK and KENWARD ELMSLIE

✠

I Stood on a Battlement the Late Eve Darkened

Ich stuont mir nehtint spate an einer zinnen

I

(*A lady speaks*)

I stood on a battlement the late eve darkened.
To a knight singing sweetly below I harkened.
'Twas the tune of Kürenberg rose amid the throng.
Either he must quit my lands or else to me belong!

(*The knight's answer is addressed to his squire*)

Now bring me hither quickly my armor and my steed,
For I must quit the lands of a lady with speed.
Fain would she compel me her dear friend to be.
She must bear the loss for ever of all love from me!

(*In the next three songs a lady speaks*)

II

When I am standing in my smock alone,
And I think of thee, noble man,
Then my color flushes, as on thorn-spray the rose,
And many a sad longing, deep within, my heart knows.

III

I reared me a falcon more than a year.
When I had tamed him and meant to keep him near,
And had adorned his feathers with gold bright and gay,
He soared aloft so proudly, and flew far away.

I saw the falcon later, flying so rarely.
Silken cords he wore became him fairly,
And his feathers were all of a red-gold hue.
God send them together, who are dear friends and true!

IV

Tears come welling up from my sad heart.
I and my comrade were forced to part.

Liars the cause of that: God give them bane!
O this were joy, could we be reconciled again!

(*In the last songs a knight is the speaker, except that the last two lines are spoken by the poet in person*)

V

Beautiful woman, now come, go with me!
Pleasure and pain, I will share both with thee.
So long as I have life, thou to me art full dear.
The ways of base lovers thou hast no need to fear!

VI

The star darkly gleaming hides its dim light.
So do thou, fair lady: when I stand in thy sight,
Then let thine eyes rest on some other man.
So none shall guess easily what we too there may plan.

VII

All the charm of womankind still goes a maid.
When to greet her from me my messenger is sped,
Were it not to her peril, I would after him go.
I know not how to praise her, I have never loved woman so.

Woman and falcon are easily made tame.
Both will come flying to a man's lure the same.
Thus did a comely knight woo a fair lady.
When I, too, think thereon, my bold heart is ready.

MARGARET F. RICHEY

DER BURGGRAVE VON REGENSBURG

All Winter I Lay Alone until a Lady Brought Me Solace

Ich lac den winter eine/wol troste mich ein wip

All winter I lay alone until a lady brought me solace.
And to our joy, summer arrived, and flowers.

The envious grew jealous. My heart is in pain,
Only a woman's love can cure me again.

"Now they tell me to avoid the knight. How I mind!
We lay hidden, happily entwined,
Secretly together. I grow weak with longing—torn
From him, our ungentle parting leaves forlorn."

RUTH YORCK and KENWARD ELMSLIE

SPERVOGEL

He Who Asks a Wolf to Dine Soon Has Cause to Wail

Swer den wolf ze huse ladet der nimmt sin schaden

He who asks a wolf to dine soon has cause to wail.
A sailor easily overloads a ship that's old and frail.
What I want to say is clear—
He who buys his wife dress after dress year after year
Buys more than that. Too vain to be mastered,
She calls him a bastard.

RUTH YORCK and KENWARD ELMSLIE

✠

Do You Know What the Hedgehog Said?

Weistu, wie der igel sprach?

Do you know what the hedgehog said?
Everyone should have his own room and bed.
Build a house, little man,
A place to live, work, and plan.
He is very badly off
Who has no home to call his own.
He will find the going rough.

Whatever the weather, snow or ice,
In the early morning, the guest must rise.
Innkeepers stay warm and dry—
The guest must leave and say goodbye
To the hearth where he does not belong.
He who has no home to call his own
Should have thought ahead while young and strong.

The rich man lives without a care,
The man in need goes everywhere
And takes what comes, both good and bad.
This must not happen to my lad,
Who longs to roam and run berserk.
He pulls my beard until I groan—
It's time I settled down to work.

RUTH YORCK and KENWARD ELMSLIE

DIETMAR VON AIST

On the Linden Overhead a Bird Was Caroling Its Lay

Uf der linden obene da sanc ein kleinez vogellin

On the linden overhead a bird was caroling its lay.
From the wood its music rang, whereat my heart was borne away
To seek a place where once it dwelled.
I saw the roses blooming there.
They call into my mind the thoughts that link me
to a lady fair.

"Methinks a thousand years are fled since
in my lover's arms I lay.
Without or cause or fault of mine he leaves me
friendless many a day.
Since the time when last I saw the flowers and heard
the sweet birds' song,

Short, alack, my joy has been and my heart-sorrow
all too long."

MARGARET F. RICHEY

✠

A Lady Stood Alone
Ez stuont ein frouwe alleine

A lady stood alone,
And looked out over the field,
And looked for her lover.
In the air above her
A falcon wheeled.
"Hail, falcon, it is well for thee!
Thou from a forest tree
Choosest what bough thou wilt
To be thy pleasure
Thus have I also done:
I chose myself a man,
My eyes did measure
And single out his beauty.
Now fair ladies envy me that booty.
O why will they not leave my love to me?
I never cared for love of theirs, but let them be."

MARGARET F. RICHEY

✠

Sleepest Thou Yet, My Sweeting?
Slafest du, friedel ziere?

"Sleepest thou yet, my sweeting?
Our night, alas, is fleeting.
A little, lovely bird but now
Flew to its perch upon the linden bough."

"I slept, nor dreamed of waking.
Up, criest thou, Dawn is breaking!

Bliss without bale, this may not be.
Whatso thou biddest, dear love, I accept from thee."

She spoke, and wept for sorrow:
"Thou goest—alas the morrow!
When wilt thou come to me again?
My joy goes with thee; I alone remain."

MARGARET F. RICHEY

FRIEDRICH VON HAUSEN

My Heart and Body Wish to Take Their Leave

Min herze und min lip diu wellent scheiden

My heart and body wish to take their leave,
Who long together now have gone their way.
The body longs to go and fight the heathen:
And yet the heart has chosen a lady
Before all others it has distressed me since that day,
One will no longer follow the other's lead.
Looking upon her has given me much grief.
God alone can settle this affray.

I thought that I had lost such misery,
When I took up the cross for God's renown.
It would be fitting that the heart were free,
But that its constancy commands a ban.
I should most surely be a living man,
If it would not behave so wilfully.
Now it is quite indifferent, I see,
For what my destiny may have in hand.

Since heart, your ways you will not mend,
And you wish to leave me with such grief,
So I pray to God that he may send
You some place where you will be well received.
Alas what will befall me when you leave!
Dare you alone with danger so contend?

Who will help you sorrow to an end
With such faithfulness as I did give?

GILLIAN BARKER and KENNETH GEE

✠

In My Dream I Saw a Woman

In minen troume ich sach

In my dream I saw a woman
Fair to gaze upon,
All night long till daybreak;
When I woke, she was gone.
Where she is now, alas,
I have no means of knowing.
That joy came not to pass
Which she was showing.
My eyes did this to me:
'Twere best, if I could not see!

MARGARET F. RICHEY

✠

If I Might Live to See the Day

Gelebt ich noch die lieben zit

If I might live to see the day
When I could greet that land so fair
Which harbors all I know of joy,
Because my lady dwelleth there,
Then no tear should vex my eye,
No man or woman hear me sigh
Or utter words of care.
Many a thing my mind would please
That used to be my mind's disease.

I fancied we were far apart
Where I should now feel very near.

In a strange land, my constant heart
Knows grief that makes old hardships dear.
Were I somewhere near the Rhine,
I'd hear the news for which I pine
Since I am planted here,
Shut off beyond the mountain screen
That stretches ruthlessly between.

MARGARET F. RICHEY

REINMAR VON HAGENAU, der Alte

I Think That Love Will Come My Way

Ich wan nur liebe geschehen wil

I think that love will come my way:
My heart lifts up towards its play,
Like the falcon in his flight
And the eagle on the wind.
Yet I left my love behind.
If only I may then discover
She is unharmed as when I left her!
It is good with her to rest.
Lord God, grant me my request
That I must see her so
And atone for all her sorrow;
If she is in distress.
That I may ease it for her
        And she may make my trouble less;
We may enjoy our love at last.
Ah the long night is gladness to me!
        How could I be downcast?

GILLIAN BARKER and KENNETH GEE

✠

You Say, the Summer Is Here Now

Sie jehent, der sumer der si hie

"You say, the summer is here now,
That joy is come to stay,
And that I am as well as once I was.
Now speak and tell me how.
Death has taken much away
So I can never overcome the loss.
What do I need then with a time of mirth,
Since Leopold lord of all joys lies in the earth,
Whom I never knew to mourn?
The world has lost by this one death
As by no other man's
So great misfortune has been borne.

I poor woman was so glad
When I thought of him
How my salvation lasted while he lived.
That this I shall no longer have,
Will with sorrow spin
Out whatever of my life is left.
The mirror of my joy is lost.
What I would have chosen to give my eyes a summer feast,
I must give up for good and all.
When they told me he was dead,
At once the blood welled red
From the heart on to my soul.

Joy has been forbidden me
By my dear lord's death
And that I must for evermore forgo.
Since there is no remedy,
Except to fight distress
So that my complaining heart is full of woe.
I am the one who still for him will grieve,

For this most hallowed man was my comfort in this life.
Now he is gone. What should I do here?
Be gracious unto him, lord God:
For a more virtuous guest
Did never in your house appear."

GILLIAN BARKER and KENNETH GEE

✠

One Thing They Say Displeases Me

Ein rede der liute tuot mir we

One thing they say displeases me:
Indeed, it almost puts me in a rage.
They keep on asking me my lady's age,
And want to know, how old is she,
Because I have been serving her so long.
They say it to incense me.
May the sweet mistress of my song
For that ill-mannered question recompense me!

MARGARET F. RICHEY

✠

The Day on Which I Took the Cross

Des tages do ich daz kriuze nam

The day on which I took the cross,
I kept my thoughts in close control,
As well beseemed that holy sign,
And as a pilgrim pure of soul.
I hoped I might so bind them to God's will
They would not swerve, nor cease His service to fulfill.
But now they tend to break away,
As they were wont, and wander free.
And this is not my case alone,
But troubles other men than me.

I well might keep my vows unscathed,
But that unruly thoughts prevail:
When I should praise the God to whom
I have sworn service, there they fail
To help me in my need, and jeopardize
My soul's salvation, harking back in treacherous wise
To those old joys whereof a taste
Lures me to do as once I did.
Maiden and Mother, give me grace,
For these I cannot all forbid!

Nor would I quite forbid free range
To thoughts (they have their own domain),
But rather give them leave to go
Thither, and straight return again.
So may they bear a greeting to our friends,
Turn back, and help me for my sin to make amends,
And may they be forgiven all
Wherewith, before, they wrought me ill!
Natheless, I fear, they are not to trust,
And often will confound me still.

MARGARET F. RICHEY

ALBRECHT VON JOHANSDORF

If I Saw One Who Could Say He Was Come from Her

Sach ich iemen der jaehe er waere von ir komen

If I saw one who could say he was come from her,
I would bless him, though he were my foe.
Had he robbed me of all else, her messenger
Should for this his punishment forgo.
He who but speaks her name
Has me to friend
From now to a full year's end.
What scathe or shame

To flay me he had wrought
Should be as nought.

MARGARET F. RICHEY

✠

This I Know, How Love Begins to Be
Wie sich minne hebt, daz wiz ich wol

"This I know, how love begins to be.
How love ends, I do not, dare not, know.
If within the heart and soul of me,
I shall feel love's kindling joy a-glow,
Spare me, Lord, the parting, which I deem
Bitterest thing of all.
This I dread beyond the heaviest dream.

"Where two loving hearts in friendship grow,
And their loves unite in one strong tie,
None shall ever part them, living so,
Till the day when one of them must die.
So with me, suppose the case my own.
If I lost my friend,
See, I should be utterly alone.

"Many an hour is needed, ere the two
Gently weld their wills and minds as one.
Should the end thereof be bitter rue,
Such I ween, were welcome news to none.
That be far from me as my own death!
And if someone there be
Who loves me, let this warn him to keep faith!"

She whom serving now, I serve for ever,
Cannot fail these words to understand.
More I must not say: this brief endeavor
Made, I yield me to her kind command.
Of her grace and goodness I have need,

And if she will, give joy
She can, and if not, I am poor indeed.

MARGARET F. RICHEY

✠

I Found without a Guard

Ich vant si âne huote

I found without a guard
The most lovely lady standing all alone.
Thus spoke his one so good:
"What are you seeking in this place alone?"
"Lady, it has happened thus."
"Say then, why are you come here? You must tell me this."

"Love sends sorrow
I complain to you, my lady sweet and kind."
"Oh, what are you saying, foolish fellow?
You would do well to give your grieving end."
"Lady, I cannot do without such tears."
"Then I will never listen to you in a thousand years."

"No, my queen, no!
My service should not go without a wage."
"You quite senseless grow,
That you can put me into such a rage."
"Lady your hate will make me as one dead."
"Who has driven you, dearest man, to such a need?"

"Your beauty has done that,
Which you have, most lovely lady."
"Your singing is so sweet
That it will wound my constant body."
"Lady, God does not so ordain."
"If I should listen, yours would be the honor; mine the shame."

"Let me yet be pleased
That to you my heart was always kindly."

"You may soon be wearied
Of hurling words against me."
"Does my speaking seem to have no merit?"
"Yes, it has given strength to my unwavering spirit."

"I too have constancy,
If you will allow me to be true."
"Be advised by me,
Give up what I can never grant to you."
"Shall I be heard then certainly?"
"God will hear you elsewhere what you desire of me."

"Shall then my singing and
All my service come to naught?"
"You may well gain your end:
You will not go without reward."
"Good lady, how should that be understood?"
"That you are more worthy for it and your spirit is renewed."

GILLIAN BARKER and KENNETH GEE

HEINRICH VON MORUNGEN

On the Heath on a Morning

Ich hort uf der heide

On the heath on a morning
I heard clear singing and sweetest song.
Thence came without warning
Sharp delight and thinking long.
To her in a throng
Wishes strong
Haled with thong.
I found her a-dancing to her song.
Freed from mourning
I leapt along.

Alone in her bower
I found her weeping tears like rain;

For only that hour
Word had reached her that I was slain.
Less hard to sustain
Old disdain
Than see plain
Her joy at my kneeling there again
Overpower
All her pain.

Alone on the tower
I found her; she made me so admire,
With ease in that hour
I could have had all my desire.
It seemed the entire
World in fire
Must expire:
Such madness her spirit's sweet attire
Had the power
To inspire.

J. B. LEISHMAN

✠

Ah Me, Shall I No Longer See

Owe, sol aber mir iemer me

Ah me, shall I no longer see,
Shining all through the night,
Whiter than snow can be,
Her body lithe and light,
Which made these eyes of mine
Unable to divine
'Twas not the bright moonshine?
Then came the dawn.

"Ah me, and shall we never see
That blessed morrow dawn,
When, as night's shadows flee,

We shall not need to mourn
'Alas, now it is day!'
As he said with dismay
When last by me he lay.
Then came the dawn."

Ah me, with kisses none could tell
She kissed me as I slept.
Hotly on me they fell,
Those heavy tears she wept.
I cheered her, though, and she
Let all her weeping be
And flung her arms round me.
Then came the dawn.

"Ah me, how often he would gaze
Like one in lunacy!
The coverlet he'd raise,
Being mad to see poor me
With nothing on at all.
It was most wonderful
How that could never pall.
Then came the dawn."

J. B. LEISHMAN

✠

Torturing Glimpses and Passions Unruly

Leitliche blicke und grôzlîche riuwe

Torturing glimpses and passions unruly
Have wasted my heart and my body for long,
Yet would I mourn my old suffering newly,
Were not my fear of the scoffers so strong.
If, then, I sing of her,
her whom I can never wrong,
Let none take falsely what I have meant truly,
I who was born for the service of song.

Some will be saying "Now hark to his singing!
How could he so if he really were sad?"
Such cannot fathom the pain that is wringing,
Such was I ever, for good or for bad.
When I stood sadly there,
little heed of me she had:
Thus it was sadness that set me a-singing,
Sadness that skills not where people are glad.

The joy and the crown of my heart is the rarest
Of all the rare women I ever could see.
Fair and so far and so fair, the all-fairest
Is she, and it glads me when others agree.
All the world shall bow,
for her beauty's sake, the knee.
Lady, reward me at last, if thou darest;
Else were such praising but folly in me.

When standing before her I gaze on the wonder
Of beauty which God made her body display,
So much is joined which elsewhere is asunder,
There I most gladly for ever could stay.
Ah me, but I must
leave her, to my great dismay;
For all of a sudden she vanishes under
A dark cloud that snatches her brightness away.

J. B. LEISHMAN

✠

Lady, Wilt Thou Heal My Smart?
Frouwe, wilt du mich genern

Lady, wilt thou heal my smart,
So let thine eyes upon me gaze.
I can no longer play this part;
This way I soon must end my days.
I am so sick, so sore at heart.

Lady, what brought me to this plight?
My eyes and thy red lips so bright.

Lady, for my pain have some care
Before indeed my days must end.
One word speak into my ear,
Turn things about, my lovely friend.
Why must thou always say: no, no—
    No no, no no, no no no . . . ?
This will break my heart in two.
Canst thou not sometime answer yes,
    Yes yes, yes yes, yes yes yes?
And thus my heart no more oppress!

HERMAN SALINGER

✠

Many a Man Has Been Bewitched by an Elf

Von den elben wirt entsên vil manic man

Many a man has been bewitched by an elf:
So am I bewitched by love so great
By the best friend man ever took to himself.
Yet she would only sneer at me for that,
And be unfaithful to me, may she then take vengeance,
And do as I beg: she would give me so much pleasure,
That my life would end for such delight.

She commands and is mistress in my heart
And is more lordly than I can ever be:
If I could have such power for my part
That she in faithfulness would stay by me
For three whole days and for as many nights!
Then I would not lose my strength and life.
Alas she is only too free of me.

So burn in me the flames her glances start
As fire kindles tinder that is dry,

And her coldness to me wounds my heart
As water forces glowing heat to die:
And her proud bearing, her beauty, and her worth,
And the wonder that is spoken of her virtues,
All that is evil and yet good to me.

Whenever her bright eyes may turn towards me
In such a way they look right through my heart,
Whoever stands between and so annoys me,
He must see his happiness depart,
For I stand and wait upon my lady
Like the little birds upon the day:
When will contentment ever be my part?

GILLIAN BARKER and KENNETH GEE

✠

She Has Wounded Me Right Through My Heart

Si hôt mich verwunt reht oldwich mîne sêle

She has wounded me right through my heart
Into the deadly pit,
For I let her see that I was suffering and distraught
For her mouth so sweet.
Once I begged of it if only it would make her serve my will
That I might steal
One sweet kiss from her, all would be ever well with me.

How I begin to hate her rose-red mouth I was sure
I never could forget!
Though it troubles me yet that a little while before
She shunned me, so obstinate.
I have grown so tired of it, that I would sooner live
In hell's abyss
And burn than any longer serve her and know no reason for it.

GILLIAN BARKER and KENNETH GEE

✠

Saw You the Ladies
Sach ieman die frouwen

Saw you the ladies
Whom you may gaze at
As they stand by the window?
The beautiful one
All she has done
Is give me sorrow.
She shines as the sun will shine
        Towards the bright morning.
Who before was in hiding:
Then I must go grieving:
I will leave her now.

Is there anyone here
Whose senses clear
He can retain?
Let him go to the fair one,
who with her crown
Has gone away;
That she may come to comfort me,
        Before I leave this life:
Love and grief
Together will lead
Me to my grave.

You should write down
Small on the stone
Which marks my grave,
She was dear to me,
Whom she would not see;
Who walks above,
May read this message
        And he will then admit
The wrong was great

She did commit
Against her love.

GILLIAN BARKER and KENNETH GEE

WOLFRAM VON ESCHENBACH

A Lady at the Watchman's Song Perceived

Den morgenblic bî wahters sange erkôs

A lady at the watchman's song perceived
Dawn's gleam as secretly
Within her noble lover's arms she lay.
Whereat she lost the great part of her joy.
Bright eyes could then not help
But fill with tears. "Alas!" she said, "O Day,
Beasts wild and tame rejoice at you
And welcome you, save I alone. What will become of me?
No longer can my lover here remain
With me: your light drives him away."

The day with might pressed in through all the panes.
They bolted many bolts:
To no avail; and thence their sorrow came.
The lady clasped her lover tightly to her
And their eyes rained down tears
On both their cheeks. Then her lips said to him:
"One body and two hearts have we,
Unparted fares our faithfulness, one with the other.
My great love is now utterly laid waste
Unless you come to me and I to you."

The grieving man then took his farewell thus:
Their fair skins in their smoothness
Came closer still. And so the day appeared:
Eyes all in tears and a sweet lady's kiss.
And there they so entwined
Their lips, their breasts, their arms, their legs
all white,

That a shield-painter picturing them
Just as they lay in that embrace would have the
perfect model.
And yet their two loves suffered grief enough.
They gave and took of love in all delight.

CHARLES E. PASSAGE

✠

It Has Thrust Its Talons Through the Morning Clouds

Sîne klâwen durch die wolken sint geslagen

"It has thrust its talons through the morning clouds,
It rises up with mighty strength,
I see it change to grey, as day will when it dawns,
The day, that from this worthy man
Would take away my company,
Whom I by night so carefully let in.
I'll bring him hence now if I can:
Great virtue in him bade me do as much.

Watchman, you sing that which takes many joys from me
And makes my grief the greater.
Tidings you bring that are, alas! unwelcome to me
Mornings toward the break of day.
These you should keep in silence from me.
To your good faith I thus command:
I will reward you if I can.
Then my beloved can remain here with me."

"He must be up and gone, and that without delay.
Take your farewell of him, sweet Lady.
Let him love you with such secrecy henceforth
That he may keep his life and honor.
He has so trusted my good faith
That I would surely bring him back.

The day has come: it was night when
You won him from me with embrace and kiss."

"Sing now, Watchman, what you will, but leave him here
Who has brought love and love received.
By your song he and I alike are terrified:
If now the morning star does not
Rise over him who came for love,
And if the daylight does not shine,
You still have often taken him
From my white arms—though never from my heart."

At the gleam that daylight darted through the panes,
And as the watchman sang his warning,
She could not fail to fear for him who was with her.
She pressed her bosom to his breast.
The knight no wise forgot his valor
(The watchman's song kept him from that);
Farewell that close and closer came
Gave them with kiss and otherwise reward of love.

CHARLES E. PASSAGE

✠

The Lament for the Love of Heroes

Der helden minne ir klage

The lament for the love of heroes
You always sang as the sun rose,
The sour after the sweet.
He who loves received
And welcome of women, though he must soon set forth,
As you forewarned them both, and then
The morning star rose, watchman, be silent, sing not of that again.

He who lies or lay
Beside his love in habit's way

Shame and concealment scorning,
Need not in fear of morning
Take himself off, he may await the day:
None need lead him away to save his life.
Such love can still be given by his own sweet wife.

GILLIAN BARKER and KENNETH GEE

✠

Bursting Leaves, Flowers Opening
Ursprinc bluomen, loup uz dringen

Bursting leaves, flowers opening
And the air of May give back their old song to the birds:
There are new songs I can sing,
When the frost is lying, good lady, even without your rewards.
The wood-singing birds and their cry
No longer rang in the ear when half the summer had gone by.

The flowers that sparkle with light
Shall be made brighter by the drops of dew,
where they are clinging:
The birds that are so fine and bright,
All the Maytime rock their children with their singing.
The nightingale was never still:
But now I am awake and sing in the valley and on the hill.

My song will seek your kindness,
Gentle lady: now help me, since I have so great a need.
Your reward should quit[1] my service,
Which I beg and beg again till I am dead.
Let me take comfort from you, then,
That my long sorrowing may have an end.

Sweet lady, can my service have success,
If your power to help will make me so content,
That my grief will surely pass

---

[1] *In the archaic sense of requite.*

And my desiring find with you its longed for end?
Your gentle ways command my song,
Day by day I sing to you both short and long.

Dear lady, your sweet goodness
And your charming anger rob me of my joy and calm.
Will you bring my heart some solace?
For one kindly word alone from you will be my balm.
Make an end of my lament,
Then the days I have to live will be so gladly spent.

GILLIAN BARKER and KENNETH GEE

✠

From *Titurel*

I Have These Many Evenings Watched for My Beloved

Ich hân nach liebem vriunde vil âbende al mîn schouwen

"I have these many evenings watched for my beloved
From out my window over heath by road and shining meadow,
And all in vain: he never comes to me.
For this my eyes must dearly pay with tears
for my beloved's love.

"Then I go from the window to the battlements
To look to eastward and to westward for a glimpse of him
Who has this long time so constrained my heart.
I may be reckoned old, not young, among the ones
who yearn.

"I journey for a while upon the raging waves;
I gaze far out, for over thirty miles I gaze
To hear, if such is possible, some word
So I may be rid of my sorrow for my fair young friend.

"What has become of my glittering joy, and how is it
That my high spirits have departed from my heart?
From both of us
A sigh must come which I thought I alone would suffer.
Yearning, I know, will drive him back to me,
However he avoids me now."

CHARLES E. PASSAGE

WALTHER VON DER VOGELWEIDE

Under the Lime Tree
Under der linden

Under the lime tree
On the heath
There our bed was,
There you can see
So fair beneath,
Broken flowers and flattened grass.
Before the forest in the valley,
Tandaradei,
The nightingale sang sweetly.

I had come
To the meadow:
My love had come before.
There I was given such welcome,
Holy Virgin! oh
I am content for evermore.
A thousand times did we not kiss?
Tandaradei,
See how red my mouth is.

There he made
So rich and fair
A bed from blooms.
There laughter stayed,

Is still heard there,
When somebody the same way comes.
On the roses, then, he may,
Tandaradei,
See where my head lay.

That he lay by me,
If it were known
(Now God forbid!), I'd be ashamed.
What he did with me,
Will be known to none
Except the two of us unnamed,
And a little bird:
Tandaradei,
Who will be the silent third.

GILLIAN BARKER and KENNETH GEE

✠

O Where Have They Vanished All My Years![1]

O weh, wie sind entschwunden alle meine Jahr!

O where have they vanished all my years!
Have I dreamed my life away, or is it real?
Did I believe in a world that was not really there?
I have slept till now and have been unaware.
Now I have woken, I do not understand
What was once familiar to me as the back of my hand.
The people and the land, there where I lived from childhood,
Are now as strange to me as if they were nothing but falsehood.
Those who were my companions, have grown heavy and old.
The field lies fallow, and the trees are felled.
Only the water flows unchanging as before,
Surely my misfortune can never be more.

---

[1] *This poem was written as part of the campaign to raise an army to go on a crusade: it was written for the Emperor Friedrich II, who had been excommunicated for his failure to keep his promise to undertake a crusade—hence the "unfriendly letters from Rome."*

Many who knew me well, now greet me wearily.
The world shows everywhere only hostility.
When I remember how many a wonderful day,
Is lost to me as if plunged deep in the sea,
Evermore I grieve.

O how pitifully the boys and girls behave
Who in time past were courteous and grave!
They care for nothing but sorrow: o why is this their way?
Wherever I turn in the world no one is gay:
Dancing, laughing, singing are acts of melancholy:
No Christian ever saw men in such misery.
Now see the women wear their jewels anyhow:
The proud knights are dressed like men from the plow.
We have unfriendly letters sent to us from Rome,
We are allowed to sorrow there is no joy at home.
My heart is weary (we lived so well those years),
For instead of laughter I must choose tears.
Even the wild birds are grieved by our lament:
Is it any wonder all my delight is spent?
O fool, what do I say in my rage and wickedness?
Who follows earthly pleasures, has lost heaven's blessedness,
Evermore I grieve.

O how we are surrounded by sweetness everywhere!
I see the gall hovering at the honey's core:
Outwardly the world is fair, white, green and red,
And inwardly so black, dark as death.
Let him be comforted, who has been led astray:
The smallest penance takes the greatest sin away.
Think of this, knights: it concerns you all.
You wear the bright helmets and the hard rings of mail,
The strong shields and the dedicated sword.
If only I deserved this honor, Lord!
Then, poor and needy, I would earn rich recompense.
I would not think of lands or nobles' opulence.
I would wear forever that hallowed crown:
The mercenary with his spear might have won.
If I could make the longed for journey over the sea,

I would sing gladly, then, and nevermore grieve,
Nevermore grieve.

GILLIAN BARKER and KENNETH GEE

✠

Children Won't Do What They Ought

Nieman kan mit gerten

Children won't do what they ought
If you beat them with a rod.
Children thrive, children grow
When taught by words, and not a blow.
Children thrive, children grow—
If you beat them with a rod
Children won't do what they ought.

Please be careful with your tongue.
That's good advice when you are young.
Push the bolt and lock the door—
No rude swearwords any more.
Push the bolt and lock the door—
That's good advice when you are young.
Please be careful with your tongue.

Please be careful with your eyes.
They show what's foolish and what's wise.
Let them see what's good and right,
And keep evil out of sight.
Let them see what's good and right,
They show what's foolish and what's wise.
Please be careful with your eyes.

Please be careful with your ears.
A fool heeds everything he hears.
Evil words, words unkind
Will do harm to a child's mind.
Evil words, words unkind—

A fool heeds everything he hears.
Please be careful with your ears.

Please be careful with all three.
Sad to say, they're much too free.
Sometimes for your peace of mind,
It's best to be deaf, dumb, and blind.
Sometimes for your peace of mind
Sad to say, they're much too free.
Please be careful with all three.

RUTH YORCK and KENWARD ELMSLIE

✠

I Sat Cross-Legged upon a Stone[1]

Ich saz uf eime steine

I sat cross-legged upon a stone,
And put my elbow on my knee bone:
I cupped my chin within my hand.
If only I could understand
This world and how therein to live:
But no advice that I could give
Would show how three things could be won,
And guarantee the loss of none.
Wealth and fame are two,
And each to each will evil do:
The third is God's good will,
Which must the others far excel.
I'd keep it under lock and key.
But it can never be,
That worldly goods and place
Together with God's grace

---

[1] *This poem was written in 1198. The Emperor Henry VI died in 1197, leaving a son who, since he was still a child, could not be elected emperor. Civil war broke out between the supporters of Henry's brother Philip, Duke of Swabia, and the supporters of Otto, son of Henry the Lion. The dispute lasted until 1208 when Philip was murdered and Otto was crowned emperor in Rome.*

Into our heart can come and rest.
The paths have all been lost:
Dishonesty is out for prey,
Violence travels on the way:
Peace and justice bear a wound.
The three can have no safety, if these two are not sound.

GILLIAN BARKER and KENNETH GEE

✠

Whoso, Lord God, Being Bold to Say

Swe ane vorhte, herre got

Whoso, Lord God, being bold to say
Thy Ten Commandments, finds a way
To break them for true love has failed to care.
Thy Fatherhood most men confess.
He who regardeth me as less
Than brother gives no meaning to that prayer.
Of the same substance we are made,
We grow alike, our daily bread
Passes into our bodies, whence we thrive.
Who then can tell the master from the man,
When their bare bones, by worms bereft
Of differing flesh, alone are left,
Though he had known then both full well alive.
Christian, Jew and Paynim serve His plan,
From Whom all living wonders life derive.

MARGARET F. RICHEY

✠

Winter Has Done Us Great Harm Everywhere

Uns hat der winter geschadet über al

Winter has done us great harm everywhere.
Field and forest are withered and bare,
Hushed every voice that made melody there.

O to see girls playing ball on the fair
Open road, and to hear songs of birds in the air!

Would I might sleep until winter were o'er!
Waking, I grieve, and my anger is sore
At his wide sovereignty dreary and hoar.
May will most surely defeat him once more.
Flowers I shall pluck where the grass lieth frore.

MARGARET F. RICHEY

✠

Lady World, You Tell the Devil
Fro Welt, ir sult dem wirte sagen

Lady world, you tell the devil
I have settled my account:
I have atoned for all my guilt;
He can write off the last amount.
His debtors all do well to grieve.
I'd rather borrow from a Jew, than owe it to the devil that I live.
He's silent until judgment day:
Then he demands a surety
Which even he cannot repay.

"Walther, there is no need for anger:
You should remain with me on earth.
Think how I have given you shelter,
Whatever you asked there was no dearth,
Whenever you begged I was glad to give.
That you seldom begged from me was my deepest grief.
Think how well your life is spent:
If you deny my words are true,
You will never be content."

Lady world, I've fed too well:
It is time that I was weaned.
Your gentleness has used me ill,

The pleasures that it gives are sweet.
When I looked into your eyes
The wonder of your beauty could always take me by surprise:
Yet within so much decays
I know the horror that's behind you,
And I will curse you all my days.

"Since you will not change your mind,
Do one thing only that I say:
Remember many days were kind,
And now and then just look my way
When there is nothing else beguiles."
I would do so most willingly, if I did not fear your wiles
That no man can yet defeat.
Lady, God give you then, goodnight:
I will set forth to my retreat.

GILLIAN BARKER and KENNETH GEE

✠

Who Slays the Lion? Who Slays the Giant?

Wer sleht den lewen, wer sleht den risen?

Who slays the lion? Who slays the giant?
Who conquers both is self-reliant,
He can control himself and tame
His limbs from wildness into calm.
False shame and manners borrowed for a day
Only to win a stranger's smile
May shine forth brightly for a while:
But the gilt's soon rubbed away.

GILLIAN BARKER and KENNETH GEE

NEIDHART VON REUENTAL

And If Some Place I Have a Home

Und han ich indert heime

And if some place I have a home,
Where may it be?
The swallow with a speck of loam
Has more than me.
For this is all she needs to form
A cot to last her through the summer warm
God give me a house with sheltering roof
By Lengenbach, and proof
Against the winter's storm!

MARGARET F. RICHEY

✠

I Never Saw the Field

Ine gesach die heide nie baz gestalt

I never saw the field
In lovelier bloom.
Sunrays the green leaves
Of the wood illume.
With joy, in both we hail the May's advance.
Maidens, now take hands,
And merrily haste to meet the summertime in
festive dance!

Praise unto May is given
By many a tongue!
From many a bank and brae
The flowers have sprung,
Where but a short while since no flowers had been.

The budding limes are green,
And gentle maids, as you have heard just now,
in the dance are seen.

They are carefree and filled
With joy's excess.
You maidens clothed with charm
And loveliness,
Adorn yourselves, and let Bavarians praise,
Let Franks and Swabians gaze
Enraptured! Lace the dainty smocks you don for
holidays!

"For whom shall I adorn me?"
A maiden said.
"The drowsy fools see nothing!
My hopes are dead.
Honor and joy the world accounteth strange;
The men seek nought but change;
Women of whom they might be proud come not
within their range."

"Not so," her playmate answered.
"We shall not need
To say farewell to gladness.
Of men, indeed,
Many there are who value women's best
And comeliest,
And I am wooed by one who can drive sorrow from
the breast."

"Let me behold that worth
To me unknown!
The girdle that I wear
Shall be thine own.
Tell me the name of him who loveth thee
With such fine constancy!
I dreamt last night thy thoughts were fixed on
one of fair degree."

"He whom they call the Squire of Riuwental.
Whose song is the delight
Of one and all,
He is my friend. Nor shall he lack reward.
For him, my heart's adored,
I will array me. Hence, and come along, the dance
is toward!"

MARGARET F. RICHEY

✠

The Season's Here!

Diu zit ist hie

The season's here!
I have seen none lovelier this many a year.
No more does winter cold and keen
Afflict the heart, rejoicing and serene
Among the woods so green.

May comes bringing
Flowers abundant and the mirth of birds a-singing.
See the field in bright array
Pranked, with hues so beautiful and gay
Its cares are driven away!

"Come now with me,
Playmate, and let us haste to the linden tree!
There shalt thou find what most thine eyes
Desire: recall last season's memories!
This game is worth a prize."

"Now let me don
My dress, for I am eager to be gone
To join the dance and join the play.
Not a word, dear Irmengart, I pray!
He will be there today."

Quicker than thought,
From the press her gayest gown was brought.
Swiftly was the girl arrayed.
"To the leafy linden tree my steps are swayed.
My troubles are allayed!"

MARGARET F. RICHEY

ULRICH VON LICHTENSTEIN

Among Sweet Tones in Forest Bowers

In dem walde süeze doene

Among sweet tones in forest bowers
songs of little birds are gay;
on the meadow lovely flowers
blossom in the warmth of May.
Now sweet joy my heart redeems
and gratefully my breast o'erflows
for the wealth of love it knows—
even as the poor are rich in dreams.

Hope it is beyond all measure
which for her sweet self I dare;
may I win this priceless treasure,
be forever free from care.
The wish alone has brought me gladness;
may God also grant to me
that my dream fulfillèd be
which so well has banished sadness.

May she, sweet one, false one never,
from deception wholly free,
let me hold this dear hope ever,
or until it's granted me.
Be this joy of long duration;
let me yet in hope awake;

do not from my yearning take
this precious dream, my consolation.

Of all my joys, I most receive
from wishes and from tenuous thought.
May her goodness not deceive
but grant reward, as lovers ought,
at least to understand me more
and give me of her own sweet bliss
a little portion, knowing this
will not diminish her own store.

Blessed May, it's you alone
who bring the world its wholesome curing;
you and all the world, as one,
bring joy almost beyond enduring.
How could you do such bounteous giving
without my very precious dear?
for it is she keeps hope so near,
the hope for which I go on living.

KENNETH OLIVER

MECHTHILD VON MAGDEBURG

Lord 'Tis Said That from the World

Herre, es heizzt mins herzen lust

Lord, 'tis said that from the world
I have held my heart's delight,
Have kept it myself
And other creatures all denied.
I may no further carry it—
Lord, where shall my delight be laid?

Nowhere shalt thy delight be laid
Save in my Godly heart,
And on my human breast;

There only art thou blessed
And with my spirit kissed.

MABEL COTTERELL

✠

Most Gladly Would I Die of Love

Ich stürbe gern aus Minne

Most gladly would I die of Love, if that might be;
For whom I love 'twas mine with my lit eyes to see
Him standing in my soul—my Love in me.

R. G. L. BARRETT

✠

Ails a Human Heart

Wie der Liebeswunde gesunde

Ails a human heart
From true Love's aching dart,
For such there is no healing art,
From those selfsame lips apart,
Whence came that eager smart.

R. G. L. BARRETT

✠

Dearest Love of God, I Pray Thee, Evermore Enfold My Soul

Eia, liebe Gottesminne

Dearest Love of God, I pray Thee, evermore enfold my soul,
My death it were with deepest woe,
If of Thee I must be free.
I pray Thee, Love, O let me not grow cool;
For dead are all the works I do,

May I not feel Thee.
O Love, dost sweetly bring to bitter grief,
To God's own children givest teaching and relief.
O strong Love-bond! Thy hand is fond,
With binding power, to hold both young and old.

R. G. L. BARRETT

DER WILDE ALEXANDER

Years Back When We Were Children

Hie vor dô wir kinder wâren

Years back when we were children
and at the stage of running
in gangs about the meadows—
here to this one, there to that one—
we picked up violets
on lucky days:
there you can now see cattle gadding about.

I still remember hunching
ankle deep in violets,
squabbling over which bunches were fairest.
Our childishness was obvious—
we ran dancing rounds
with our new green wreaths.
So time passes.

Here we ran swilling strawberries
from oak and pine,
over hedges, over turnstyles,
as long as day was burning down.
Then a gardener
rushed from an arbor:
"O.K. now, children, run home."

We came out in spots
those yesterdays, when we stuffed on strawberries;

it was just a childish game to us.
Often we heard
our herdsman
hooing and warning us;
"Children, the woods are alive wth snakes."

One of the children, breaking
through the sword grass, grew white
and shouted, "Children, a snake
ran in there. He got our pony.
She'll never get well.
I wish that snake
would go to hell."

"Well then, get out of the woods!
If you don't hurry away quickly,
I'll tell you what will happen—
if you don't scurry away
from the wood by daylight,
you'll lose yourself;
your pleasure will end in bawling.

Do you know how five virgins
dawdled in the meadows,
till the king slammed his dining room door?
Their shouting and shame were outrageous,
their jailer tore everything off
down to their birthday suits;
they stood like milk cows without any clothes."

ROBERT LOWELL

JOHANNES TAULER

There Comes a Ship All Laden
Es kumpt ein schiff geladen

There comes a ship all laden
Right up to highest board.

It brings the Son of the Father,
The true eternal Word.

Upon a calm still ocean
The little ship is borne
It brings us richest treasure,
The noble Heaven-Queen.

Maria, thou Rose so precious,
A branch of every bliss
Thou lovely blossoming crocus[1]
O free us from our sins!

Quietly the ship doth move,
Rich burden unsurpassed,
The sail is tender Love
The Holy Ghost the mast.

MABEL COTTERELL

HANS ROSENPLÜT

He Who Scrubs a Raven White
Wer baden wil ein Raben weiss

He who scrubs a raven white
And works at this with all his might—
Who wants the sun to parch the snow,
A chest to lock up winds that blow,
To sell bad luck, or so he hopes,
Who wants to bind all fools with ropes,
To shear bald men, though they're not hairy—
He loves what is unnecessary.

RUTH YORCK and KENWARD ELMSLIE

---

[1] *A play upon words in German cannot be reproduced: the word "crocus" also means "timeless, beyond time."*—Translator's Note.

ANONYMOUS

Nuns' Drinking Song
Trienklied der Nonnen

Let us sing and all be gay
        In the roses
With Jesus on this happy day
Who knows how long we're here to stay
        In the roses

Let the wine of Jesus flow
        In the roses
That is where we all should go
Then with joy our hearts will glow
        In the roses

For us He'll pour out cypress wine
        In the roses
We'll all be drunken from the wine
And from our love, sweet and benign
        In the roses

Let us raise our glasses high
        In the roses
Let's drink up, and drain them dry
The wind is the Holy Ghost who sighs
        In the roses

Let the wine be passed around
        In the roses
Soon we will be homeward bound
Filled with the timeless joy we've found
        In the roses

RUTH YORCK and KENWARD ELMSLIE

NOTES AND BIOGRAPHICAL SKETCHES

Very little remains of Germany's lyric poetry prior to the twelfth century, although there actually existed a substantial body of elegies, heroic poems and gnomic and erotic verse. Included here are such remnants as *The Lay of Hildebrand* (*Hildebrandslied* [c. 700]), which illustrates the rugged attitude of Germanic tribesmen moving into the collapsing world of the Roman Empire; and several spells, which reflect the pre-Christian mentality endeavoring to control the forces of Nature by magical means. From the charming "Thou Art Mine, I Am Thine" a tender note seems to announce, like a propitious dawn, the arrival of the *minnesang*—the love poets.

ALBRECHT VON JOHANSDORF (fl. 1197), a Bavarian minnesinger of noble descent, served under the Bishop of Passau and participated in a crusade, perhaps that of 1197. Among his forty-three poems, there are sixteen songs and two crusading songs—reflecting his personal experiences and admirable poetic gifts.

DIETMAR VON AIST (c. 1150-1170), an Austrian nobleman from Mauthausen, a town by the Aist, a tributary of the Danube, lived through the transition period between the somewhat crude Austro-Bavarian verse and the newer courtly convention of the *minnesang*. In addition to the lovely "A Lady Stood Alone," in which he used, as did *Der Kürenberg* (q.v.), alternate stanzas for knight and lady, he is remembered for his "Sleepest Thou Yet, My Sweeting?" the oldest *alba* (*Tagelied*) in the German language.

FRIEDRICH VON HAUSEN (c. 1150-1190), a Rhenish minnesinger, was born toward the middle of the twelfth century near Kreuznach, in Worms. He served the Archbishop of Mayence in 1175 and when a decade later Henry VI went to Italy he formed part of his retinue. Later he accompanied Frederick Barbarosa in the third crusade (1189) and was killed at the battle of Philomelium (Syria) on May 6, 1190. He left some fifty-five poems which despite their echoing at times Bernart de Ventadorn (q.v.) and Conon de Bethune (q.v.), show him to be a highly sensitive, inspired and original poet.

HEINRICH VON MORUNGEN (d. 1222), born in the Sangerhauser region of Thuringia, served in the court of Dietrich von Meissen, whom he accompanied in 1197 to the Holy Land. He retired to the monastery of St. Thomas in Leipzig where he died and where he is buried. In the thirty-eight pieces extant—*lieder, albas, pastourelles*—the troubadour influence (especially Bernart de Ventadorn's [q.v.]) is discernible, but nonetheless his masterful control of his art, his rich imagery, his expressive language, places him as the greatest of the minnesingers, with the one exception, perhaps, of Walther von der Vogelweide (q.v.).

KÜRENBERG, DER VON (c. 1150-1160) derived from the Austrian family of the Kürenberger that lived near Linz, on the Danube. Fifteen of his poems have been preserved. Because of his *Nibelungenlied* type of stanza, totally free from Provençal influences, some critics have wanted to attribute to him the German epic poem, the *Nibelungenlied.* Best known among his works is *The Falcon* (*Falkenlied*), the falcon symbolizing the hero, and thereafter, the inconstant lover—an ever recurring literary symbol (cf. Kriemhild's dream in the *Nibelungenlied* and also songs of Dietmar, Reinmar, Heinrich von Mügeln and Meinloh von Sevelingen).

MECHTHILD VON MAGDEBURG (c. 1207-1285), mystic writer best known for her *Das fliessende Licht der Gottheit,* after her novitiate in Magdeburg entered the Cistercian convent in Helfta, near Eisleben, where she died. Her verse fuses the qualities of the *Canticles* with those of the *minnesang,* expressing adequately her intense religious feelings.

NEIDHART VON REUENTAL (c. 1180-1250)—Reuenthal means "Valley of Cares," a name given to him because of his incurable penury—was born in the region of Landshut, in Bavaria, of noble parentage. During his youth he sojourned at the court of the Duke Louis of Bavaria and participated in

1217-1219 in Leopold's expedition to Syria. Toward 1230, having lost Duke Ottoman II's favor, he served Frederick II of Austria. Little or nothing is known about him after 1237. By depicting, and often burlesquing, the life and manners of the peasantry in his dance-songs (*Tanzlieder*), Neidhart discovered a new vein which grew in popularity, to the detriment of the *minnesang*.

REGENSBURG, BURGGRAVE VON (c. 1147), Danubian minnesinger of noble lineage, was probably the son of Burggrave Heinrich III, who died in 1177, and brother of Burggrave von Rietenberg, who also wrote poetry. In Regensburg's work the folkloric mixes with the world of chivalry.

REINMAR VON HAGENAU, *der alte* (c. 1155-1210) was born in the Alsatian town of Hagenau, not far from Strasbourg, and lived for a long time at the court of Duke Leopold IV, whom he accompanied in the crusade of 1190. He left several *lieders* and *albas* and a crusading song, and all his work is characterized by a sweetness and tenderness suggestive of Petrarch, to whom he has been compared. Gottfried von Strassburg called him "the nightingale of Hagenau."

ROSENPLÜT, HANS (XVth century), also known as Hans Schnepperer, was a Nuremberg armorer who, championing the rising middle class, waged a bitter struggle against the powerful lords then headed by Markgraf Albrecht Achilles of Brandenburg. A precursor of his fellow townsman Hans Sachs, he wrote satires, plays, political songs, crude for the most part but quite arresting.

SPERVOGEL (c. 1170), pseudonym of a minstrel-knight, a writer of didactic poems, folksy, humorous.

TAULER, JOHANNES (c. 1300-1371), Dominican friar, a disciple of Meister Eckart, was active in Basel, Cologne and Strasbourg, his native city. In addition to his sermons, eighty of which are extant and which show him as a popularizer of the ideas of the great mystics, he wrote some lovely religious lyrics.

ULRICH VON LICHTENSTEIN (c. 1200-1275), Styrian knight from Lichtenstein, led an adventurous life colored by the ideals and madness of Don Quixote. His autobiography in verse, *Vrowendienst* (c. 1255), presents a panoramic view of life at the end of the *minnesang* and of knight errantry. Ulrich wrote also over sixty lyrics: dance-songs (*Tanzlieder*), love songs, and *albas*. The charming "Among Sweet Tones in Forest Bowers" was set to music by Mendelssohn.

WALTHER VON DER VOGELWEIDE (c. 1170-1230) has been considered the greatest lyric poet in the German language before Goethe. Born in the Austrian Tyrol, he probably studied in a religious school where he learned the art of poetry, making his literary debut toward 1190. In Vienna he served in the court of Duke Leopold V, competing there with Reinmar von Hagenau (q.v.). After Leopold's death (1194) he continued in the service of Leopold's son, Frederick I, who met an untimely death in the Holy Land (1198), and after that Walther roamed the land—now following the son of Frederick Barbarosa, now Othon of Brunswick. When Pope Innocent III excommunicated Othon, Walther sided with Othon and rose violently against the Pope. Toward 1220 Frederick II granted Walther a fief in Wurzug, where he lived until his death. It is not at all certain that he took part in the Sixth Crusade (1228-1229). Walther left approximately 200 pieces: *lieder, pastourelles,* gnomic poems and much political verse—some of which are among the loveliest lyrics in the German language.

WILDE ALEXANDER, DER (late XIIIth century), i.e., the wandering Alexander, is the pseudonym of a commoner from Southern Germany, a rather enigmatic figure, who delighted in allegorical and gnomic poems. One of his singular contributions, unique for his times, was children's poetry.

WOLFRAM VON ESCHENBACH (c. 1170-1217), considered the greatest epic poet of medieval Germany, was born in Eschenbach, near Ansbach, and served as counselor to various lords, among others Count von Wertheim and the Landgrave Hermann of Thuringia. His major work was *Parzival.* His lyrics, some eight *lieder* and five *albas* or *Tagelieder,* are characterized by their dramatic and sensuous qualities.

BIBLIOGRAPHY

Adams, H. *Mont-Saint-Michel and Chartres.* Garden City, N.Y.: Doubleday Anchor Books, 1959.

Auerbach, E. *Mimesis.* Garden City, N.Y.: Doubleday Anchor Books, 1957.

Barker, E. *The Crusades.* New York: Oxford University Press, 1923.

Barraclough, G. (ed.). *Mediaeval Germany.* 2 vols. Oxford: Blackwell, 1938.

Bethurum, D. *Critical Approaches to Medieval Literature.* New York: Columbia University Press, 1951.

Chadwick, H. M. and Nora K. *The Growth of Literature.* Vol. I, *The Ancient Literatures of Europe.* New York: Macmillan, 1932.

Chaytor, H. J. *From Script to Print.* Cambridge University Press, 1945.

——— *The Troubadours.* New York: Macmillan, 1912.

Cheney, E. P. *The Dawn of Modern Europe.* New York: Harper, 1936.

Closs, August. *The Genius of the German Lyric.* (Revised edition.) London: The Cresset Press, and Philadelphia: Dufour Editions, 1962.

Cotterill, H. B. *Medieval Italy.* New York: Stokes, 1915.

Coulton, G. C. *Life in the Middle Ages.* Cambridge University Press, 1930.

——— *Medieval Panorama.* Cambridge University Press, 1939.

Crosland, J. *Medieval French Literature.* Oxford: Blackwell, 1956.

Crump, C. G. and Jackobs, E. F. *The Legacy of the Middle Ages.* Oxford: Clarendon Press, 1926.

Curtius, E. R. *European Literature and the Latin Middle Ages.* New York: Pantheon, 1953.

Dawson, C. H. *The Making of Europe.* New York: Sheed & Ward, 1932.

—— *Medieval Essays*. New York: Sheed & Ward, 1954.
—— *Mediaeval Religion*. New York: Sheed & Ward, 1934.
Duckett, E. S. *The Gateway to the Middle Ages*. New York: Macmillan, 1938.
Emerton, E. *Mediaeval Europe*. Cambridge, Mass.: Harvard University Press, 1934.
Evans, J. *Life in Mediaeval France*. New York: Oxford University Press, 1925.
Ford, B. *The Age of Chaucer*. Penguin, 1954.
Gaspary, A. *A History of Early Italian Literature*. London: Bell & Sons, 1901.
Gilson, E. H. *The Spirit of Medieval Philosophy*. New York: Scribner, 1936.
—— *Reason and Revelation in the Middle Ages*. New York: Scribner, 1938.
Harman A. *Mediaeval and Early Renaissance Music*. London: Rockliff, 1958.
Hearnshaw, F. J. C. (ed.). *Mediaeval Contributions to Modern Civilization*. New York: Barnes & Noble, 1949.
Huizinga, J. *The Waning of the Middle Ages*. Garden City, N.Y.: Doubleday Anchor Books, 1958.
Jackson, W. T. H. *The Literature of the Middle Ages*. New York: Columbia University Press, 1960.
Jarrett, B. *Social Theories of the Middle Ages*. London: Benn, 1926.
Ker, W. P. *The Dark Ages*. New York: New American Library (Mentor), 1958.
—— *Epic and Romance*. New York: Macmillan, 1922.
—— *Essays on Medieval Literature*. New York: Macmillan, 1908.
Lewis, C. S. *The Allegory of Love*. New York: Oxford University Press (Galaxy Book), 1958.
Lewis, E. *Medieval Political Ideas*. New York: Knopf, 1954.
MacKinney, L. C. *The Medieval World*. New York: Farrar, Straus, 1938.
Magnus, L. *European Literature in the Centuries of Romance*. London: Kegan, Paul, 1918.
Morey, C. R. *Mediaeval Art*. New York: Norton, 1942.

Painter, S. *French Chivalry*. Baltimore: Johns Hopkins University Press, 1940.

——— *Mediaeval Society*. Ithaca, N.Y.: Cornell University Press, 1951.

Power, E. *Medieval People*. New York: Houghton Mifflin, 1935.

Powicke, F. M. *The Christian Life in the Middle Ages*. London, 1935.

Rand, E. K. *Founders of the Middle Ages*. Cambridge, Mass.: Harvard University Press, 1928.

Reese, G. *Music in the Middle Ages*. New York: Norton, 1940.

Reinhard, J. R. (ed.). *Mediaeval Pageant*. New York: Harcourt, Brace, 1939.

Richey, M. F. *Essays on the Medieval Love-Lyric*. Oxford: Blackwell, 1943.

Rickert, E. (ed.). *Chaucer's World*. New York: Columbia University Press, 1948.

Stephenson, C. *A Brief Survey of Medieval Europe*. New York: Harper, 1941.

——— *Mediaeval Feudalism*. Ithaca, N.Y.: Cornell University Press, 1942.

Taylor, H. O. *The Medieval Mind*. 2 vols. New York: Macmillan, 1930.

Thompson, J. W. *An Introduction to Medieval Europe*. New York: Norton, 1937.

Tilley, A. *The Dawn of the French Renaissance*. Cambridge University Press, 1918.

——— *Medieval France*. Cambridge University Press, 1922.

Valency, M. *In Praise of Love*. New York: Macmillan, 1958.

Villari, P. *Medieval Italy*. London: Unwin, 1910.

Vossler, K. *Medieval Culture*. 2 vols. New York: Harcourt, Brace, 1929.

Wendell, B. *The Traditions of European Literature*. New York: Scribner, 1920.

Williams, H. F. *An Index of Mediaeval Studies*. Berkeley, Calif.: University of California Press, 1951.

INDEX OF *Poets*

INDEX OF *Translators*

INDEX OF *Titles*

(Titles that are also first lines are indicated in Roman type)

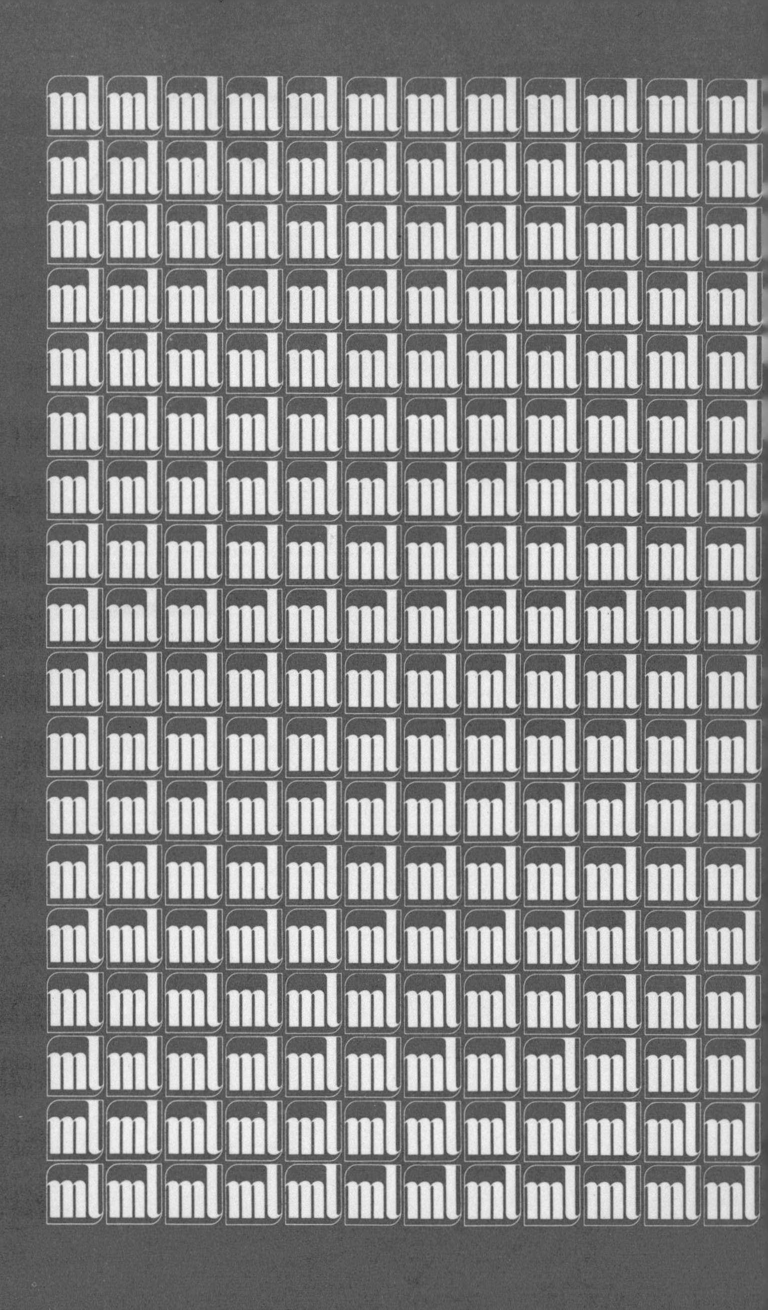